Republic of Drivers

# Republic of Drivers

## A Cultural History of Automobility in America

Cotten Seiler

The University of Chicago Press | Chicago and London

Cotten Seiler is associate professor of American studies
at Dickinson College.

The University of Chicago Press, Chicago 60637
The University of Chicago Press, Ltd., London
© 2008 by The University of Chicago
All rights reserved. Published 2008
Printed in the United States of America

16  15  14  13  12  11  10  09  08      1  2  3  4  5

ISBN-13: 978-0-226-74563-3 (cloth)
ISBN-13: 978-0-226-74564-0 (paper)
ISBN-10: 0-226-74563-5 (cloth)
ISBN-10: 0-226-74564-3 (paper)

Library of Congress Cataloging-in-Publication Data

Seiler, Cotten.
    Republic of drivers : a cultural history of automobility in
America / Cotten Seiler.
        p. cm.
    Includes bibliographical references and index.
    ISBN-13: 978-0-226-74563-3 (cloth : alk. paper)
    ISBN-13: 978-0-226-74564-0 (pbk. : alk. paper)
    ISBN-10: 0-226-74563-5 (cloth : alk. paper)
    ISBN-10: 0-226-74564-3 (pbk. : alk. paper)
1. Automobiles—Social aspects—United States—History—
20th century. 2. National characteristics, American. 3. Social
values—United States—History—20th century. 4. United
States—Social conditions—20th century. 5. United States—
Civilization—20th century. I. Title. II. Title: Cultural history of automobility in America. III. Title: History of automobility in America. IV. Title: Automobility in America.
    HE5623.S42 2008
    303.48'320973—dc22

                                    2008006413

For Harriette Seiler and John Seiler

# contents

# acknowledgments

I believe it was E. L. Doctorow who, responding to an interviewer's question on the logistics of writing something as long and intricate as a novel, used the analogy of driving through dark country at night: your headlights won't let you see very far, but they will get you all the way there. Having arrived at the end of a book, I like this analogy more and more. But headlights by themselves are not enough; and I would not have made it without the many navigators who rode with me, and watched my transit from above.

My mother, Harriette Seiler, and my father, John Seiler, have been reservoirs of support and love all my life. I can't begin to thank them. My grandmothers, Gabrielle Nye and Elizabeth Seiler, were exemplars of kindness, grace, and joy. My affection and respect for my brother Casey, my sister-in-law Rachael, my sister Margaret, and my brother-in-law Dan Engler go unsaid most of the time; but I hope they know how much they have enriched my life, and how dear they are to me. Ben Seiler, my favorite eight-year-old nephew, thinks he can take me to school on the basketball court, but I assure the reader I have at least another year of supremacy.

At the University of Kansas, Barry Shank and Bob Antonio both provided models of what a scholar and teacher ought to be—smart, but not at the expense of being compassionate; rigorous and serious, but never without levity (especially regarding oneself). Norm Yetman's kindness and resourcefulness gave me not just a template for how one chairs an academic department, but a code for living the academic life. At Dickinson College, Sharon O'Brien, Lonna Malmsheimer, and Amy Farrell welcomed me into an American studies department whose camaraderie, commitment to students, and intellectual energy make it a pleasure to go to work. Wonderful colleagues such as Victoria Sams, Adrienne Su, Jen Blyth, Marc Mastrangelo, Chris Francese, Melinda Schlitt, Pauline Cullen, David Hernandez, Karl Qualls, Kirsten Guss, Jerry Philogene, Ashley Finley, Norm Jones, and Ebru Kongar helped me weather rough times and celebrate good ones.

The early phases of the project received much-needed financial support and morale boost via fellowships from the Eisenhower World Affairs Institute and the Graduate School of the University of Kansas. Later, grants from Dickinson College's Research and Development Committee made it possible to complete archival research and to write. A Fulbright Award at the University of Hong Kong in the spring of 2007 enabled me, as I finished the manuscript, to consider American automobility from afar, even as China itself accelerates into something of a People's Republic of Drivers. At the University of Chicago Press, Doug Mitchell guided the project with the verve and thoughtfulness of a fine jazz drummer; and Michael Koplow, my manuscript editor, was as thorough as he was kind to this rookie author.

The completion of *Republic of Drivers*—and my happiness—would have been impossible without the following people: Mike Elliott and Ana Chucair, Scott Davis and Krista Hanni, Jeff Johnson, Tim and Angela Welsh, Dirty Bird Brown, Dave and Becky Richeson, Mike Ezra, Jamie Smith and Maria Blackburn, Janet Rose, Lewis Seiler, Natalie Dykstra, Elizabeth Duffy, Brandon Burke, Aaron Ketchell and Marcia Fisher, Guy Stevens, Michael Warner, T. R. Johnson, Anna Neill, Betsy and John McDonald, Jo-Anne Bruce and Frank Snelgrove, Steph Owen, David Krause, Mike Monti and Anne Baldwin, Ed Snajdr and Shonna Trinch, Ellen Faris, Jo Anne Brown, Robert Vodicka, Catherine Siegel, Ryan Johnson and Anne Dean, Jan Emmenegger, and my students at Dickinson College, the University of Kansas, and the University of Hong Kong.

I ask all of my family and friends what Walt Whitman asked his ever-expanding crew of companions in *Song of the Open Road*: "will you come travel with me? Shall we stick by each other as long as we live?"

# Automobility and American Subjectivity

You road I enter upon and look around, I believe you are not all
    that is here.
I believe that much unseen is also here. —Walt Whitman[1]

Almost from the moment of the Interstate Highway System's authorization in 1956, historians, sociologists, geographers, political scientists, urban planners, journalists, cultural critics, and artists have ruminated on
the far-reaching effects of cars and highways on transportation and work
patterns, the environment, social customs, and popular culture. The resulting body of work ranges in rigor from treatise to frolic, and varies
in tone from outraged to elegiac to resigned to celebratory. Nearly all of
it, however, characterizes the Interstate Highway System as an agent of
epochal rupture. As the historian Tom Lewis tells his readers in the introduction to *Divided Highways*, "This is the story of consequences, how for
better and worse the Interstates have changed our lives."[2]

Beyond this common thesis, however, these works tend to cleave down
a predictably partisan line, their titles promising evidence of how the interstates built or ruined the nation, empowered or enslaved its population. In finding in the momentous coming of the interstates either trium-
phant progress, liberation of the self, destruction of the environment and
society, or the loss of national innocence, the authors of these emotive
works reproduce, implicitly or explicitly, the ideology of American excep-

tionalism: the Interstate Highway System, they argue, made or unmade a singular and heroic nation, depicted alternately as earthly kingdom or withering Eden.[3]

I am after a different narrative. Readers expecting a travelogue, a polemic, a technical history of highway design, or a romp through "our love affair with the car" will be disappointed by this book. Its essential questions are cultural, philosophical, and political, not automotive nor technological nor even psychological, narrowly defined. Its objects of inquiry are the *affect* generated by driving, and the instrumentalization of that affect under shifting regimes of liberalism and capitalism in the twentieth century.

Given this focus on the ways driving has made Americans feel, think, and act, *Republic of Drivers* sees continuity where other works have diagnosed rupture. It argues, for example, that the Interstate Highway System merely dedicated a larger share of resources to a covenant with automobility that was many decades old. More properly speaking, this study sees the interstates and the practices of automobility as the products of a highly specific conception of what it means to be modern and free. What follows is the story of how and why that conception became dominant, and the role of automobility in illustrating it and shoring it up.

The scope of years examined here may seem arbitrary, but there are some compelling reasons for situating automobility's ascent and zenith between 1895 and 1961. Primitive self-propelled vehicles (with internal combustion engines fueled by steam, hydrogen, coal, and gasoline) had been developed in Europe since the late eighteenth century. Determining the date and inventor of the first automobile depends on semantics— what, precisely, constitutes an automobile?—not to mention nationalism: French accounts tend toward engineer Joseph Cugnot's 1769 steam-powered wagon or inventor Edouard Delamare-Debouteville's 1883 four-stroke engine; Americans may cite Oliver Evans's 1789 patent for a steam vehicle; most automotive historians claim German engineer Karl Benz's 1885 four-wheeled horseless carriage as the prototype for contemporary cars. Yet the "automobile age" in the United States begins in 1895, the year of the organization of the first automobile-manufacturing concern in the United States, the Duryea Motor Company; the submission of over five hundred auto-related applications to the U.S. Patent Office and the latter's award of the "road engine" patent to George Selden; the first scheduled automobile race in the United States, in Chicago (won by Frank Duryea); the launch of the trade magazines *Horseless Age* and *Motocycle*; and the introduction of the noun *automobile* (adapted from the French) to American English.[4] The year 1961 marks the departure from office of the Eisenhower administration, facilitator of the Interstate Highway System and thus of automobility's full fruition, and the beginning of a national awareness of automobility (a term resuscitated in 1961) as a system with profound cultural, economic, political, and environmental consequences. Between 1895 and 1961—a period that also saw the rise of the United States to global military, political, economic, and cultural power—automobility emerged as a shaper of public policy and the landscape, a prescriptive metaphor for social and economic relations, and a forge of citizens.

This study pays particular attention to two key periods within this span of years. It focuses first on the early decades of automobility, from 1895 through the 1920s, during which automobility became entrenched in political institutions, the economy, the landscape, and cultural life more generally. From there it moves to an account of what we might call automobility's high-modernist moment in the 1950s, when the discursive spaces of politics and social and economic life found symbolic expression in the limited-access interstate highway, and the horizons of citizenship came to look very much like those of driving. Each of these eras saw automobility surge in terms of auto sales and growth of infrastructure. Each also saw major crises in and/or renegotiations of American individualism. Seeking to understand the reasons for automobility's expansion, this study examines the formulations of dominant, and therefore implicitly white and male, selfhood visible in the social science, industrial management theory, popular culture, cultural and intellectual history, and literary scholarship of each era. I argue that, in these moments of danger that threatened capitalist-liberal hegemony by destabilizing its narrative of selfhood, automobility performed a crucial restorative role by giving that selfhood a vital form conducive to the existing arrangement of power.

A central aim here is to describe the *subjectivity*—simply put, the way of being in and perceiving the world around us—organized and reinforced by driving.[5] My use of this term follows from the poststructuralist claim that language and other cultural discourses are the origins and lathes of identity. The consequences of this claim are not merely intellectual (they never are with ideas), but political and ethical as well. The concept of subjectivity challenges, as it reveals, the ideological nature of the construct of "the individual." This figure—sui generis, autonomous, ahistorical, prior to language, endowed with reason and natural rights, and transparent to itself—emerged out of the religious and political upheavals of the sixteenth and seventeenth centuries and provided the axiomatic justification of the liberal and capitalist revolutions of the eighteenth and nineteenth.

Under the regimes those revolutions emplaced, the principle of the individual as the fundamental unit of society continues to anchor hegemonic political, legal, and economic theory and practice, as well as commonsense worldviews more generally. The ideology of individualism, which has held sway in the United States at least since the early nineteenth century, has justified and naturalized the prevailing arrangement of social, economic, and political power by making that arrangement appear the aggregate of innumerable acts of choice and consent on the part of free individuals.[6] Attempting to describe the past outside the terms of this ideology, historical accounts drawing on theories of subjectivity situate their human protagonists in contingent, historically and culturally determined processes of meaning and power. Individuals, according to the ideology of individualism, produce themselves; subjects, by contrast, are produced through discursive practice, and act within specific historical frames, which themselves undergo inevitable transformation.[7]

Subjectivity is socially determined. Language is principal among the discourses and practices by which we come to recognize and represent ourselves as belonging to specific categories of personhood—women, Latinos, consumers, middle class, Americans—and to speak and act from those subjectivities. However, the Copernican kernel of the theory of subjectivity—the rejection of "the individual" as primal or ahistorical—does not preclude belief in the capacities for consciousness, communication, and other types of agency that were the heroic and essential characteristics of the figure of the "autonomous individual." The difference lies in the theory of subjectivity's insistence that it is our very fashioning as subjects that equips us with agency.[8]

This theoretical perspective informs the following investigation of one of the most quotidian of American practices, automobile driving. More precisely speaking, this book analyzes the act of driving and all of those components that make driving possible, practical, empowering, fun, salutary, and imperative, and which together compose the entity called *automobility*. At least one etymological account places the origin of this term as early as 1903, after which it seems to have dropped from common usage.[9] In 1961, the historian John Burnham argued that the gasoline tax, implemented nationally in the 1920s, "stands as evidence that Americans are willing to pay for the infinite expansion of their automobility."[10] Used in this basic sense, the term names a pattern of individualized mobility made possible by the self-propelled mechanical vehicles that became increasingly available to consumers from the close of the nineteenth century forward, and operating simultaneously and, at least at first, in competition with modes of transport organized around locomotives and horses. Implicit in Burnham's usage is an attitude toward that mobility characterized by entitlement, an implication the historian Mark Rose captures in his definition of automobility as "the conviction of most that motor vehicles and fast-flowing expressways [are] good in their own right."[11]

These senses of automobility—as both a mode of movement and a conscious attitude toward it—are fundamental to the more capacious definition I want to develop here. The historian James Flink assesses automobility as "the combined import of the motor vehicle, the automobile industry and the highway, plus the emotional connotations of this import for Americans."[12] I will return to Flink's curious addendum "for Americans" presently; but his inclusion of a broader array of signs, institutions, objects, practices, and feelings opens onto a fuller conception of automobility as a composite entity consisting of more than simply cars and roads. The sociologist John Urry argues that "automobility can be conceptualized as a self-organizing, autopoietic, non-linear system that spreads worldwide, and includes cars, car-drivers, roads, petroleum supplies and many novel objects, technologies and signs"; the literary scholar Sidonie Smith has characterized it as "the configuration of people, machines, landscape, urban geography, and culture that attends the increasing dependence upon the gas engine for transport in industrial and postindustrial societies"; and the sociologist Jörg Beckmann writes of a "sociocultural phenomenon" and a "mobility paradigm."[13] More helpful still is the environmental scientist Sudhir Chella Rajan's interpretation of automobility as "a mammoth social institution . . . less an abstract agglomeration of certain forms of individual behavior than a contingent social enterprise with a specific history responsible for its institutional and ideological sustenance. It is a remarkable motif woven from several social and spatial elements."[14]

With this emphasis on its historicity and its multiple, heterogeneous, intersecting components, I propose that we comprehend automobility as what Michel Foucault called a *dispositif*—a concept somewhat impoverished by its English translation to "formation," "grid of intelligibility," or, the term I will use, "apparatus." Used by Foucault to name a multifaceted, coordinating network of power, an apparatus bridges the ground between the more textual "discourse" and the materiality of practice; it incorporates both discourses and practices, as well as their crystallized effects. Foucault elaborated the concept as

> firstly, a thoroughly heterogeneous ensemble consisting of discourses, institutions, architectural forms, regulatory decisions, laws, administrative measures, scientific statements, philosophical, moral and philanthropic propositions—in short, the said as much as the unsaid. Such are the elements of the apparatus. The apparatus itself is the system of relations that can be established between these elements. Secondly . . . the nature of the connection that can exist between these heterogeneous elements. . . . Thirdly, I understand by the term "apparatus" a . . . formation which has as its major function at a given historical moment that of responding to an *urgent need*. The apparatus thus has a dominant strategic function.[15]

More than merely a set of policies or attitudes cohering around cars and roads, automobility comprises a "multilinear ensemble" of commodities, bodies of knowledge, laws, techniques, institutions, environments, nodes of capital, sensibilities, and modes of perception.[16] This apparatus has channeled power in both the productive and repressive senses of the word: it has regulated, legislated, aided, and compelled the motion of bodies mechanical and human; it has established and delimited a horizon of agency, social relations, political formations, self-knowledge, and desire. As the philosopher Giorgio Agamben asserts in his exegesis of Foucault's term, apparatuses "must always involve a process of subjectivization; they must, that is, produce their own subject."[17] Moreover, as I will argue below, automobility emerged during and as a strategic response to the crises precipitated by the transition from proprietary to corporate capitalism in the United States.

Can we name the subjectivity produced by the apparatus of automobility? With some apprehension, I propose calling it *American*. To return to Flink's definition of automobility as "the combined import of the motor vehicle, the automobile industry and the highway, plus the emotional connotations of this import for Americans," one might ask, why only for Americans? Is this apparatus exclusive to the United States? The long history of automobility outside North America and its current flourishing in Asia make such a claim dubious.[18] Nevertheless, Flink is on to something with his emphasis on the American-ness of automobility.

As mentioned above, this study will not attempt to limn the "real America" that automobility has either enervated or animated; but it will argue for automobility itself as an apparatus that coincided with, facilitated, and illustrated the United States' spread across its continental borders and its imperial rise. Moreover, it asserts automobility as essential to shaping the dominant meanings of "America" and "American" in the twentieth century. These terms have become vexing for scholars (if not for politicians), and rightfully so. Decades of struggle over their descriptive ambit have established their decidedly ideological character. Of course, the terms designate, minimally and not unproblematically, geographical origin or placement in what is or what has become the territory of the nation-state known as "the United States." While this sense of "America" and "American" is important to the analysis that follows (unfolding as it does in this national space), more pertinent is these terms' ability to signify myth, transmit ideology, and confer power.

From this perspective, the central question is not what the interstates have done to America/ns, but to what ends and in the service of whose interests that adjective and those nouns have been deployed. The enterprise of assigning the honorific "American" to events, people, institutions, landscapes, works of art and literature, and values has been bound up with legitimating particular regimes of accumulation and policies of exclusion, assimilation, and conquest throughout the nation's history. In the mid-twentieth century, for example, social scientists and humanities scholars in the United States mapped a constellation of qualities—newness, self-reliance, innocence, mobility, idealism, authenticity, pragmatism, renewal, dynamism, and modernity—that were ostensibly distinctive to the national citizenry (coded as white and male). As I will discuss below, this set of virtues, figured heroically as the "American character" and invoked by a range of hegemonic institutions, justified the quest for national supremacy over alternative regimes—especially Soviet communism—and the imposition of a U.S.-modeled template of political economy on the developing world. Succeeding generations of scholars and activists rightly assailed the fictiveness of this figure, the exclusionary violence it enacts, and the political programs it ideologically funds.

It is therefore not without anxiety that I report that this study attempts a similar, and equally impossible, specification of "American" qualities and behaviors. I hope that the difference between my invocation of the "American character" and that of an earlier generation of scholars will be clear to readers. In summoning the repressed to return, so to speak, this study aims to historicize rather than aggrandize, to demystify rather than reify. However, the assertion that the "American character" was and remains an ideological chimera is not tantamount to a denial of its normative power. In fact, despite its scholarly debunking over the past few decades, the individualistic "American character" has endured as a vital hegemonic exemplar, as the most cursory dip into the intertwined discourses of contemporary mainstream politics and popular culture will confirm.[19] The historian David Potter, one of the scholars who crafted and advanced the "American character" paradigm, noted that "without attempting a verdict on the historical veracity of this image of the American as individualist and idealist, it is important to bear in mind that this image has been partly a portrait, but also partly a model . . . an idealization of what is best in Americanism, and of what Americans should strive to be."[20] Used in this way, the antonym of "American" is not "foreign" but, as in the notorious formulation of the congressional committee charged with ferreting out subversion, "Un-American."

That said, the inquiry that follows will necessarily use the term "American" in conventional ways. That is, the adjective will delineate basic national belonging and origin, as in "Ford is an American company"; and the noun will name the status of this belonging, as in "Frank Duryea was an American." Yet I also intend another sense of the noun and adjective that elaborates a set of tendencies, identifications, behaviors, and affective attachments and antipathies (that is to say, a subject) along the lines of Potter's reminder, or as in Hector St. John de Crevecoeur's 1781 query, "What then is the American, this new man?"[21] To venture an answer to Crevecoeur, "American" describes, in the analysis that follows, a condition of amenability to a regime of control that characterizes its particular compulsions as "freedom."

Some readers might object to this use of "American," with its apparent connotations of determination and manipulation. What I am after here, however, is a description of a particular subjectivity and not of the architecture of a conspiracy. I understand that subjectivity's ethos, freedom, as a "formula of rule" within liberal-capitalist hegemony; yet despite freedom's effectiveness as an ideology for the governing and managing of individuals and groups, it has also proven remarkably volatile, inspiring powerful challenges and revisions to that hegemony.[22] Others might protest that this usage of "American," even emptied as it is here of its more blindly affirmative or jingoistic connotations, simply recapitulates American exceptionalism. But it is precisely this exceptionalism (typified, for example, by Leon Mandel's assertion that "what so clearly differentiates the American from his global fellows is his mobility") that I want to evoke with this formulation, to trace out the performances and disciplinary imperatives of belonging in a nation that narrates itself as novel, singular, and in forward motion.[23] In a sense, my aim with these two terms, "automobility" and "American," is to collapse them into one another: to be American is to claim automobility as one's habitat and *habitus*. As the literary scholar Mark Simpson has suggested, mobility has entailed a "method by which inhabitants of the United States managed to name, to circulate, to represent their representability as American subjects."[24]

In the twentieth century, to drive was to assume the performative contours of the generic "American"—a conduit and effect of those dispositions and habits, institutional structures, natural and built environments, and flows of power and capital that developed (in this nation) during the Second Industrial Revolution. The pages below plumb what Jean Baudrillard referred to as "this spectral form of civilization which the Americans have invented [and which] suddenly seems the best adapted to the probability—the probability only—of the life that lies in store for us."[25] The implication here, of course, is that "American" and "driver" in this sense name a capacious, supranational, even imperial subjectivity organized by the apparatus of automobility, and therefore inhabitable by Germans, Chinese, Australians, etc. The driving subject moves along grooves created, surveyed, and administered by that apparatus, and is also *legible* to it through the various modes of enumeration—driver's licensing and insurance, for example—connected to the nation-state and corporate capitalism.[26] Hence we might think about the current controversy over the licensing of undocumented immigrants in the United States as expressing both state and corporate anxieties over legibility, safety, and security and xenophobes' fears of ascribing immigrants even the symbolic "American" identity of the driver's license.

Though driving expresses a dominant subjectivity, its practice is inflected in countless ways. The various car subcultures in the United States that date at least to the 1960s, such as largely white and working-class "hot rod" or "stock car" enthusiasts and Chicano/Latino and African American "lowriders," as well as the more recent Asian-American "import street racer" culture, illustrate the dominance of automobility even in the fashioning of distinctive "ethnopolitical identit[ies]."[27] While these groups' expressive appropriations of the ultimate standardized commodity of late modernity is certainly significant, more striking, perhaps, are the driving styles these cultures promote. The disdain these cultures show for the efficiency and regulation of postwar automobility shows not only in the cars themselves, but in the excessive speeds of street racing and masterful, unhurried torpor of cruising, both of which are outside the law or at least the conventions of "good driving." Nevertheless, in characterizing these cultures, I would stress the theorist Raymond Williams's understanding of "alternative" as representing an inflection of, rather than a challenge to, dominant hegemonic practice.

What follows will use "American" in some places as this descriptor of subjectivity and in other places as a marker of national origin or situation—I hope that the context will make the distinction clear, and that it's safe to do what I do now, which is take American out of quotation marks.

*Republic of Drivers* attempts to describe the apparatus of automobility as limned in government documents, middlebrow print media, drivers' manuals and guidebooks, automotive trade magazines, philosophy, advertising, cultural criticism, scholarship in the humanities and social sciences, industrial and commercial films, highway engineering studies, photographs, literary works, and popular music. It also draws upon, as it tries to bridge, five main bodies of scholarship from the past few decades: automotive history, cultural history of the twentieth-century U.S., social history of the automobile, analyses of the "politics of mobility," and what I will call the sociology of automobility. Each has provided invaluable perspectives, tools, and data; but I hope that this study, as it draws from these bodies of scholarship, complements them too, by suggesting ways around their individual blind spots and shortcomings.

I am indebted first to studies of the automobile, highways, and automotive industries. The work of James J. Flink, Mark Rose, John B. Rae, and several others provided a crucial background on the industrial and technical innovations, personages, companies, and political entities that built the machines, policies, and landscapes of automobility in the United States.[28] While this work documents richly the chronological rise of cars and highways, it tends to ignore, or to attribute to human nature or self-evident "national values," the socially constructed dispositions and historically specific exigencies that underlie the desire to drive and to pave.

In arguing for a consideration of automobility as a shaper of subjects, this study joins provocative, often contentious debates among cultural and intellectual historians on conceptions of individual selfhood and their political significance. Works by James Livingston, T. J. Jackson Lears, Ellen Gruber Garvey, Alan Trachtenberg, Gail Bederman, Charlene Haddock Seigfried, and Barry Shank, to name just a few, describe the cultural, political, intellectual, and economic conditions out of which automobility took root and flourished.[29] At the same time, their analyses of proletarianization, corporate capitalism, consumption, and the crises of American selfhood these developments occasioned lack substantial treatment of automobility as a response to those crises.

This study also engages pioneering literature in the social history of automobility by Virginia Scharff, Clay McShane, Kathleen Franz, Peter Ling, Michael L. Berger, David Gartman, and others. These studies improve upon earlier and/or more conventional automotive history by attending to the ways in which social and national identities and ideologies have influenced or determined people's zeal for and access to the agency of driving and technology itself.[30] Narrating the multiple experiences of automobility through the lenses of gender, race, class, region, and nation, this work problematizes the unitary driver assumed by automotive historians. It also helpfully places into historical and cultural context the "will to automobility" that automotive history has glossed as timeless and universal. Yet the social history of automobility has not delved deeply enough into how mobility itself informs and structures modern liberal subjectivity, the contested "prize" that its disparate groups seek to realize through the practice of automobility.

This deeper investigation of mobility as a source and performative resource of the modern subject has been undertaken from various disciplinary perspectives and methodologies. As a result, it is difficult to name the fourth body of scholarship with which this work engages, one informed by literary studies, cultural studies, political philosophy, and geography, among others. Its common object of inquiry is the "politics of mobility," a concept recently investigated by Mark Simpson. Mark Seltzer, James Clifford, Sarah Jain, Eric Leed, Sidonie Smith, Wolfgang Schivelbusch, Kris Lackey, Patricia Fumerton, Kristin Ross, and Jeffrey Schnapp have also produced provocative accounts of mobility's histories, mythologies, and pathologies with an eye to the stakes of mobility in regard to subjectivity.[31] These works convey a sense of mobility as both a disciplinary technology and a form of capital; they emphasize that power forces people to move or to remain immobile, that it "hails" them as particularly empowered (raced, classed, gendered, and national) subjects. The corollary is that the capacity of individuals and groups to move freely serves as an index of their power; and hence mobility is an arena of contest and performative display. Moreover, such works help us see how experiences of mobility become textualized, and how textual forms have been affected by mobility.

At the same time, works interrogating the politics of mobility and their textualization have paid less attention to the ways in which the power relations and subjectivities of mobility have been enacted and systematized in the environments of contemporary life. For this foundation I turn to the fifth and final body of scholarship of which this study avails itself, which I call the sociology of automobility. Over the past decade, Mimi Sheller, John Urry, Jeremy Packer, Sudhir Chella Rajan, Jörg Beckmann, and others have elaborated the specific seductions and compulsions of the spaces and practices of automobility, attempting to map the larger social and political formation that automobility represents. If these analyses have lacked substantive historical or textual components, they have nonetheless developed a set of descriptive concepts that historians and scholars in the humanities have not yet employed in any consequential way (perhaps because of the newness of the subfield).[32]

I hope that this study draws together these resources and sets of questions and encourages more discussion of the relation between mobility and subjectivity in worlds past and present. This discussion strikes me as especially valuable at a moment in which mobility (both actual and virtual) expands in tandem with systems of surveillance and control deployed by state and commercial entities to ensure the legibility, tractability, security, and productivity of subjects.

The first chapter, "Individualism, Taylorization, and the Crisis of Republican Selfhood," examines the turn-of-the-century context of automobility's emergence. Automobility was the product and anodyne of an era in which patterns of labor and economic organization were undergoing tremendous change. A range of commentators viewed the phenomena of proletarianization and industrial consolidation with suspicion and trepidation, for these phenomena appeared to contract or eliminate the spaces and institutions that had sustained the venerable ethos of yeoman and artisanal autonomy that had formed the ideological basis for American political economy. The scientific management theory of Frederick W. Taylor, which radically altered the experience of work, registered with many as particularly egregious—not merely disempowering, but emasculating. Taylorism and corporate capitalism had the potential to debilitate and call into question the ideological figures and narratives that served to orient and reconcile male and white workers to their places under the current regime, and thereby threatened to bring about the unraveling of liberal-capitalist hegemony itself.

Yet this unraveling never occurred. By the 1920s, the older ideology of individualism stood in critical tension with a newly articulated ideology—also called "individualism"—that more effectively justified the regimes of corporate capitalism and consumer culture. Its imperatives were cooperation (as opposed to resistant independence), distinction within corporate bodies (which were in turn increasingly seen as facilitating rather than frustrating selfhood), and expression and fulfillment of a unique inner self through commodified leisure and consumption (as opposed to the denial of self-interest). This new "expressive" individualism, developed and articulated in mainstream politics and advertising, responded to and effectively absorbed the critique of liberal selfhood (and therefore of the political and economic status quo) leveled by reformers and social scientists. The subject that emerged in expressive-individualist texts—I discuss the example of Herbert Hoover's *American Individualism* (1922)—merged a spectacular and loudly bruited "freedom" with political quiescence; its cardinal practice was automobile driving.

Chapter 2, "Workmen's Compensation, Women's Emancipation: The Promise of Automobility, 1895–1929," examines the ways in which the automobile was heralded as both the instrument for the performative recuperation of the "sovereign self" of the republican past and the facilitator of the blithely masterful new subjectivity of the consumer-citizen. The chapter argues for a revision of the dominant "thesis of utility" in explaining mass automobility's rise. It proposes that we consider the *act of driving*, rather than the utilitarian and status-conferring automotive object, as the crucial compensation for apparent losses to the autonomy, privacy, and agency registered by workers under the transition to corporate capitalism, and therefore as an important ideological tool for the preservation of hegemony.

This ambivalence of automobility—its offer of transgression and transformation, its ultimate amenability to the status quo—is strikingly evident in its relationship to gender, one focus of this chapter. As many feminist scholars have pointed out, the "open road" celebrated by Walt Whitman and others is in fact a gendered space of—to borrow a highway engineering term—"limited access." It is commonly understood that from the advent of automobility, patriarchal social formations discounted women's competency behind the wheel—a metaphor for their fitness for republican citizenship—and discouraged or prohibited them from driving. Yet this story of women's automobility, while generally accurate, does not fully convey how ambiguous the gender of automobility initially was. Nor does it attend to how specific gendered modes of automobility crystallized as the latter developed as an apparatus, extending its reach into law, politics, the economy, art, literature, public health, the built environment, and the patterns of everyday life. Drawing on early motor touring narratives, automotive magazines, and promotional materials, I argue that the heroic, revivifying, and individuating automobility that became the province of men was initially taken up by "new women" as well. By the 1920s, however, women were ascribed to an automobility organized around domestic tasks, consumption, and ornamental femininity.

The chapter closes with a discussion of the construction of the apparatus of automobility during these first decades of the twentieth century. I am interested in the ways in which, as automobile use grew to the point where it became a *problem* to be solved or managed, automobility became a discursive field for the expansion of what Foucault called *governmentality*. This term refers to the goals of the modern, liberal system of power (which includes but also subsumes "the government") and the *style* in which it rules. These goals can best be summarized as the scrutiny, classification, and management of populations with an eye to their improvement, broadly understood.[33] In the early twentieth century, the physical threat posed by the automobile to public welfare justified the enterprises of roadbuilding, driver licensing, vehicle registration, codification of traffic law, insurance underwriting, and the expansion of police agencies. As automobility achieved sway over the practices of everyday life and transportation policy, it simultaneously provided to powerful institutions a myriad of new techniques by which they could know, and therefore shape and manage, subjects. Most importantly, automobility emerged as a "technology of the self," organizing a compelling mode of self-government anchored in liberal notions of freedom.

Themes of subjectivity, policy, and the built environment feature prominently in chapter 3, "Crafting Autonomous Subjects: Automobility and the Cold War," which connects the authorization of the National System of Interstate and Defense Highways to early cold war anxieties concerning American selfhood, feminization, and conformity. The 1950s saw a range of powerful institutions extol driving as an antidote to an alleged "crisis of the individual"—which was also a crisis of patriarchy—and an illustration of the superiority of the "American way of life." Social scientists and artists such as David Riesman, William Whyte, Jack Kerouac, and John Steinbeck, as they lamented the decline of the masculine individualism of the American past, suggested the open road as the site of its renewal. A similar preoccupation with the sovereign individual could be seen in the propaganda of the postwar state. American propagandists, keen to avoid dogmatism, foregrounded material examples of the individualism that the nation claimed to champion; ever-expanding automobility provided one such example.

Challenging as incomplete the standard explanation of the Interstate Highway System as simply a product of the postwar boom and a military necessity, the chapter argues for a consideration of the interstates as an instance of domestic propaganda. Further, it argues that this massive commitment to automobility represented an attempt, on the part of a number of powerful institutions—not least among them Eisenhower's avowedly anti-statist state—to forge and sustain a specific subject, one who *performed* freedom even as he lived acquiescence to the social and political status quo. As it had done earlier in the century, driving represented this subject; yet what was distinct about the idealized automobility of this cold war era was its highway character. Interstate automobility, with its speed, ease, standardized environments, disconnection from the landscape, and, most important, limited access and egress, offered a rich set of linguistic, behavioral, and visual metaphors for citizenship during the early cold war.

The racial politics of automobility are the focus of chapter 4, "'So That We as a Race Might Have Something Authentic to Travel By': African American Automobility and Midcentury Liberalism." This chapter measures the import of driving to struggles for racial equality in the twentieth century through an analysis of *Travelguide (Vacation & Recreation Without Humiliation)* and *The Negro Motorist Green Book,* midcentury guidebooks that directed black drivers to nondiscriminatory roadside lodging, dining, and mechanical assistance. Published between 1936 and the early 1960s, when racial inequality became an impediment to American global hegemony, these guidebooks mediated between Jim Crow and civil rights sensibilities, and between a traditionally white mode of individualism and the appeal to collective action that would power the civil rights movement. I argue that the periodicals' vehement arguments against discrimination on the highway were underpinned by a firm belief in automobility as a cardinal practice of the citizen-in-full.

One unanticipated result of the interstate highway era was the increasing superfluity of these guidebooks. Somewhat ironically, the federally overseen "nowhere" space of the highway, disconnected from its immediate environment and serviced by standardized hotel, gasoline, and restaurant chains, offered its black drivers an opportunity to *pass* as the blank liberal subject—the citizen of the "republic of drivers," with all of its privileges and limitations.

I take up this species of citizenship more fully in chapter 5, "'How Can the Driver Be Remodeled?': Automobility and the Liberal Subject," which also revisits and expands upon the theme of governmentality introduced in chapter 2. The chapter pays particular attention to the technical discourse of midcentury highway engineering, a key concern of which was the corrigibility of the driver. What interests me here is the political analogue of the engineers' desires for measurability, efficiency, and manageability in the human elements of automobility. Drawing upon recent critiques of liberal individualism as encouraging withdrawal from political engagement and submission to ever-larger concentrations of power, this chapter inquires into how the practices and environments of postwar automobility express specific visions of social and political organization and formulations of citizenship.

The belief in self-directed motion as an agent of liberation, cleansing, edification, and nationalization is powerful and venerable in American culture. "Everything good is on the highway," Ralph Waldo Emerson wrote in his 1844 essay "Experience," five decades before the automobile would embark on its conquest of everyday life in the United States; nearly a century before the coming of the limited-access highway, and a century and a half before the first petroleum war was fought.[34] In what follows I argue that we have heeded Emerson well, not least by scoring the landscape with highways; but, more crucially, by investing our habitation of the social world with the character of driving, and according others the status of anonymous, potentially hostile units of traffic.

# chapter one

# Individualism, Taylorization, and the Crisis of Republican Selfhood

As much recent work in cultural history has shown, the turn of the century—the time of automobility's emergence—produced a discourse of anxiety and uncertainty surrounding the perceived loss of a subjectivity, described as "sovereign selfhood" or "autonomous individuality," ideologically crucial to the legitimacy of American political economy. This discourse responded to a shift in the mode of capitalist production and organization that threatened to undermine the credibility and the compulsory force of the ideology of individualism.

The regime of "scientific management" developed by Frederick Winslow Taylor and his disciples plays prominently in my reading of the rise of automobility, though not as the former has been typically cast, as the intellectual blueprint for the productive revolution of Fordism. While Taylor's theories were essential to developing the modern assembly line and thereby accelerating productivity, my interest here is the ways in which, as the sociologist Mark Bahnisch puts it, "the minute division of labor characteristic of Taylorism, and the alienated work which is its consequence, have become a floating signifier written into central narratives and myths of the 20th century."[1] Taylorization made automobility possible, but it also made it necessary.

## possessive individualism and republican selfhood

The religious, political, and economic revolutions of the Enlightenment derived their legitimacy from the figure of the "autonomous individual." "Individualism," a new conception of the origins and nature of the self and society, emerged from the theological dissent of the Reformation and the political revolts of post-Restoration England, developing by the late eighteenth century into a coherent theoretical foundation for the new institutions of government, justice, production, and exchange in modernity. "Possessive" individualism, which posits the individual as "essentially the proprietor of his own person or capacities, owing nothing to society for them," radically challenged an earlier view of human beings as divinely shaped and situated within formations of power (i.e., monarchy) that were themselves divinely ordained.[2]

As articulated by Enlightenment thinkers, possessive individualism legitimated a liberal political economy founded on "the conception of the individual as a private being."[3] Liberalism's origin myth of autonomous, rational individuals entering into contract with one another to protect their property ("contract theory") underwrote the revolutionary political system of eighteenth-century republicanism, which is perhaps best understood as tempering liberalism's more centrifugal tendencies. The republicanism crafted in the United States conceived of selfhood as deriving from labor; economic autonomy (ownership of oneself and the yield of one's labor) stood as the guarantor of virtue, and hence the criterion of citizenship.[4] As it undermined the bases of the *ancien régime*, republican contract theory provided modern citizens and subjects of capitalism with a new set of justifications for the emerging arrangement of power. The goal of this explanatory system, ideology, was the naturalization and reproduction of that arrangement of power without the need for coercion. Animating this ideology were "freedom," "liberty," and "self-determination," idealized concepts that obscured the new systems of disciplinary control that surpassed those of premodernity in scope and effectiveness.[5]

And yet, possessive individualism assumed a capacity and necessity for the mobility of individuals that the premodern order, predicated on stasis and fixity, would have found intolerably corrosive. As I will discuss more fully below, mobility was a key practice by which the autonomous individual enacted his political identity. I use the pronoun "his" intentionally here: possessive individualism, it must be noted, was not necessarily incompatible with ascriptive and hierarchical structures of social organization. In colonial America and the early republic, for example, the denial of personhood to women and nonwhite people revealed individualism to be practicable only by a small minority. This exclusion was less a blind spot than an enabling condition. As several contemporary scholars have noted, individualism as a social imaginary *required* that some people be denied the elemental self-possession of the autonomous individual, the latter demonstrated in the ability to own and control one's laboring capacity and issue, and to move oneself outward across geographical space or upward through socioeconomic strata.[6] Haunting the republican imagination was the condition of dependence, which, according to Jefferson, "begets subservience and venality, suffocates the germ of virtue, and prepares fit tools for the designs of ambition."[7]

Racialized slavery and gendered dependency—both conditions of immobility—ensured, as they threw into relief, the independence of white, propertied, and male freeholders. The slave had no proprietorship in his own body—that first component of liberty—and hence was rendered incapable of securing and defending the property rights that anchored possessive individualism. The condition of being owned represented in republicanism "only a more dramatic, more bizarre variation of the condition of all who had lost the power of self-determination."[8] Women's status in republican ideology, as Linda Kerber and others have shown, was a distinctively complex and in some senses empowered one; yet ultimately woman's supposedly biological and emotional traits attenuated her independence, hence her virtue, and hence her fitness for citizenship.[9] For white men of few means, the ideology of possessive individualism compelled securing one's independence through productive labor, and eventually assuming the figure of the paterfamilias that anchored the "political culture" of republicanism.[10] The remarkably durable model of subjectivity conceived in the early republic established a standard for future models; most, as we shall see, have been found wanting in comparison.

## emersonian individualism and market culture

Individualism was conceptualized retrospectively, beginning with the self-conscious discourse on the new—and by most accounts deleterious— social ethic developed in the Atlantic world in the early nineteenth century. Visiting from France in 1831, Alexis de Tocqueville noted with dismay Americans' propensity to think of themselves as "standing alone," owing nothing to ancestors or contemporaries. The pejorative neologism "individualism" described the atomizing tendencies in American democracy at odds with the classical republican ideal of the virtuous citizen. Tocqueville admonished against this "mature and calm feeling, which disposes each member of the community to sever himself from the mass of his fellow-creatures; and to draw apart with his family and friends; so that, after he has thus formed a little circle of his own, he willingly leaves society at large to itself." In the decades that followed, however, philosophers and theorists of political economy in the United States began to affirm individualism as a basis for a just social order.[11]

For example, the romantic transcendentalist doctrine developed by Tocqueville's contemporary Ralph Waldo Emerson asserted individualism as the proper ethic of the authentic and autonomous self. Adding an emphatically American perspective to European Enlightenment thinkers' philosophical and political privileging of the "natural individual," Emerson limned an idealized modern disposition that twentieth-century historians and cultural critics would echo with theorizations of "the sovereign self," "the American character," the "nineteenth-century mind," or "inner-directed man."[12] Emerson's work, with its "extravagant claims for the powers of the individual," spoke to the leveling impulses emergent in Jacksonian America.[13] Responding to a protean nineteenth-century America—unmoored from premodern custom by industrialization, urbanization, and the rise of mass ballot democracy, and struggling with the odious practice of chattel slavery—Emerson spun a "doctrine of the infinitude of the private man" as a resource for both engaging and escaping contemporary life.

Emerson's individualist exhortations were well suited to a burgeoning market culture that weakened traditional forms of association and restraints on individual desire and ambition.[14] Absent these centripetal forces, how would morality and society be maintained? "The great man," Emerson wrote in his 1841 essay "Self-Reliance," "is he who in the midst of the crowd keeps with perfect sweetness the independence of solitude." Indeed, the society that emerges in the essay is baleful and constricting, a corporate juggernaut "in conspiracy against the manhood of its members."[15] Yet implicit here, and growing in emphasis in Emerson's later thought, is the paradoxical belief that the self-reliant individual who preserves his solitude simultaneously generates social unity and harmony. In Emerson we see the archetypal individual and social imaginary of liberalism, the atomic, mobile, and acquisitive energies which republicanism mitigated. And yet the individualism that develops in Emerson's thought achieves a strangely centripetal character, as it convenes a social formation that "enforces conformity at the very moment it extols individuality."[16]

Later in the century, liberal thinkers such as John Stuart Mill, William Graham Sumner, and Herbert Spencer exalted individualism and advocated for the state a minimal role as the guarantor of formal negative freedom and the enforcer of contract relations. These patterns of thought owed much to Adam Smith's eighteenth-century elaboration of the "invisible hand"—a natural mechanism that naturally orders and balances the seemingly chaotic actions of self-interested individuals—and to the evolutionary theory of Charles Darwin. Darwin provided a biological analogue of the liberals' fundamentally atomistic social universe, in which the exceptional individual was the lever of all economic, intellectual, and ethical progress.[17]

## modernity's mobile individuals

The historian Frederick Jackson Turner's 1893 essay "The Significance of the Frontier in American History" attributed the nation's democratic characteristics to its vastness and purported emptiness, and the consequent high degree of mobility of its people. Even as Turner sounded the elegy for the frontier, he looked to mobility for the continuation of American exceptionalism. "He would be a rash prophet indeed," he wrote, "who should assert that the expansive character of American life has now entirely ceased. Movement has been its dominant fact, and, unless this training has no effect upon a people, the American energy will continually demand a wider field for its exercise."[18] Commentators before and after Turner have also found in mobility—especially its volitional form, travel—the genius of modernity and the signature of the sovereign self.

The geographer Eric Leed, for example, has analyzed "travel as a demonstration of freedom and means to autonomy," arguing that

> the right to travel had entered into the Western definition of the
> free autonomous individual whose associations to others are
> a result of conscious acts of connection, of allegiance and con-
> tract. . . . [T]he voluntariness of departure, the freedom implicit
> in the indeterminacies of mobility, the pleasure of travel free from
> necessity, the notion that travel signifies autonomy and is a means
> for demonstrating what one "really" is independent of one context
> or set of defining associations—remain the characteristics of the
> modern conception of travel.[19]

The past four centuries of Western thought abound with examples to corroborate Leed's claims. Marx and Engels famously pointed out that the narratives and practices of obligation and fixity (in space and class) that had characterized premodernity gave way in modernity to an emancipatory lexicon of rights and mobility; the eighteenth-century English jurist William Blackstone included "'the power of locomotion' free of arbitrary restraint" in his enumeration of English constitutional rights. As Emerson had proclaimed that everything good is on the highway, Walt Whitman paid more thorough tribute to the open road:

> From this hour, freedom!
> From this hour I ordain myself loos'd of limits and imaginary lines,
> Going where I list, my own master, total and absolute,
> Listening to others, considering well what they say,
> Pausing, searching, receiving, contemplating,
> Gently, but with undeniable will, divesting myself of the holds that
>     would hold me.[20]

More recently, the political scientist Leslie Dale Feldman has identified a particularly American strain of liberalism derived from the work of Thomas Hobbes that conceives of the freedom to *move* as primary and essential to a range of other rights. The historian James Oliver Robertson describes a similar linkage in American culture in his assertion that "a free American in pursuit of happiness . . . is *mobile,* is, has been, will be, in motion"; as does the sociologist Gerald L. Houseman, who argues that "the intrinsic relationship between movement and personal freedom is verified by historical experience which ranges from feudalism to the contrasting conditions of black and white settlement in America, from Horatio Alger dreams of maximum mobility, social as well as physical, to the hopeless finality of Dachau."[21]

Mobility's status as a right—liberalism's conceptual stock in trade— also owes to capitalism. Raymond Williams historicized mobility as "essentially an impulse formed in the breakdown and dissolution of older and smaller kinds of settlement and productive labor."[22] Inasmuch as capitalism has depended upon the availability of a large pool of labor willing to move across distances small and great, mobility has been extolled culturally as a salutary and enriching characteristic. Indeed, capitalism communicates its ethos using tropes of motion, as in the capitalist who "hustles" for profit and cultivates the image of himself as a "mover" (an image that, as Benjamin Franklin pointed out, is itself a form of capital). Acts of production, consumption, and commodification—even the worker's alienation of her labor power and her sale of it—are ultimately acts of transport.

Mobility is ostensibly a universal right; yet it has been and remains a perquisite of social, political, and economic power, insofar as its true goal is "not movement as such; it is *access to people and facilities.*"[23] As Mark Simpson points out, "To the extent that mobility is not so much a common resource as a social and material resource crucial to the production and reproduction . . . of national, raced, engendered, classed subjectivities, it becomes the locus of contest."[24] The volitional mobility of the knight-errant, pilgrim, entrepreneur, or tourist—"someone who has the security and privilege to move about in relatively unconstrained ways"— throws into relief the unsanctioned motion of vagrants or tramps (those in possession of the volatile, expansive subjectivity the historian Patricia Fumerton distinguishes as "unsettled"), the coerced mobility of the nomad, undocumented worker, or refugee (as in the forced removal of Native Americans), and the circumscribed mobility of the disabled, racial others (as in the Black Codes and Jim Crow statutes), the poor, and women.[25] As a component of male prerogative, mobility has traditionally depended, Leed and others have observed, on "the sessility of women."[26] Scholars such as Clifford, Doreen Massey, Janet Wolff, Annette Kolodny, and Sidonie Smith have further explored mobility as a deeply gendered practice and form of capital, asking how and why, in Smith's words, "'the traveler' has remained endurably 'masculine'" and "modes of motion [are] identified with masculine competencies."[27]

## consolidation and the challenge of the social self

Disciples of individualism held that, in the words of one 1900 author, Evander Bradley McGilvary, "there is a core of selfhood in each person, which is not constituted by relation to anything else outside."[28] This claim was fundamental to a political economy rooted in yeoman self-reliance, artisanal production, and proprietary capitalism. Yet much of the philosophy and rising social science of the nineteenth century mounted an epistemological, political, and ethical challenge against individualism and the liberal view of society as nothing more than an aggregation of individuals who were themselves presocial "uncaused causes."[29] For example, Robert Owen's 1813 *A New View of Society,* perhaps the first sustained articulation of socialism, denied the doctrine of possessive individualism and affirmed a rigid determinism, insisting that the individual "never did, nor is it possible he ever can, form his own character."[30] Karl Marx and

Friedrich Engels gave this assertion increased scope and sophistication, insisting that individuality was "an expression and confirmation of *social life*," and that "the more deeply we go back into history, the more does the individual . . . appear as dependent, as belonging to a greater whole." The natural individual, Marx maintained, had been conjured by bourgeois philosophers as the embodiment and vehicle of their theories of economic order and political sovereignty; it was imperative that this ideological figment "be swept out of the way, and made impossible" as part of the *telos* of historical materialism.[31] In the United States, the Turner thesis reached, by an alternative route, the same conclusion of many social scientists and radical philosophers; namely, that individual autonomy was not primal but rather required specific historical, social, and even geographical conditions for its exercise—conditions that were now vanishing.

A forceful critique of individualism responded to the conditions created by postbellum consolidation—the concentration of political power in the federal government and of economic power in large industrial firms backed by finance capital. The entrepreneurial capitalism plied and justified by the figure of the autonomous individual stagnated in the 1870s as the capital gains brought by proletarianization shrunk, leading firms to merge and vertically integrate, and to lower workers' wages. The years between the end of the Civil War and World War I saw some of the most violent and consequential confrontations between labor and capital in U.S. history, as workers organized to challenge the lowering of wages and the deskilling and mechanization of work. Yet despite American labor's radical collective struggle, its rhetoric remained well within the hegemonic frame of eighteenth-century political economy, evincing what a number of scholars have called "working-class republicanism."[32] The 1890s saw consolidation's discontents express their resistance politically in populism, which, recapitulating republican fears of dependency, sought to restore Jefferson's utopia of sovereign selfhood anchored by artisanal production and decentralized institutions of government and finance. Yet the challenge mounted by labor groups and populists over the last two decades of the nineteenth century failed to stop consolidation, which, as one political scientist noted in 1897, "menace[d] seriously the stability and permanence of the individual as a social unit."[33]

The manifest interdependence of American life at the end of the nineteenth century inaugurated a sweeping cultural discourse elegizing the autonomous individual. "The principle of individualism . . . has been forced to abdicate its seat of authority," wrote the economist Henry C. Adams in 1887. The next year, the philosopher Thomas Whittaker began an overview of current American political economy by asserting the "theoretical and practical . . . movement away from what is called 'Individualism.'" [34] Social science during this time turned "from the idea of the individual as a solitary being" toward a focus on the determining agency of environmental contexts. [35] Such a conception derived from the antifoundational epistemology of American pragmatism and feminism, radical ways of thinking that challenged "the historic premise of the innate stability of the individual" with "a new social psychology that derived personality from the close contexts of society." [36] Theorists such as William James, John Dewey, Jane Addams, George Herbert Mead, Jessie Taft, Charles Peirce, Josiah Royce, and Charles Horton Cooley asserted communication and association as the matrices from which the self emerges and grows. [37] Like the individualists, subscribers to this new view of self-formation found corroboration in Darwinian evolutionary theory, specifically the claim that the form and fate of an organism are shaped by its immediate environment. Although pragmatists rejected individualism's axiomatic claim of the primacy of individual subjectivity, they preserved in their prescriptive analyses the liberal emphasis on the human capacity for freedom.

## taylorism and the demise of sovereign selfhood

Even as individualism's decline disrupted settled patterns of thought and practice, a growing chorus of business and political elites heralded a new political economy based not on independence but cooperation. Many elites enthusiastically repudiated the gospel of individualism that had, ironically, legitimated their imperial position. William Graham Sumner, for example, had by 1900 made a striking volte-face from his earlier defense of liberal individualism, proclaiming the "more perfect integration of all societal functions" under the aegis of the corporation. George Perkins of J. P. Morgan lectured Columbia University students in 1908 on the backwardness of the "wholly self-seeking and ruinous" individualism of the past, and its replacement by "constructive and uplifting" cooperation among individuals under the aegis of the corporation. "The day of the combination is here to stay," declared John D. Rockefeller. "Individualism is gone, never to return." Articulating his early political values, Woodrow Wilson affirmed in 1906 socialism's capacities to counterbalance an obsolete individualism that, he wrote, "has much about it that is hateful, too hateful to last." [38]

Frederick Winslow Taylor's scientific management theory, developed over the last two decades of the nineteenth century and first publicized in 1895, made explicit the fading of individualism. Taylor sought to increase productivity through precise delineation, measurement, surveillance, and enforcement of workers' activities. The engineer regarded his proposed reduction of the laborer to an interchangeable machine part without much pathos: "In the past," he wrote in *The Principles of Scientific Management* (1911), "man had been first; in the future the system must be first." Contemporary economic life, he stressed, required "cooperation, not individualism."[39] Taylorism may be seen as the culmination of the trajectory of alienation from work, and hence from one's authentic self, that began with proletarianization. Reaching beyond the spaces of industrial work, Taylorism spread, in the twentieth century, to a variety of institutions, offering techniques of management and observation that had as their end the construction and governance of efficient and flexible subjects.

Scientific management replaced the erstwhile regulating structures of craftsman autonomy and workers' guild codes with rationally determined standards monitored by a new class of university-trained bureaucratic managers allied with ownership. The authority of science, the economist Robert Hoxie wrote in his excoriating 1915 critique of Taylorism, "put the individual worker at a disadvantage in any attempt to question the justice of the demands made upon him."[40] Workers' resentment over their disempowerment, loss of autonomy, and coercion into more rapid and precise work was offset by monetary incentives such as Ford's eight-hour, five-dollar workday (implemented in 1914), and, as a number of scholars have argued, by the material satisfactions of a nascent consumer culture created and sustained by the increasing availability and affordability of mass-produced goods.[41]

Taylorism's transformation of the spaces and nature of work salted the earth in which the ideological models of selfhood—the autonomous individual of liberalism and the virtuous citizen of republicanism—were rooted. As the British economist Sidney Webb observed in 1891, heteronomy, not autonomy, characterized the contemporary laborer: "from a self-governing producing unit, he passed into a mere item in a vast industrial army over the organization and direction of which he had no control."[42] If self-directed productive labor was the font of the self, what species of self would emerge from Taylorized labor? Taylor himself likened workers to oxen and incorrigible children, a stubborn mass that cared mostly about retaining its own control and working as little and as slowly as possible; and yet, one of the ironic effects of Taylorization was the *individualization* its careful prescriptions of motion and speed effected in each laborer. This phenomenon, which Mark Seltzer has described as "disciplinary individualism," isolated the worker from collectivities as it brought bodies and dispositions under more rigorous managerial control, not so much immobilizing them as setting them into motion determined by the system.[43] Although, as several theorists have pointed out, workers resisted this control regime, its ultimate achievement was internalization by workers, which managers lauded as "responsible autonomy" (a concept I will examine in detail below). The Taylorized factory (and white-collar office) culminated the shift between an institutional mode Foucault distinguished as the "discipline-blockade"—peripheral, local, charged with "arresting evil"— and that of the "discipline-mechanism"—in which universal surveillance and "subtle coercion" are internalized.[44] Indeed, Taylor averred, in an adage long preceding Foucault, that the "product of a factory is not materials, but men."[45]

But what type of men? The price of Taylorized labor appeared to be manhood itself. One of the reasons male workers who were identified as white—those most readily "hailed" as the sovereign selves of republicanism—resisted the implementation of conditions of surveillance and timing was the latter's resemblance to the regime under which women and people of color labored. Taylor's infamous dialogue with "Schmidt" in *Principles of Scientific Management,* in which he explains to a hypothetical, presumably immigrant worker that the way to higher wages (becoming a "high-priced man") requires submission and obedience to the manager, rehearses the dynamics of slavery. "If you are a high-priced man," Taylor tells Schmidt, "you will do exactly as this man tells you to-morrow, from morning till night. . . . Do you understand that? When this man tells you to walk, you walk; when he tells you to sit down, you sit down, and you don't talk back at him."[46] The control by managers of Schmidt and his brethren made their assumption of republican personhood impossible. Such abjection was likely on the mind of Edward Cadbury, the chocolate producer and critic of Taylorism, who in 1914 characterized the workplace scientific management had shaped as one in which "initiative and judgement and freedom of movement are eliminated."[47]

If, as the theorist Rey Chow has written, "one of the chief sources of the oppression of women lies in the way they have been consigned to visuality," the crisis of subjectivity occasioned by consolidation was simultaneously a crisis of male and white superiority.[48] Under the auspices of Taylorism, critics asserted, male white workers were evacuated of their formerly and naturally authoritative, robust, creative, and mobile traits, and reduced to the stereotypical docility, sessility, and subservience of women and slaves. Period sources and labor historiography abound with vignettes of male workers' resentment of and resistance to Taylorist humiliations, both on the shop floor and in management's intrusion into home life, leisure, and even sexual practices in the name of legibility and corrigibility. Accounts of the Taylorization of the factory work of women, provisionally white immigrants, and/or people of color, however, tend to convey a labor sensibility so accustomed to being scrutinized, hectored, and driven by bosses that the rational domination of scientific management constitutes nothing terribly new, and may even bring relief.[49] Drawing on psychoanalytic and literary theory, James Livingston has characterized the imaginary inaugural moment of Taylorized labor as a "primal scene" in much American historiography. This moment of male workers' reduction to automatons brings not merely disempowerment, but emasculation and ocular "penetration," or at the very least a politically debilitating effeminacy.[50]

How significant was Taylorization? It certainly altered the conditions of labor for skilled white male workers in the United States. Yet as Hindy Lauer Schachter has suggested, the "Golden Age" of craftsman autonomy before 1840 is at least in part an embellishment on the part of workers' organizations, historians, and Marxist labor-process theorists. She and other scholars have cast doubt, moreover, on the degree to which actual Taylorist management, as opposed to Taylor's *theories*, found purchase in American industry, and whether work has in fact been degraded and deskilled under corporate capitalist mass production.[51] While such critiques are valuable, they tend, like the labor process theory they oppose or modify, to forestall the tragedy of republican subjectivity—autonomy is still within workers' reach, or Taylorization really wasn't so bad—rather than to historicize it.

My purpose here, however, is not to uphold or refute the account of lost producer autonomy developed in the late nineteenth century (and rehearsed by the historians and cultural critics more or less ever since), but to mark its ubiquity, persistence, and generative power.[52] Like the world-historical concept of possessive individualism itself, the significance of the declension narrative of sovereign selfhood depended not on its historical verifiability but on its capacity to evoke a utopian vision, or register its impossibility. I am less interested in whether or not Taylorization actually effected such a diminution of republican selfhood and masculine prerogative (and with them national distinction) than in the proliferation of its primal scene as cultural text—as, to paraphrase Clifford Geertz, a story we tell ourselves about ourselves. Specifically, my interest is in the ways in which the trauma of Taylorization necessitated the ideological production of a new, compensatory subjectivity characterized by self-determination.

## toward a new individualism

By the early 1900s, an uneasy consensus that social selfhood expressed the reality of subjectivity had formed. On an ideological level, however, the social self appeared to threaten the sustainability of American capitalism and liberalism, the legitimacy of which derived from the presocial, self-interested individual's contractual consent to their laws, practices, and structures. As the sovereign self lost its justifying force, could the social self step into the breach? Or would the new conception of the self license a socialist shift?[53] A broadly construed reformist sensibility informed by social selfhood was shared by those legal, social, and political theorists, philosophers, and activists loosely affiliated under the banner of progressivism. Antagonistic to laissez-faire ideology and the ways in which it both justified and occulted the monopolistic developments in economic life, progressives rejected the species of individualism that superintended market society and procedural politics. However, beyond shared suspicion of concentrated capitalist power and confidence in the modern state's ability to remedy social and economic problems, progressives were, generally speaking, split between those who advocated more totalizing mechanisms of social control and those who sought to refurbish individual freedom by cultivating institutions committed to social justice and democracy.[54]

Progressives struggled with the question of what a post-individualist society would look like. Given the dominance of the republican model of selfhood—which defined citizenship as the coefficient of productive labor and the stewardship of its fruits—in both hegemonic and counterhegemonic political practice, it was difficult to imagine what type of politics might be sustained by the social self. Many regarded that entity as capricious, irresolute, and easily gulled, a feminized creature of consumer culture, advertising, mass media, and the deskilling of labor. To what could it consent? To what *wouldn't* it consent? Walter Lippmann, for example, decried the "intellectual ascendancy of the collectivist movement" that had promulgated the social self model. This lament, echoing Jefferson's condemnation of dependency, dovetailed with Lippmann's assertion of the tractability of public opinion: to the degree that the self was social, he felt, it also tended to be mediocre, ill-informed, and subject to the seductions of product advertisers and demagogues; a nation of "mass men" therefore required not more democracy but more meticulous control of information and the political guidance of mandarins.[55]

A more hopeful strain of progressivism, which included the pragmatists, emphasized the democratic potentials of a more corporate (which they tended to inflect as "cooperative") society, seeing proletarianization as, in James Livingston's interpretation, "an irreversible historical fact that multiplies the possibilities of subjectivity."[56] They remained optimistic about the potentials for individuality in such developments as urbanization, bureaucratic organization, immigration, and communication and transportation technologies—the new associational structures of modernity. At the same time, these progressives leapt to the defense of the individual against the new and immense combinations of power. Hence William James's sentiments in an 1899 letter: "The bigger the unit you deal with, the hollower, the more brutal, the more mendacious is the life displayed"; and Woodrow Wilson's similar assertion, in 1914, that "law in our day must come to the assistance of the individual."[57]

Indeed, as Otis L. Graham noted, progressives were "individualists at heart—the word 'individualism' appears hundreds of times in their literature."[58] The individualistic idiom was evident in works such as Herbert Croly's influential *The Promise of American Life* (1909). Croly sought to replace the destructive and narrowly economic and "Jeffersonian" individualism of the past with a more democratic and "constructive individuality," in which the individual realized himself not through isolation and escape, but through action that effects some type of "social amelioration."[59] Croly's contemporaries, among them James, Dewey, Cooley, Lewis Mumford, and Charles Beard, similarly reconceived individualism to emphasize the individual's fulfillment through participation in various types of communities, replacing the narrowly negative conception of freedom with a more substantive form predicated on the satisfaction of physical, intellectual, and emotional needs.

As they repudiated the corrosive "pecuniary culture" and a narrowly procedural politics of abstract rights, pragmatist philosophers sought to pour a new and vital social ethos into individualism's rhetorical vessel. Yet a satisfactory prototype was elusive. As Jeffrey Sklansky has observed of Charles Cooley's thought, "The central social problem in an age of capital was not that economic self-reliance was increasingly unattainable for a majority of Americans, but that they nevertheless clung to that idea in the absence of any clearly conceived alternative."[60] Like Croly, Cooley disparaged the "lower 'individualism' of our time," advocating instead an understanding of individual freedom as the "*opportunity for right development, for* development in accordance with the progressive ideal of life that we have in conscience." [61] Rendering a compelling image of that freedom posed a dilemma, a consequence of the pragmatists' insistence on the priority of the social to the subject: they could not begin their reconstruction of society as the Enlightenment *philosophes* had—with a proleptic subjectivity—if subjectivity was in fact the product rather than the basis of society. Elaborating the "new individualism" flummoxed Dewey, who wrote in his 1929 treatment of the issue, "I am not anxious to depict the form which this emergent individualism will assume. Indeed, I do not see how it can be described until more progress has been made in its production." [62]

Articulating a viable new subjectivity was paramount to both progressive reform and the legitimacy of a corporate capitalist regime. Commentators of all stripes agreed that the denouement of sovereign selfhood had brought about a state of, in Geertz's words, "conceptual confusion, in which the established images of political order [had] fade[d] into irrelevance or [were] driven into disrepute." [63] Yet as James, Dewey, and other pragmatists struggled to describe the new and propitious forms of subjectivity that might emerge in corporate society as an element of their more ambitious and radical project of democratic reconstruction, an alternative and ultimately more successful effort was being mounted by business corporations, advertisers, and consumer sociologists. These figures and institutions shared with pragmatists a sense of proletarianization's obdurate presence and an enthusiasm about the consequent decentering of republican selfhood. Yet in contrast to the pragmatists' iconoclasm, these proponents of consumer modernity sought to reproduce the familiar and heroic individualism of the past, the symbols and narratives of which remained rooted in republican ideology. Aiming for an analogue of the autonomous individual and virtuous citizen for the age of the corporation and consumer culture, this approach had the more conventional objective of justifying things as they were.

## the unashamed individualist

The proliferation of Taylorism and bureaucracy in the early twentieth century failed to diminish what William H. Whyte would describe in 1956 as "the public worship of individualism." [64] But individualism's implacability and ubiquity in Progressive Era public discourse obscured how the concept had been altered. These years saw the republican creed of self-reliance refigured as an ethos compelling performative self-expression and distinction, reconciling the subject to membership in the organization and promoting acquiescence to social and political norms. This transformation was well under way by 1908, when Theodore Roosevelt (himself a progressive of sorts) adamantly defended a creed that if voiced only two decades earlier would have sounded oxymoronic—the "wise and regulated individualism" that anchored the platform of the Republican Party.[65]

The boom years of the 1920s saw a myriad of analyses and defenses of individualism issuing from social science, popular literature, political rhetoric, the pulpit, and journalism.[66] One remarkable example was Herbert Hoover's 1922 treatise *American Individualism,* which combined a rearguard defense of an anachronistic creed with a prescription for accommodation to the corporate age. In it Hoover doggedly upheld "the actual permanent and persistent motivation of our civilization," individualism, one of the "five or six great social philosophies" currently battling for global supremacy. Though the text largely rehearsed truisms about national equality of opportunity and the incentive to achievement, it is striking for its polemic against "those theorists who denounce our individualism as a social basis." Hoover reiterated the claim that "intelligence, character, courage, and the divine spark of the human soul are alone the property of individuals. These do not lie in agreements, in organizations, in institutions, in masses, or in groups. They abide alone in the individual mind and heart." Having absorbed the hard lessons of recent history, "the backwash and misery of war. . . . economic disintegration . . . social disintegration . . . political dislocation," Hoover proclaimed that "from it all, I emerge an individualist—an unashamed individualist."[67]

Yet Hoover advocated no simple return to laissez-faire liberalism. In crafting a viable analogue of the pioneer ethos of the nineteenth century, Hoover exemplified the strategy of adaptation and cooptation with which capitalist hegemony responded to the legitimation crisis brought about by consolidation and its symptom, social selfhood. Though *American Individualism* championed what Dewey, Croly, and others condemned as the dominant "pecuniary culture," Hoover distinguished the current enlightened version of capitalism from the predatory and anarchic capitalism of the past. He noted approvingly how under a capitalism that stressed "cooperation," one saw "the initiative of self-interest blended with a sense of service."[68] If one component of classical republicanism had been an insistence on self-reliance, Hoover stressed the more civic strand of the individual's fulfillment through and responsibility to collectives, wedding the affective power of individualism to the organization, to which the former was no longer oppositional.

Here was Dewey's new individualism, without the ambivalence or the radical critique. Hoover's formulation made the republican (and progressive) claim that individuals achieve true selfhood only in the context of service to community equivalent to the Taylorist subsumption of individuals to the corporate productive enterprise. Hoover's individualism—he added the prefix "rugged" while on the presidential campaign trail in 1928—turned, in Walter Benn Michaels's words, "the independent individual's disruptive energies into the organized individual's ambitious energies." Michaels stresses the growing propensity, over the early decades of the twentieth century, to conceive of the organization as granting rather than diluting individuality. Yet that individuality, once defined by the inflexible self's autonomy from and resistance to Emerson's "joint-stock company" of the social, became increasingly the index of one's difference and distinctive place within an organized system.[69]

Yet for all his enthusiasm for a subjectivity that looked a great deal like the social self, Hoover did not title his text *American Socialism*. Rather, he and other fabricators of the new individualism marshaled an older heroic and nationalist language. Hence Hoover's avowals of his own "unashamed individualism" (presumably in contrast to the ashamed variety), speaking individualism back into relevancy as a "social basis" despite its dubiety. Even as Hoover and others bade farewell to the autonomous individual of the past, they affirmed the continuing vitality of that subjectivity's cardinal trait of self-determination. If the spaces of work no longer made "individuals" in the archaic sense, modernity offered a wealth of opportunities for the fashioning and performance of something like a sovereign self: independence could be reclaimed in practices that evoked the hardship and "ruggedness" of the pioneer past; and autonomy could be retrieved through acts of consumption.

## expressive individualism and consumer culture

*American Individualism* thus participated in a many-named process described by historians, social scientists, philosophers, and literary artists over the past hundred years; that is, the transition from a nineteenth-century "mode of subjection" preoccupied with the hewing of "character" to those based in the elaboration of "personality"—from "self-determination" to "fulfillment"; from "salvation" to "self-realization"; from "inner-directed" to "other-directed" patterns of "social character"; or from "utilitarian" or "economic" to "expressive" individualism. This latter term is, perhaps, redundant: all strains of individualism are expressive inasmuch as they depend on rhetoric, spectacular practices, and institutions for their performative iteration.[70] Each form, however, sanctioned different performances and goals: in contrast to the utilitarian individualism of proprietary capitalism, propelling the individual upward through strata of wealth and power, expressive individualism emphasized, as Winfried Fluck writes, "the search for self-realization. Its major issues were no longer those of economic success or the promise of the social recognition of one's probity, but the assertion of personal difference, that is, the ability of the individual to assert his or her own uniqueness and otherness against the powers of cultural convention and encroaching disciplinary regimes."[71]

Whence this uniqueness and otherness? In an era of standardization, the crucial project of the self was that of exteriorizing interiors, giving expression to the unexpressed, making visible the unseen. The political scientist Char Miller has observed that the alienating discipline of the Taylorized workplace (and barracks and classroom) led, ironically, to the cultivation of "a secret, hidden self, scarcely elaborated in action and capable of possessing unseen emotions and desires."[72] Antonio Gramsci, in *The Prison Notebooks*, described a similar scenario, whereby a work regime of "mere mechanical routine" fosters in the worker "a state of complete freedom."[73] Beneath a strictly enforced yet superficial conformity, people's interiors were singular and not (yet) legible to "disciplinary regimes." As the sociologist Irene Taviss Thomson has shown, the social criticism of popular periodicals and advice books of the 1920s fairly obsessed over the individual's need to express an inner self over against the dictates of society. The encouragement of self-expression, Eugene Dimnet advised in the best-selling *The Art of Thinking* (1929), "ought to be our chief concern."[74] Yet this expression of the distinctive inner self was to have a centripetal rather than a centrifugal effect. Presaging the social criticism of the cold war, the criticism of the 1920s hypothesized the good society as that which enabled the healthy "rebellion" of its members.

That rebellion was to be a depoliticized one. Expressive individualism, with its emphasis on feelings, difference, and fulfillment, discouraged a conception of self, and therefore a politics, based on productive labor and class identity. The regimented shop floor and bureaucratic office seemed ill-suited to expressive individualism; rather, that ethos held that "realizing one's full humanity required some escape from work."[75] Instead, the rising consumer culture provided the resources for the construction and performance of a distinctive individual identity, a message sounded incessantly by an increasingly sophisticated advertising industry. Coming into its recognizably modern "scientific" form by the 1920s, that industry called forth in consumers fundamentally political anxieties—regarding class status, gender identity, and agency—which advertisers depicted as soluble through consumption. Indeed, consumer capitalism's genius lay in its apparent ability to meliorate politically significant polarities of wealth and access to goods, and to open to workers new avenues to the good life.[76] According to many elites, the "industrial democracy" of the early twentieth century had made class-based political action unnecessary. By the 1920s, media celebrations of newly arrived members of the middle class, their combative politics exchanged for creature comforts and respectability, testified to the happy demise of a labor movement seeking anything more than its slice of the pie.[77] Here consumption offered a direct link to republican citizenship, understood as a material stake in the stability of the current order.

In one sense, then, citizenship was conflated with owning; in another, the essential practice of the citizen was that of choosing. Yet the act of choosing, if the consumer was to be heroized, had to carry with it a political valence; it had to be represented as an exercise in sovereignty rather than the effect of manipulation. As discussed above, the social self of consumer culture met with disdain for its association with stereotypically feminine traits of mercuriality, vanity, malleability, and visibility. However necessary to the current order, this creature was no *citizen* in the republican sense. The solution lay in adapting the crucial political attribute of (masculine) self-determination to a world of abundance. To this end, as the historian Charles McGovern has argued, early advertisers established a figure of the "sovereign consumer" in an effort to divert "emphasis from the freedom from state power over lives and property to freedom for self-cultivation and, ultimately, freedom of choice among already selected brands and goods."[78] This figure, featured in advertisements for a myriad of products from soap to clothing to automobiles, merged the expressive individual of the marketplace with the autonomous individual of republican political culture, offering reassurance that a subjectivity distinguished by self-determination had survived the transition from the old to the new regime of accumulation. It was a social self, but it looked like a sovereign self. Its characteristics were mobility and choice; and its embodiment was the driver.

chapter two

# Workmen's Compensation, Women's Emancipation: The Promise of Automobility, 1895–1929

As long as motor cars were few in number, he who had one was a king: he could go where he pleased and halt where he pleased; and this machine itself appeared as a compensatory device for enlarging an ego that had been shrunken by our very success in mechanization.
    —Lewis Mumford[1]

## accounting for automobility

In 1900, there were some eight thousand registered automobiles in the United States; by 1929, the number was over 23.1 million.[2] Whence the demand for the automobile? It seems strange even to ask the question, since in the United States the automobile, in the words of the historian Kristin Ross, has been for so many years "completely integrated into the banality of the everyday"; it presents itself as one of the "goods whose habitual use effectively removed them from the discursive realm."[3] Still, the question remains worth posing. Even the authoritative texts analyzing the first decades of automobility have either ignored it or answered it too summarily. Assumptions of inevitability permeate most accounts of the rise of automobility, occluding the cultural exigency that I want to emphasize here.[4]

The first motorists in the United States were Gilded Age elites, whose desire for display was fulfilled by staging exclusive races, auto gymkhanas, and extravagant auto shows. Depictions of the automobile in the press of the era reveal an uncertainty about the machine's significance. Was it the harbinger of new era, or simply proof of the infantility and effeminacy of the rich? In 1899, *Harper's Weekly* reported that

> this season, for the first time, we have become familiar with the lighter types of self-propelling vehicles, guided on the streets by their owners or their owners' servants, and used for pleasure or private convenience. There is a new, expensive toy in the world, which is handy and amusing, and which the well-to-do will proceed to experiment with, while their less opulent brethren congratulate themselves in being able to go without it without inconvenience or serious regret.[5]

Almost immediately after its appearance, however, the car was identified as the focal point of an increasingly anxious and strident class politics, as well as an exacerbator of urban/rural tensions and a threat to public health.

Like the bicycle before it, the automobile's entry into established urban and rural traffic patterns had an imperiousness about it. The low number of auto-related fatalities at this time (1900 saw 96) belied the offense it caused among the "less opulent." Woodrow Wilson commented in 1906 that "nothing has spread socialistic feeling in this country more than the use of automobiles. To the countryman they are a picture of arrogance of wealth with all its independence and carelessness." The same year, Tennessee Representative Thetus Sims channeled rural and working-class antipathy to the horseless carriage in his House-floor tirade against the "rich, reckless, dare-devil young men, driving automobiles simply for pleasure." A 1904 production of Theodore Kremer's play *The Great Automobile Mystery* was lauded for its exploitation of its audiences' hatred for the automobile. Working-class audiences seemed particularly impressed, a reviewer suggested: "up in the gallery you can curse the machine even harder for twenty-five cents." Noting a critic's comment that "I do not like motor cars and never will until I am able to own one," a 1906 issue of *Town & Country* dismissed the "prejudice against motor cars" as "some persons always look[ing] with suspicion at that which they are too poor to possess."[6]

This populist vitriol peaked in 1906; after that, automobile sales began to increase sharply. In 1907, the same *Harper's Weekly* that had, eight years earlier, registered its amusement at the plaything of the rich predicted that the automobile would become "the ready, tireless and faithful servant of man throughout the world where civilization has a home or freedom a banner."[7] By 1910, the 458,500 automobiles registered in the United States provided some credence to *Outing* magazine's claim that there existed "two great divisions of the civilized human race, those who owned machines and the others who would like to."[8]

In explaining the automobile's astronomical growth in the first decades of the twentieth century, most historical works put forth a thesis of utility; they stress (or simply assume) the automobile's facilitation of transport of goods and people in the context of *work* as the key to its adoption. When demand is understood simply as a result of the public's knowledge of the automobile's capacities for work (as a "servant," to borrow from the *Harper's Weekly* quote above), the sharp increase in purchases after 1906 is easily attributed to more efficient production and falling prices, and to the dissemination of this knowledge. James Flink, John Rae, and Michael L. Berger, for example, have argued that the early populist-accented condemnation of the automobile was soon tempered by its increasing use and ownership by farmers and rural doctors, whose association with work and practicality authorized the automobile's transition from trifle to helpmeet, thereby ensuring its entrenchment in American life.[9] Other factors, of course, were the introduction, in 1908, of the low-priced Ford Model T—a machine whose contours and maker fairly radiated utilitarian values—and the perfection of the assembly line in 1913.

The utility thesis finds support in the fact that the earliest automobile advertising stressed product reliability and ease of use rather than the empowering diversions of motoring. The first automobile advertisement in a non-trade publication, for the W. E. Roach Company in a 1900 *Saturday Evening Post,* claimed only that Roach automobiles "give satisfaction."[10] Yet the banality and technical focus of such ads do not necessarily prove that utility was the automobile's selling point; they just as plausibly reflect the advertising and automobile industries' fledgling condition. As the historian Pamela Walker Laird has argued, early automobile advertising amounted largely to product information. It was not until the 1920s, when General Motors chairman Alfred Sloan transformed the auto industry by diversifying GM's product line, making annual stylistic changes to its models, and marketing to niche consumers, that advertising explicitly invited consumers to link the sovereignty, speed, and thrill of the automobile to the expression of their gendered and classed identities. "It seems anomalous," Laird writes, "that the automobile industry should have dragged its heels so in promoting what we now buy—whether we care to admit it or not—as dream machines and components of our personalities."[11]

Another factor in the traction of the utility thesis was the focus of most historical treatments of early automobility on the workshop and the boardroom. These have tended to privilege the interpretation of the automobile by its creators and industrial producers. The pioneers of the auto industry, as portrayed in most historical accounts, saw cars as mechanisms for transport, not as vehicles for the affirmation of the self; and they represented themselves as technicians, not revolutionaries. Given the inventors' and entrepreneurs' self-representations and their rehearsal in most standard works of automotive history, it is not surprising that the earliest automobile advertising would focus on the technical and demur on the cultural and philosophical meanings of driving and car ownership. Significantly, most of these works display the ideological predispositions and elisions common to contemporary business history—its individualistic worldview, the assumption of the overall rectitude of corporate capitalism, and relative inattention to class and other inequalities.[12]

If advertisers and their industrial clients were initially disinclined to make grand claims about the promise of automobility as an instrument of democratization and individual regeneration, they were virtually alone in their reluctance. As Laird has observed, "apparently automakers did not feel the need to prove that automobility was exciting."[13] In fact, their hardship lay in proving that it was *mundane*. As I will discuss below, automobility's thrilling nature had been established during its earliest years by a myriad of literary and visual artists, journalists, philosophers, and commentators. Much of the thrill these sources described, however, came in the unwanted form of the accidents or breakdowns through mechanical failure or poor performance; hence the industry's early public emphasis on the quality, safety, dependability, and facility of use of its products.

Other analysts of automobility's rise and reign have deployed, instead of or alongside the thesis of utility, explanations stressing the compatibility of the automobile with a transcendent human nature or a slightly less transcendent national ethos. James Flink, for example, characterizes automobility as "rooted in basic human drives." In a similar vein, the popular author M. M. Musselman mused that "the human race is well named. One of its primary emotions seems to be a powerful interest in contests having to do with going from here to yonder in the shortest space of time."[14] In this way historical accounts of automobility resemble nothing so much as the numerous historical accounts of capitalism that see the latter as the culmination of innate human drives and desires, and the present order as the maturity of an "embryo" that always existed.[15]

A variant on the human-nature thesis explains automobility as a natural expression of self-evident and dehistoricized national values. The political scientist James Dunn sees the reign of the automobile as representing "the kind of individualist equality particularly well suited to American values"; by extension, he writes, "the kind of planning, land-use, and auto-restrictive powers needed to stem the tide of automobility are literally, un-American." Leslie Dale Feldman accounts for the automobile's rise by asserting that "any technological invention which facilitated freedom of movement was certain to be prized in America, where Hobbesian atomism and the conception of liberty in terms of freedom *from* impediment were two basic tenets of society."[16] Like the thesis of utility, these claims may not be untrue; but they are insufficient, begging questions of interpretation and historical context. Even if the desire for ever-expanding mobility is in fact universal (or at least an essential component of "American values") we must still attend to how mobility emerges "as a powerful part of social narratives of one kind or another in specific times and places."[17]

In 1895, the first issue of the automotive journal *The Horseless Age* asserted that "those who have taken pains to search below the surface for the great tendencies of the age, know what a giant industry is struggling into being here. All signs point to the motor vehicle as the necessary sequence of methods of locomotion already established and approved. The growing needs of our civilization demand it; the public believe in it, and await with lively interest its practical applications to the daily business of the world."[18] The same year, the *Chicago Times-Herald* predicted that "persons who are inclined . . . to decry the development of the horseless carriage . . . will be forced . . . to recognize it as an admitted mechanical achievement, highly adapted to some of the most urgent needs of our civilization."[19] These statements inaugurate what would become the dominant mode of naturalizing automobility in American life: testifying to its fulfillment of pressing, presumably economic, but at the very least utilitarian needs. But the "urgent needs of our civilization" were also ideological.

Two works analyzing the rise of mass automobility in the United States, the sociologist David Gartman's *Auto-Opium: A Social History of American Automobile Design* and the historian Peter J. Ling's *America and the Automobile: Technology, Reform, and Social Change,* pay particular attention to its social and economic matrix. Insisting that we look to "cultural motives beyond mere utility" in the process of the automobile's adoption, Gartman's Marxist social history depicts automobile consumption by the middle and working classes in the early twentieth century as an important means to those groups' fulfillment of "true needs for self-determining activity."[20] Ling similarly asserts that "any attempt to comprehend the historical significance of the automobile's introduction must also consider its cultural as well as functional appeal."[21]

Both authors recognize, as I do, the automobile as a meliorative response to the crisis of legitimacy in turn-of-the-century capitalism brought about by the Taylorist transformation of production. Gartman's and Ling's theses jibe with recent work on early twentieth-century consumer culture that asserts consumption as the practice through which workers recovered a depoliticized analogue of republican selfhood, thereby preserving the hegemonic order. According to Gartman, corporate capitalists' strategy entailed "culturally integrating the working masses into the realm of private consumption pioneered by the bourgeoisie. . . . The personal autonomy lost at work was recuperated in the realm of consumption, where the proliferation of product brands, models, and styles offered consumers a wide range of choices."[22] To this end the mass-produced but endlessly reconfigured automobile, the culture's most powerful signifier of identity and status, did invaluable work.

Without denying the importance of consumption and ownership to this republican reconstruction, I contend that the crucial practice is *driving*. Ling alludes to "motoring . . . as a therapy which adjusted individuals to the strains of modern life while tying the people concerned more tightly to the existing order" and "as an activity which relied upon personal initiative, gave a sense of independence, and permitted willful individualism."[23] Yet he and Gartman ultimately locate the automobile's "amnestic and compensatory function" in its capacity to sublimate the desire for economic and political change to the promise of individual transformation.[24] Superseding the automobile's utility or its induction of workers into "industrial democracy" were driving's sensations of agency, self-determination, entitlement, privacy, sovereignty, transgression, and speed; these were instrumental in establishing automobility as a public good and thereby ensuring its growth as an apparatus.[25]

Driving provided the means by which the transition described in the previous chapter—from character to personality; from inner-direction to other-direction; from utilitarian to expressive individualism; from sovereign to social selfhood—could be both dramatized and expiated. To the white elites that were automobility's first beneficiaries, driving offered opportunities for the traditional crafting of character through expedition and hardship, even though such crafting took place within a culture of leisure. To middle-class and working-class white men, driving appeared able to deliver an analogue of the sovereign selfhood attenuated by Taylorization and bureaucratic regimentation, and to masculinize consumer identity more generally. For women, immigrants, and people of color, groups whose automobility would be as contested as their fitness for citizenship, the driver's seat beckoned as the crucible of that fitness and as the vantage of the American-in-full. In the United States at the turn of the century, driving a car promised not only transportation, but transformation.

## a lovely activity

What, exactly, happens when one drives? In a 1997 essay, the philosopher Loren E. Lomasky argues that automobility is

> complementary with *autonomy*: the distinctively human capacity to be self-directing. . . . An autonomous being is not simply a locus at which forces collide and which then is moved by them. Rather, to be autonomous is, minimally, to be a valuer with ends taken to be good as such, and to have the capacity as an agent to direct oneself to the realization or furtherance of these ends through actions expressly chosen for that purpose. This is what motorists do. Therefore, insofar as we have reason to regard self-directedness as a valuable human trait, we have reason to think well of driving automobiles. . . . Because automobility is a mode of extending the scope and magnitude of self-direction, it is worthwhile.[26]

Drawing from the same rhetorical well as most automobile advertising after 1920, Lomasky rehearses here the commonsense notion that an individual's operation of a car facilitates freedom and self-improvement. Transportation analyst Melvin Webber concurs in his essay, "The Joys of Automobility": "there can be no question about the automobile's virtues . . . as an instrument of personal freedom." "On the road," echoes the writer Ruth Brandon, "we are transformed: winged, invincible—free." Sam Kazman, an attorney at the neoliberal Competitive Enterprise Institute (with which Lomasky is affiliated), similarly asserts that "convenient as driving may be, it is much, much more than that. It is a lovely activity, and a moral activity." A *Boston Globe* columnist echoes with the claim that "at the deepest level, our cars are a tangible expression of our most important values. Freedom. Choice. Privacy. Individualism. Self-reliance."[27]

The rhetorical affinity with advertising is not surprising given that most of these texts represent a rearguard public-relations campaign, funded directly or indirectly by the automobile and/or petroleum industries, to reaffirm automobility at a time in which its social, economic, and political costs appear intolerably high. Yet they are deeply interesting for the way they reintroduce into discourse the early claims of the promoters of automobility, long after automobility has become a habitual, even compulsory, practice of everyday life. These contemporary evaluations of automobility as "lovely," "moral," and decidedly "worthwhile" to the individual confirm driving's function as what Foucault called a "technology of the self"; that is, a practice that "permit[s] individuals to effect by their own means or with the help of others a certain number of operations on their bodies and souls, thoughts, conduct, and way of being, so as to transform themselves in order to attain a certain condition."[28] The condition developed through this particular technology of the self is a mode of modern self-governance known as *freedom*.

At the turn of the century, even more than today, driving replicated an ancient gesture discussed in the first chapter, that of *moving* to represent oneself as an unfettered and self-directing agent. Early drivers were everywhere assured that, in the words of the historian Warren Belasco, "everything was up to *you*; everything was open, like the road itself."[29] *Outing*, for example, enthused that "this freedom, this independence, this being in the largest possible degree completely master of one's self, constitutes one of the greatest charms of country travel by automobile." "There's nothing in the world to equal travelling on a motorcar," wrote two 1902 motorists, "you're as independent as a bird." Also in 1902, another writer declared that the car had enabled drivers "to really travel again, as free men, free to decide, in the free air." A 1909 *Harper's Weekly* identified the central charm of automobility as "the feeling of independence . . . the ability to go where and when one wills." The same year, an Ohio congressman driving back to his district averred that "it is the independence and . . . the lust for pushing on that are elements in the pleasure of travelling by automobile." "The prospect of new and varied roads," mused Theodore Dreiser as he motored through Indiana in 1916, "appears to make a man independent and give him a choice in life."[30]

These more sanctioned attractants of driving, however, were complemented by the more baneful elements lamented by critics such as Woodrow Wilson. Especially for the working-class and middle-class white men who would acquire automobility with the advent of the low-cost Ford Model T in 1908, driving's compensatory value depended on cars being what the early critics (and more recent ones) maintained they were: instruments for the display of blithe, arrogant, potentially destructive power—"insolent chariots," as one later author would put it.[31]

*Speed* was a particularly important element in this regard, as it conferred immediate distinction. The elites who were the first adopters of automobility deployed speed as a marker of social power and distinction, both on public roads and in organized races. "You can't go by a Houpt-

**figure 1.** The anonymous, autonomous driver. Courtesy of BFRC.

Rockwell," claimed one early ad, "so go buy one."[32] As automobility trickled down the class structure and technology improved, the increasingly available commodity of speed functioned as an equalizing agent, an intoxicant, and an occasion for the performance of mastery. The literary scholar Jeffrey T. Schnapp has observed that advances in transportation technology in the mid-eighteenth century, notably the development of lightweight *cabriolet* carriages, increasingly made it "possible to envisage speed as a kind of drug, an intensifier, an *excitant moderne*."[33] Various commentators testified to the salubrious effects of the cabriolet's horseless descendent. William Howard Taft, for example, the first motoring president, likened the sensations of motoring over fifty miles per hour to "atmospheric champagne." A 1916 writer had it on good authority from "one of the greatest nerve specialists in America . . . that for relieving the strain on the brain of the busy executive of today . . . there was nothing to compare with the automobile." This was, however, an egalitarian elixir: "One does not have to be in the multi-millionaire class to experience the relief of having the cool sweet breath of evening brush our cares and sorrows away."[34]

Intoxicating and anodyne automotive speed was also an occasion for the demonstration of one's control over the vehicle and oneself. As the historian Miriam Levin has observed, the contemporary meaning of "control" emerged with industrial modernity; it initially "refer[red] to the apparatus by means of which a machine, [such] as an airplane or automobile . . .

was made to perform. By century's end the term had already come to refer to mastery of the self."[35] As the automobile propelled people at unprecedented, ever-greater velocities, it resisted, and occasionally overthrew, human control. Automobility's tumult supplied ready analogies for the landscapes of capitalist modernity, and as the historian Kurt Möser suggests, one's competence behind the wheel indicated the capacity to thrive in capitalist modernity. The qualities of "independence . . . resourcefulness, calm behavior under stressful conditions, cold-bloodedness, fast reactions, the ability to concentrate and to anticipate other road users' moves" describe *homo economicus* as delineated by Benjamin Franklin or Max Weber.[36]

The powerful conjunction of self-determination, speed, and mastery informed the common and durable trope of driver-as-monarch—a symbolic identity that merged masculine potency and charisma. Preceding by a quarter-decade Lewis Mumford's statement that opens this chapter, E. B. White reminisced in 1936 that "the driver of the old Model T was a man enthroned" (fig. 1).[37] In addition to promising transgressive thrills and speed, advertisers enticed and flattered consumers with images of power and distinction, as in Oldsmobile's 1920s "Autocrats of the Road" campaign. Other sources emphasized, however, motorized regality's heavy crown: after cataloguing the pleasures of "a sport fit for kings" ("a man can sit in his own carriage and fly over the country roads at a speed limited only by law") a 1902 *Outing* warned that "there are in the world, alas, too many individuals who, not content with the possession of a giant's strength, must needs use it like a giant." The same magazine had cautioned drivers that "you are the most absolute monarch locomobility ever produced—until something happens."[38]

Early twentieth-century popular culture, art, and political philosophy also celebrated the car as a force-multiplier of the self, facilitator of a gratifying, thrilling transgression, and a fosterer of self-control. In Kenneth Grahame's popular 1908 children's novel *The Wind in the Willows*, for example, the character Toad is transformed behind the wheel into "Toad at his best and highest, Toad the terror, the traffic-queller, the Lord of the lone trail, before whom all must give way or be smitten into nothingness and everlasting night." Similarly, the glamorous Jordan Baker in Fitzgerald's 1925 novel *The Great Gatsby* justifies her recklessness behind the wheel with a social imaginary in which other drivers, not she, must be careful. A 1913 *Scribner's* article on automobility's maturity hailed the contemporary motorist: "you yourself . . . have seen the speedometer needle hang at 50 or 60, and have come unscathed through adventures which, when you think of them in cold blood, bring a creepy stirring to your spine." At the vanguard of this cult of risk and power were the Italian poet F. T. Marinetti and his fellow Futurists, for whom the desire for automotive speed, indeed, for collision and even injury, marked a driver as one of "the *living* men on earth."[39]

The flattering image of the automobile entailed, in turn, a general disparagement of the automobile's ancestor and erstwhile rival, the locomotive. Like its predecessor apparatus, automobility organized a historically distinct mode of perceiving natural and built environments.[40] By the end of the nineteenth century, the perceptual revolution wrought by the locomotive was all but exhausted. Rail travel, which insulated the passenger from the landscape, weather, wildlife, and humanity rushing past the windows, offered no proving ground, but only an unchanging procession of many-seen vistas toward which the passenger's attitude might be either passive fascination or drowsy apathy. "The steel-walled Pullman," etiquette maven Emily Post noted dismissively, "carefully preserves for you the attitude you started with."[41] Moreover, there was no agency to rail travel. Circumscribed by track, schedule, and the standardized comforts and technological advances that marked rail's industrial maturity (Pullman and dining cars, upholstery, air brakes, etc.), the passenger enjoyed the privilege and endured the impotence of never being the engineer. In a sense, rail travel set the same restrictions on the enterprise of travel as Taylorism imposed on the process of work. "A man in a train," sniffed English auto enthusiasts Lord Montagu and F. Wilson McComb, "is a man in a straitjacket."[42]

The automobile, by contrast, offered to challenge and fortify travelers, to reintroduce, as Phil Patton writes, "the values of the frontier by making movement a permanent state of mind."[43] The disorientation and difficulty of moving through a not-yet-automobilized landscape was narrated as tonic. In a 1902 issue of *The Automobile*, for example, engineer Hiram Percy Maxim described a ramble around Pittsburgh as "about as strenuous a ten-mile automobile ride as one can find available in any of our large cities. Taken just before business it serves as an admirable awakening for a busy day and repeated after business gives an exciting finish."[44] Indeed, the automobile resembled not the experience of riding a train but that of riding a horse, which, in the words of one 1837 author, "vary their form and movement in a thousand ways," and through which the "the rider's nerves are strung, his senses are quickened; eye, hand, and ear are alike on the alert; the blood rushes through the veins, and every faculty is aroused."[45] There was a horselike willfulness and unreliability to early automotive technology, which broke many a starter-cranking wrist and oversteered many automobiles into ditches; but the experiences of mobility by horse and train only approximated automobility's novel perceptual mode. The surfeit of representations of driving during the early twentieth century suggest a pressing need to narrate, and thereby assimilate, that mode.

## pioneering automobility

As stated above, the driver was an analogue of the "sovereign consumer." More properly speaking, driving powerfully expressed the dispositions and themes of consumer culture, specifically those of choice, self-determination, and self-transformation. Yet driving's rugged, exhilarating, and transgressive character cast it as shopping's more propitiously masculine analogue—the practice, as it were, of the "unashamed individualist" in the Hooverian mold. In the first generation of motor touring narratives, we see automobility sanctioned as a vehicle of individual and national renascence—a means to resuscitate republican selfhood and reopen the frontier. These texts, which were authored mostly by white elites, many of them women, emphasized the driver's patriotic communion with America—figured as a pristine and uninhabited yet historically significant landscape—and heralded the dynamic and sovereign driver as a national ideal. Many of these travelers were sponsored in one way or another by auto companies, who promoted the journeys as "reliability tours" demonstrating the quality of a particular make or model.

These accounts exemplify what scholars have called the experiential mode of tourism, understood, Erik Cohen's words, as "the search for 'experiences': the striving of people who have lost their own centre and are unable to lead an authentic life at home to recapture meaning by a vicarious, essentially aesthetic experience of the authenticity of others."[46] As Jackson Lears and others have argued, the dilemma of modern subjectivity registered forcefully with elites. Steeped in the ethos of republican virtue and self-making, many encountered in industrial modernity a hitherto unknown and deeply troubling ease of life. Exempt from labor but afflicted with a debilitating anxiety, they bemoaned the loss of the Protestant virtues of self-denial and work as they simultaneously noted those virtues' increasing superfluity. Just as industrial workers interpreted proletarianization as traumatic displacement (and emplacement), so too did elites characterize modern material luxury, with its disconnection from "real things" such as the land, as spiritually, morally, and physically enervating. One response to the decline of character-through-work was a desire for "authentic" (which often meant anachronistic and rustic) experience, and the development of more strenuous, rigorously governed, and character-building forms of leisure, such as long-distance auto touring.[47]

Authors of early touring narratives conflated journeys past and present, pretending to and simulating the tribulations of pioneer crossings of the continent. "If we overlooked the fact of our own motor car," marveled Emily Post, making the coast-to-coast trip (as a passenger) in 1916, "we could have supposed ourselves crossing the plains in the days of the caravans and stage coaches." Edith Wharton, in her account of driving through France, remarked that "the motor-car has restored the romance of travel. . . . It has given us back the wonder, the adventure, and the novelty which enlivened the way of our posting grandparents." The sight of so many hale and intrepid motor tourists in western hotels made *National Geographic* editor William Showalter, traveling by rail in 1923, wonder if the motorists "pity me for my effete love of ease."[48]

These authors, male and female alike, invoked a wilder America, put themselves and their machines in it, and, so positioned, claimed fellowship with the generation of white conquerors that had preceded them. Chas. G. Percival, writing in 1913, estimated his military "experiences in Central and South America . . . free[ing] my little brown brothers" to have readied him for his cross-country trek.[49] Of course, these latter-day white pioneers traversed a landscape domesticated through genocide, and perforce characterized in literature, historiography, art, and popular culture by elegy. The common threats to white motorists at the turn of the century were generally no graver than impassable roads, flat tires, and overheating radiators; and the emptied land appeared once again a horizon of possibility for revitalizing the self, and conjuring a national community.

In 1915, journalist Newton A. Fuessle, in his celebration of the newly completed Lincoln Highway, averred that "one may whirl across the continent a score of times as a railway passenger and never sense the slightest fraction of the feeling of nearness to the States and cities traversed. . . . The Highway affords an incomparable inspirational course in Americanism."[50] Others remarked on automobility's ability to engender a national fellow-feeling that bordered on the socialistic. "Automobiling is democratic," the sociologist Charles Horton Cooley wrote in his journal after running out of gas in rural Michigan in September of 1923, "because it brings all sorts of people face to face, and mostly under fellowship conditions. You constantly have recourse to give and receive courtesy and help. The inconvenience of running out of gasoline was nothing to the pleasure I had from the kindness of the country people near Chelsea. I would like to erect a monument to the Unknown [American] Farmer who has so often been kind to me in every conceivable difficulty."[51] Another sociologist, Harvey W. Peck, praised the exploratory nature of driving, which facilitated in the citizenry "that modicum of political intelligence which is necessary for democracy." After affirming the compatibility of automobility with "traditional social, political, ethical and aesthetic values," Peck ended his evaluation of "civilization on wheels" with a similarly approving assessment of automobility's potential benefit to a socialist transformation.[52]

Articulating those more traditional values were the motorist advocates of the "Good Roads" movement (begun by bicyclists and manufacturers in 1880), who made explicit in their promotions of roadbuilding the patriotic narrative and consanguine national whiteness made possible by the American road. Marguerite Shaffer has discussed, for example, the 1911 Daughters of the American Revolution–published pamphlet *The Old Trails Road: The National Highway as a Monument to the Pioneer Men and Women*, which exhorted its readers, "Men and Women of today: With the blood of such historic stuff coursing through your veins, build a national highway from ocean to ocean over these old trails." Appeals such as this one were predicated on the growing belief that "auto tourists could not only vicariously reenact the nation's pioneer history but also embrace the democracy and independence of the open road . . . thus reaffirming their true American character."[53]

In 1924, M. H. James of Pennsylvania's Department of Highways concluded his robust defense of automobility with an elaboration of a heroic figure:

> The greatness of the United States was simply taken for granted before the automobile enabled citizens to see for themselves the extent of this country. But now unhampered the average citizen drives from coast to coast, from Canadian to Mexican border. He sets up his camp trailer, or his pup tent, or he parks his car in the Adirondacks or the Alleghenies; or he finds him a sandy beach along the ocean in New Jersey; or he avails himself of a municipal camping site. He has had a full and enjoyable day. He has climbed mountains and floated down hill. He has passed through timberlands or across farming country or the wastelands left by careless toilers who took toll of nature. He has cooked his own meals beneath the sky, or he has found moderately priced subsistence along

the way. And so at close of day, with an enjoyable tomorrow just ahead, he sinks into slumber with a satisfaction never equalled in the covered wagon days.[54]

Throughout the 1920s, proponents of motor touring in the United States deployed this "average citizen" who had been revitalized, fortified, made resourceful, and tethered to the history and progress of the nation through his automobile travels.[55]

## fair woman as a motorist

There must be women with check books (or access to their husbands'), who love the outdoor life, crave exercise and excitement, who long for relief from the monotony of social and household duties, who have said, "I wish I were a man." Why don't you tell them that your motor car is the solution to all their troubles.

    −Unnamed "letter writer," Ford advertising pamphlet *The Lady and Her Motor Car* (1911)[56]

Given driving's association with masculine prerogative and ruggedness, it seems curious that women were among the first to attempt and document cross-country motor journeys. These pioneering narratives, however, tended to issue from the passenger's rather than the driver's seat (Emily Post, for example, was chauffeured by her son).[57] Nevertheless, these women represented themselves as adventurers seeking to be remade through trial, as bellwethers of the land's domestication, and as members of the upper class: they and their accounts illustrate the ambiguously gendered status of automobility in its first decades.

A number of historical studies, foremost among them Virginia Scharff's illuminating *Taking the Wheel* (1991), emphasize the painstakingly maintained equation of automobility with masculinity from the earliest years of the car culture. "The auto," Scharff writes, "was born in a masculine manger, and when women sought to claim its power, they invaded a male domain."[58] The automotive journalist and writer Denise McCluggage has suggested that a gendered division of labor obtained in the maintenance of transportation tools before the automobile: women cared for the living horses while men tended to the inanimate wagons. The horseless age relieved women of their duties, and hence their agency in matters of mobility; and automobiles were further gendered male by their association with "the status group of the rich. Cars were playthings, they had not yet become utilitarian, they were still toys—men's toys."[59]

Though, to be sure, automobility has been a vital compensatory practice and exclusionary discourse of American men in the twentieth century, white women have been among its participants at least since Genevre Delphine Mudge of New York became the "first recorded woman driver" in 1898.[60] The next three decades saw the image of the woman driver undergo repeated renegotiation as the automobile itself made, in Scharff's words, "the transition from toy to tool."[61] The gendered images and rhetorics of driving from this era help us chart this changing perception of the automobile; but they also help us narrate the changing status of American women. The historian Sarah Jain has written that, at the turn of the century, the question surrounding the automobile was "what did it have the potential to become?"[62] It was a question equally applicable to women, as an emergent "New Womanhood" challenged dominant representations that marginalized women as weak and submissive, and as women fought for, and attained, suffrage.

Ultimately, early women's automobility is best understood as a site of negotiation at which a traditional idealized femininity was reconciled with the more progressive, if not subversive, New Womanhood.[63] As the car became a literal instrument of women's deliverance from the spaces of domesticity, women used images of driving (such as those in the touring narrative discussed above) to conceive a more intrepid modern femininity, one that was politically significant. Through advertising, producers of automobiles and related commodities embraced this femininity. During and directly after women's struggle for the franchise, advertisers flattered women with an identity of "sovereign consumer," celebrating, in often explicitly political language and images, women's capacities to make informed choices and to "accept no substitutes."[64]

However, women's newfound agency was forcefully contested by those distrustful of empowered and mobile women; hence the standard sexist assertions of women's weakness, vanity, irrationality, and pretensions to masculinity rehearsed in the popular discourse of the "woman driver." Reactionary opponents to women's automobility were vocal and numerous. A 1905 correspondent in the British magazine *Autocar*, for example, fulminated against "these would-be men," and made clear his desire that "the controlling of motor cars will be wrested from the hands of such persons."[65] At least as abundant, however, were those voices, many of them issuing from the most steadfastly hegemonic institutions, urging women to take the wheel. We must consider women's participation in early automobility as not so much curtailed as *shaped*. This requires examining the type of driving to which women were directed and the imaginary relationship with the car and the highway they were encouraged to develop.

American culture in the 1890s, as mentioned above, perceived the automobile as a *toy*—an expensive whirligig produced for the amusement of the effete rich. Early motorists demonstrated, through driving and display, their class power; yet it does not necessarily follow that the automobile always and everywhere denoted the gender power of hegemonic masculinity. In fact, the elite provenance of the automobile called its gender status into question, as the effeminacy of wealth stood as a common trope in republican political culture. From the 1890s to the first decade of the 1900s, the purchase and operation of automobiles was viewed as an element of the "high society [that] is largely a feminine affair."[66] An 1899 *Harper's Bazar* speculated that

> automobiles promise to be even more fashionable than bicycles. In Newport so many are now used by women and men of fashion that their horses have to be exercised by the coachmen. . . . One watches with no little concern the present attitude of the fashionable world on both sides of the water to this new invention. Still, no one is safe making predictions about fads, especially when those who can afford to pay the cost of every change of fashion and whim have adopted them.[67]

The "women and men of fashion" identified here typified not the republican selfhood of the heroic past, but the irresolute social self of the consumerist present—a subjectivity associated with the feminine.

"Since the automobile has come into fashion," asserted the caption of one early image, "it is interesting to know that it is quite as good taste for a lady to drive as for a gentleman" (fig. 2). One reason for this equality was the limited range of most early cars. In the first decade of automobility, the large portion of automobiles were powered by electricity and steam, with gasoline a distant third. The historian Kurt Möser has observed that the fashionable milieu of turn-of-the-century motorists had its own gendered divisions, which he describes as "a *flâneur* culture, often linked with women's use of cars in big cities like Paris, and a male-dominated speeding and dangerous racing culture, on the 'open road.'"[68] The urban gadabouts tended to drive electric cars, which, though also driven by men, were cast due to their limited range and speed as "ladylike." Scharff and others have argued that the auto industry's marketing of lightweight and smaller electric cars to women reflected normative assumptions regarding feminine

**figure 2.** The automobile as fashion accessory, late 1890s. Courtesy of NMAH.

competency and the propriety of women's gallivanting.[69] Prior to World War I, however, American women also participated in races, auto clubs, and "gymkhanas"—obstacle course competitions requiring driving skill, dexterity, and improvisation—and, as we have seen, took to the open road on cross-country reliability tours in the faster and more cumbersome gasoline-powered cars.

Many historians positing early automobility as masculine point to the technical expertise and physical strength that were evidently the primary necessities of the first drivers. Clay McShane, for example, has written that, in the face of the turn-of-the-century decline of male individualism, "the corporate bureaucrat could find the emotional equivalent of the skill, autonomy, and strength of the idealized farmer, traditional craftsman or small entrepreneur with his knowledge of cars and their upkeep."[70] A number of owners may well have possessed such technical proficiency. But the unreliability of the first automobiles, the lack or high cost of the specialized tools for their maintenance, and the poor conditions and natural hazards of early roads, put at least as many if not more operators—male and female—in a state of feminized dependency. Moreover, given the class status of early drivers, those without the physical strength required to start and drive a car (and to get it out of mud and around obstacles) and the technical knowledge and skill to fix it, could always hire someone with these qualities.

Insofar as its use conveyed fashionability and consumption rather than values of remunerated *work,* and its ownership was confined to hedonistic elites, the automobile remained, if not feminine, at least indeterminately gendered. Its connotations of effeteness likely led Theodore Roosevelt, preoccupied with putting up a manly and populist front, to disdain the automobile in favor of the horse.[71] As automobility "trickled down" to the lower classes, however, it would necessarily be accorded a more masculine character; but driving would retain traces of its early associations with feminine mercuriality and frivolity, even as later car culture, as Sarah Jain notes, "manifested a performative hypermasculinity verging on overcompensation."[72]

For women as well as for men, the promise of automobility was that of transformation—yet at issue was the *type* of transformation automobility would effect in women. Early advertisements and media that promoted women's automobility foregrounded the ornamental allure of the car itself and the clothing and accessories that went with it. A 1906 *Town & Country,* for example, included "The Vogue of Motoring for Women," a photo page that featured society women at the wheels of their cars.[73] The communications scholar Michele Ramsey has argued that such images "specifically divorced Woman's role in society from political or economic independence and promised women a type of social status that could be garnered through the purchase of an automobile."[74] Through figures such as "the Automobile Girl," posing (with or without a male companion) by or at the wheel of a car and clad in the latest motoring fashion, product marketers and purveyors of images underscored automobility's potential to attract both other women's envious looks and male suitors' gazes—the essential components of glamour. Such depictions privileged the seductive power of the car as a commodity over driving; indeed, the glamour of such images inhered in the female driver's stillness rather than her motion, and

**figure 3.** Scorching. Courtesy of NMAH.

thus did not contradict those who maintained that women had no business operating a car. In 1914, for example, *Outing* complimented women on "motoring chapeaux . . . [that] frame a pretty face enchantingly" but, citing their weakness under strain, judged them unfit to drive.[75]

Women, however, challenged their relegation to the ornamental, perceiving in automobility more profound capacities. The bicycle craze of the 1880s, in which middle-class women were avid participants, supplied a lexicon for and a set of dispositions toward mechanized, mobile modernity.[76] "To be mistress at the wheel of her own motor car," declared the 1911 advertising pamphlet, *The Woman and the Ford*, "is an ambition that appeals strongly to most young women."[77] Images of mobile women, such as the 1901 print "Scorching" (a term for speeding coined by bicyclists or their blown-by pedestrian antagonists) which depicts two women and a dog hurtling down a country road (fig. 3) suggested an agency beyond the power of glamour. Responding to *Outing*'s trivializing compliment, one reader asserted in 1914 that "even in New York there are women sufficiently plucky and expert to take a machine into that wonderful tangle of traffic that makes Fifth Avenue one of the show thoroughfares of the world."[78] Like their male counterparts, the first female drivers relished driving's sensations of mastery, freedom, thrill, and self-determination.

If working- and middle-class white men found in driving an antidote to the surveillance and confinement experienced in Taylorized and bureaucratized workplaces, to white women of the same classes driving represented liberation from the household. "Learning to handle the car has wrought my emancipation," wrote home economist Catherine Frederick in 1912.[79] Insofar as such emancipation increased sales, even the most socially conservative advertisers endorsed and hyped it. "It is woman's day," trumpeted The Woman and the Ford. "No longer a 'shut in,' she reaches for an ever wider sphere of action—that she may be more the woman. . . . [The automobile] has broadened her horizon—increased her pleasures—given new vigor to her body . . . It is a real weapon in the changing order."[80] Ford and other companies were not calling for gender revolution but emphasizing the automobile as the proper conveyance for middle-class women's shopping and leisure forays, as it enabled women to move through public space without being subject to the glances and touches of men of other races and classes (a hazard of streetcar and rail travel).

The theme of emancipation dominated literary representations of female drivers, such as the series of Motor Girls, Automobile Girls, and Motor Maids novels marketed to girls and young women between 1910 and 1917. As the historian Kathleen Franz and the literary scholars Sherrie Inness and Nancy Tilman Romalov have observed, these texts introduced young women to transportation technology, and, in inspiring them to master it, encouraged a more general sense of competency and autonomy. Franz describes these fictional female drivers as "transitional figures" who upheld ideals of domestic femininity even as their automobility "contained feminist accents."[81] Several scholars have also pointed to the significance of driving in early women's adventure films that suggested (or threatened) a new female agency outside the boundaries of domesticity and marriage. Such films, argues the literary scholar Sara Parchesky, "construct[ed] the woman driver as an image of not merely professional competence but also uninhibited desire and active resistance to patriarchal constraints."[82]

Moreover, the transgressive component of driving took on a more directly sexualized character for women. Automobility granted women access to a form of technology that was not (yet) a tool of domestic labor. In using that technology, many women derived a type of pleasure different in nature from the fulfillment of a gender imperative. Noting the ubiquity of women in automobile advertisements and exhibits, Robert Sloss asserted in 1910 that "the woman at the wheel is no allegory." Sloss's article, noteworthy for its forceful defense of women's ability not only to drive but also to perform maintenance, even suggested a female erotics of automobility:

It is a curious fact that, if she goes at motoring seriously, woman's natural intuition puts her into closer touch with her car than a man seems to be able to get with his. She acquires the "feel" of the mechanism more readily, she detects more quickly the evidence of something out of adjustment, and altogether she drives more gently and with more delicate technic—all of which adds peculiarly to her pleasure and satisfaction in motoring.[83]

The characterization of woman as more attuned to the "feelings" of the car was in keeping with the nurturing stereotype of True Womanhood; but there was a fine line between sensuous and sensual. "Fair Woman as a Motorist," a 1904 article by Luellen Cass Teters in *Motor* magazine, ventured an explanation for women's adoption of this "highly masculine pleasure" that implied a sort of ravishing by nature and machine:

There is a charm of independence about the automobile that strongly appeals to one; in face of its almost rakish unconventionality, the quiet respectability of equine flesh commands no attention except among the timid, and disciples of antiquated forms of locomotion. . . . Motoring leaves its perceptible ravages in disheveled locks, dusty garb, and tanned countenance, [but] there are few who would exchange this Atalanta form of traveling for the sedate maneuvers of a horse.[84]

The popular representations of the automobile as an aphrodisiac, a means to privacy and seclusion, and an enclosed space for unsanctioned sexual contact, identified it as an instrument both of male potency and illicit female desire. The 1905 song "In My Merry Automobile," for example, has "Johnny Steele" teaching "Lucille" how to drive the car they use to go "sparking" in the "dark old park": the sheet music cover features Lucille steering as Johnny sits beside her.[85] Such images of "the car [as] an extension of the self—a sort of powerful prosthetic device" were cause for both titillation and anxiety.[86] As the automobile added to the sexual allure of a Johnny Steele, it threatened to eclipse and supplant him as the object of female desire. A 1913 article that advised women to "get your instructor to show you the gentle art of cranking a machine without effort" hinted at an independence of a problematically sensual variety. "There is a great satisfaction in being thus independent of the services of some masculine biceps."[87] Fears of male irrelevancy were likely exacerbated by technological advances, such as the electric starter (developed in 1912) and the closed car (widespread by the 1920s), which removed many of the physical barriers to a woman being alone with her car.

## the domestication of automobility

Of course, such self-determination and competence suggested a political analogue. It is not surprising that American women's claims to automobility arose alongside their increasingly forceful demand for the franchise. An embodied expression of self-governance and agency, driving stood as a compelling metaphor for republican citizenship. Republicanism requires that the citizen enter the public sphere as a blank figure, divested of his particularities, and thereby empowered to speak and act as an abstract, "disinterested" member of the public. This self-abstraction of the citizen, as the literary scholar Michael Warner has argued, disembodied political agency, even as it ensured that only those with specific types of bodies could assume it.[88] In the United States, driving, as a public performance of freedom, has generally been governed by this same tacit ascriptivism and bad faith. Assuming the figure of the driver required resources of class (the means of car ownership and upkeep), gender, and race (the largely male and overwhelmingly white prerogatives of free mobility), despite a dominant rhetoric of universality and uniform access.

Therefore, by driving, women (as well as people of color, whose relationship to automobility I discuss in detail below) affirmed their fitness for citizenship and legal equality with men. Women's self-representations of driving in long-distance touring narratives, serial novels, films, and magazine articles such as "Fair Woman as a Motorist" can be read, then, as parables of political competency; just as the disparagements, in both popular and "expert" culture, of women's (and nonwhites') driving abilities cast universal suffrage, civil rights, and immigration as suspect. Indeed, the rise of mass automobility offered a pretext for calling subordinate groups' claims to citizenship further into question, with doubts about "safe driving" standing in for political fears.[89] Yet whatever the perceived threats to the republic posed by women's entry into the driver's seat (and the voting booth), by the 1920s women's automobility had been incorporated as an essential, as opposed to a merely tolerated, element of a reengineered patriarchal and capitalist order. The years surrounding World War I mark the absorption or redirection of the more potentially radical energies released by women's driving.

Not surprisingly, this period also marks the emphatic masculinization of automobility. The rise of mass automobility between the 1908 advent of the Model T and the saturation of the auto market and the economic collapse of 1929 reshaped the social, political, economic, and military landscape in powerful ways, and transformed the automobile's whirligig image to that of an implement of commerce and progress. "Millions now recognize the automobile as a necessity," proclaimed a Portland Cement Association advertisement in a 1924 *Motor*. "It is no longer a luxury for the few. Sixty per cent of its use is for business."[90] World War I—the first motorized war—confirmed the vehicle as an instrument for the extension of an aggressive masculinity. Kurt Möser quotes a 1924 German commentator asserting that "the enemies of the automobile are identical to pacifist and weakly men . . . At the wheel one will find therefore the cold-blooded, the energetic, in short: the sane men."[91]

The domestication of automobility is illustrated by the example of the actress and stuntwoman Anita King's 1915 solo journey from Los Angeles to New York (the first such trip by a woman driving alone). King, dubbed "The Paramount Girl" by that studio's press agents, told a California newspaper that she would make the trip "to show the men folk the sturdiness of what they call the weaker species when it comes to grit and perseverance."[92] Though she was followed or preceded along her route by Paramount's agents, King—self-reliant, glamorous, sexually "free" (and therefore armed with a pearl-handled revolver)—was presented to readers as a thrilling embodiment of New Womanhood. Yet King's adventures as narrated by Paramount, in keeping with mainstream popular culture's mitigation of potentially disruptive acts and figures, reaffirmed rather than destabilized traditional gender models. King's spokeswomanship for hegemony was exemplified in an article in *Sunset* magazine telling of her encounter with a young rural girl who begged the actress to take her to Hollywood, far away from her homebound existence in Wyoming. Listening to the movie-struck girl's story, King's "soul awoke to a responsibility" compelling her to advise the girl to stay home and assume a domestic role.[93]

Popular culture treating women's automobility such as the adventure films and serial novels mentioned above deployed a similar strategy of inciting transgression before ultimately prescribing accommodation. According to Nancy Tilman Romalov, a cardinal achievement of the Motor Girls genre was "to reconcile greater freedom and fitness for girls with their continued subordination to a patriarchal, genteel order." Kathleen Franz notes a similar strategy in Sinclair Lewis's 1919 novel *Free Air*, in which a courageous and capable young female driver is compensated for quitting her peregrinations with an idealized companionate marriage to a young mechanic.[94] Advertisers, and their clients too, struggled to hew to a domestic ideal as they pressed into service dynamic images of emancipated women; the dilemma was especially acute after women's achievement of the franchise.[95] Though these forms rewarded symbolically their heroines for their mobile agency (and their heroes for their respect for the latter), they also organized a happy attenuation of that agency in the heroines' ultimate consent to a role that we might call "New True Womanhood."

This model of femininity was predictably tethered to the household, though it affirmed an "independence" that had "less to do with political and economic emancipation than it [did] with leisure and wealth," and which could be realized through the good offices of automobility among other "labor-saving" technologies.[96] It could be distinguished in advertisements for the "second car" aggressively promoted by manufacturers who feared the exhaustion of the auto market in the 1920s. This car was to be primarily the wife's helpmeet in the fulfillment of her daily tasks, and secondarily a means to her wholesome, beautifying enjoyment of "the outdoors." Two Ford closed-car advertisements from 1924 (figs. 4 and 5) conveyed the joys of a thoroughly feminine automobility that expanded women's abilities to serve husbands, children, and the consumer economy (through shopping and chauffeuring) *and* provided opportunities to "recharge the batteries" through pastoral respite.

Achieving a sort of stasis by the late 1920s, women's automobility was thus, as I mentioned earlier, shaped rather than curtailed. The same, however, can be said for men's automobility, which manufacturers, advertisers, and cultural producers continued to affirm through an ethos of transgression against a stultifying and confining world (often itself cast in gendered terms). However, though more clearly and forcefully presented in the discourse of women's automobility, the interpretation of freedom as empowered participation in the reproduction of capitalist-liberal hegemony would come to structure automobility more generally.

## building the apparatus

I think men's minds are going to be changed in subtle ways because of automobiles; just how, though, I could hardly guess. —Booth Tarkington[97]

Here I want to sketch out a theme pursued more fully in later chapters; namely, automobility as a forge of subjects as well as a rationale and a means for expanding governmentality in the twentieth-century United States. Governmentality can be defined as a modern disposition of power

**FREEDOM**

*for the woman*

*who owns a Ford*

To own a Ford car is to be free to venture into new and untried places. It is to answer every challenge of Nature's charms, safely, surely and without fatigue. ⟨Where a narrow lane invites or a steep hill promises a surprise beyond, a Ford will take you there and back, in comfort, trouble-free.

⟨Off and away in this obedient, ever-ready car, women may "re-charge the batteries" of tired bodies, newly inspired for the day's work

FORD MOTOR COMPANY, DETROIT, MICHIGAN

CLOSED CARS

**figure 4.** New Womanhood, automobilized. Courtesy of BFRC.

geared toward the management of individuals and populations with an eye to their health, security, productivity, and safety. In order for something to become an object of governmentality, it must be figured as a *problem*, both in terms of its being a hazard and obstacle to the goals above and an opportunity for the extension of control.[98] As a problematic modern prac-

Getting the Most
Out of
Every Day

To the woman at the wheel of a Ford car,
every road seems straight and smooth; hills
melt away and rough places are easy. This
is because of care-free confidence in its re-
sponsive, sure performance. When a woman
hesitates to manage a heavy car; when she
needs an extra one for personal or family use,
or when her means forbid the drain of high upkeep cost, she should
have the easily handled, easily parked, reliable service of a Ford. She
finds, also, that comfort and perfection of motor have not run away
with cost and she can make unlimited use of her car without anxiety
of care or upkeep.

FORD MOTOR COMPANY, DETROIT, MICHIGAN
TUDOR SEDAN, $590  •  FORDOR SEDAN, $695  •  COUPE, $525  •  (All prices f. o. b. Detroit)

Ford
CLOSED CARS

**figure 5.** True Womanhood, automobilized. Courtesy of BFRC.

tice and discourse, automobility resembled nothing so much as sexuality. Like sexuality, automobility's emancipatory pleasures and destructive
potential called for the construction of an apparatus, consisting of legal,
technical, medical, cultural, economic, political, ethical, and architec-
tural/spatial elements, that would simultaneously enable and constrain,

cultivate and regulate, *govern* and *license* it. And, like sexuality, automobility provides a crucial medium for the performance of a normative modern subjectivity of freedom.

Building the apparatus of twentieth-century American automobility occupied a myriad of actors across a multitude of discursive fields. As many scholars have pointed out, the automobile inflicted trauma on established patterns of rural and urban life, and on the bodies of the people accustomed to these patterns.[99] It is perhaps difficult for inhabitants of the twenty-first century, for whom the abundance of auto-related deaths and injuries appears a regrettable but otherwise unremarkable fact of life, to grasp the public horror at the carnage wrought by early motorization, especially the deaths of children and elderly pedestrians. H. H. Bliss was American automobility's first pedestrian victim, in New York City in 1899; and by 1906 fifteen states had recognized auto accidents as a hazard to public health. "The recent trend . . . of automobile fatalities has been so definitely and consistently upward," asserted two economists in 1928, "that it is difficult to avoid raising this issue: What can we expect from the automobile as an instrument of death in the near future?"[100] The lethal capacities of the automobile provided the rationale for various projects, initiated by the state, industry, and advocacy groups, intended to shape the behavior of drivers as well as pedestrians, establish legal codes and monitoring mechanisms, and transform and regulate the built environment.

Roadbuilding was the most prominent of these projects. In modernity, the proliferation of roads had paralleled the rise of the "public" as a social and political abstraction in the eighteenth century. Situated between the authority of the state and the responsibility of that state to "private" citizens, the public emerged as a category of enterprise geared toward the improvement of places and populations, and gave rise to a stratum of bureaucratic professionals charged with managing those projects.[101] The mapping and navigation of the continent were integral to the exercise of state power, in terms of marking and regularizing territory as well as establishing patterns of movement.[102] The nineteenth century saw massive arterialization of the American landscape—turnpikes cordoned and trails beaten, tracks laid, canals, passes, and tunnels carved. While the wagon was an important personal and commercial conveyance and forger of roads, the locomotive more indelibly inscribed the physical and political patterns of American transport.

The bicycle, which began to be produced and sold in large quantities in the United States, was another agent of transformation, performing, in the words of the sociologist Sidney Aronson, "the dirty work for its mechanical successor." In addition to giving initial expression to "that new type of mobility which became so characteristic of the twentieth century," the bicycle was responsible for much of the early political agitation for road improvement.[103] In concert with rural farmers, early motorists, and their respective industrial and political advocates, bicyclists' groups pressed the government for the improvement and expansion of the generally abysmal road system. The resulting Good Roads movement, financed by industrialists such as bicycle (and later automobile) manufacturer Albert Pope, achieved its first victory in 1891, when it convinced the New Jersey legislature to provide one-third of the funds for county road projects. By 1893, the movement was powerful enough to be granted "advisory" status within the Department of Agriculture as the Office of Road Inquiry (ORI).

As the historian Owen Gutfreund has argued, early pro-automobility agents cannily construed their interests as public interests, thereby ensuring that the costs of roadbuilding would be borne by the public and not only by road users.[104] The push to aggrandize automobility and to discredit transportation alternatives was augmented by an increasingly influential cadre of highway engineers, who, the historian Bruce Seely has shown, cloaked their technocratic ambition in a rhetoric of necessity, progress, and public service.[105] The Federal-Aid Road Act of 1916, which approved $75 million in matching funds for distribution among the states, signified the first substantial federal commitment to automobility. Its largesse was to be administered by the ORI's successor agency, the Bureau of Public Roads (BPR) under its autocratic commissioner, Thomas H. MacDonald. During the 1920s MacDonald and his engineers increased the number of hard-surfaced miles of highway to over 400,000. From the limited range of roads and communities entitled to federal roadbuilding aid in the early years—generally rural farm-to-market roads and towns with fewer than 2,500 inhabitants—the succeeding decades saw the extension of federal funds to roads that connected and passed through larger municipalities, and to high-speed multilane highways.[106]

Roadbuilding projects were increasingly articulated and pitched to the public in a rhetoric that stressed crisis, progress, safety, democratic processes, and freedom, yet at the same time forcefully rejected the legitimacy of "planning" and collectivity more generally.[107] Beginning in the 1920s, transportation policy makers rejected as outmoded or futile the expansion of long-distance passenger rail systems and the revitalization of urban mass transit. By contrast, an aura of inevitability and promise clung to automobility. The prevailing view held that the people had chosen the car, and the car was annexing urban space, which in turn needed to be reconfigured—there was no alternative.[108] Automotive industries and their political familiars began in the 1930s to dismantle the rail infrastructure as they more fully automobilized the American landscape, and continued to develop the legal and behavior codes and supporting institutions of automobility.[109]

In this network of paved public roads that emerged in the 1890s and culminated in the National System of Interstate and Defense Highways in the 1950s, one glimpses the liberal state's growing sense of automobility as a means to governing populations. Road networks, the political scientist James Scott has recently argued, "have long reflected the centralizing ambitions of local lords and the nation's monarchs"; desiring traffic patterns that it can measure and control, the state eradicates, if it can, "routes *not* created by administrative fiat."[110] Roadbuilding has been integral to the larger enterprise of creating what the philosophers Gilles Deleuze and Felix Guattari call "striated space," a physical network in and through which the social, economic, and juridical elements of an apparatus of power operate.[111]

For its drivers, the striated space of the road sought *legibility*—the condition of being knowable, classifiable, and predictable; hence between 1899 and 1954, each American state instituted mandatory vehicle registration (and taxation) and driver evaluation and licensing. The state-issued driver's license—currently held by 87 percent of United States residents of driving age—has become the basic means of authorizing and verifying not merely driving ability, but individual identity and—as the recent controversy over licensing undocumented immigrants shows—national belonging. The geographers Martin Dodge and Rob Kitchin observe that "the driving license as both a material token of identification that can be displayed on request and as a verifiable record in a governmental database has become one of the most valuable 'codes of life.'"[112] In addition to licensing and registration, the state and industry created a host of mechanisms to further striate the public space of early automobility and enumerate its drivers. Motorized state highway patrol agencies spread after Connecticut established one in 1903; industrial and citizens' advocacy groups such as the National Safety Council, the Highway Education Board, and the American Association of National Highway Officials proliferated after 1913; 1927 saw liability insurance required by Massachusetts law; and driver education began in public schools in Pennsylvania in the early 1930s.[113]

To return to a question posed earlier: what happens when one drives? We might contrast the celebrations of automobility by its more unabashed supporters past and present with the essayist John Jerome's assessment:

> The basis for the appeal of the private automobile has always been a kind of mystically perceived total freedom. In practice, it is the freedom to go wherever one wants to go (wherever the *roads* go, which opens up another sociological can of worms), whenever one desires to go (whenever the car is ready, when one has paid the price in preparation and maintenance, in taxation and legal qualification, whenever one has the wherewithal to feed the machine), at whatever rate one desires to go (assuming the traffic will allow, that congestion eases—and at rates up to but not beyond the arbitrary standards established to protect one from the dangers of excessive use of his own freedom).[114]

The sociologist André Gorz, whose work has focused on the reduction of workers' autonomy, finds a similar paradox in the promise of automobility:

> It appears to confer on its owners limitless freedom. . . . [Yet] unlike all previous owners of a means of locomotion, the motorist's relationship to his or her vehicle was to be that of user and consumer—and not owner and master. . . . The apparent independence of the automobile owner was only concealing the actual radical dependency.[115]

More recently, Sarah Jain has observed that "enveloped in a rhetoric of freedom, the automobile concentrates the most astonishing hyper-regulation"; Dodge and Kitchin note that "with the transition from novel sight to ubiquity, drivers and vehicles have been increasingly drawn into the orbit of governmentality through successive layers of monitoring, identification, and regulation"; and the U.S. government reported in 1968 that "the average American citizen [has] more direct dealings with government through licensing and regulation of the automobile than through any other single public activity."[116]

Can we still call driving "a lovely activity"? In its ability to produce the proper subjects and citizens for the political and economic landscapes of contemporary American life, there is none lovelier. The increasing scope and sophistication of automobility's apparatus should not be interpreted simply as *foreclosing* on driving's promise to the "shrunken egos" (to borrow Lewis Mumford's phrase) of Taylorized modernity. Rather, we need to see the emerging apparatus of automobility as evidence of a hegemonic desire to facilitate, expand, and regularize the ideological valuable experience of freedom that driving offered. In contrast to the sensations and structures of the factory floor and the bureaucratic office that reminded workers of the imperatives of control, driving still *felt* and *looked* like freedom. It therefore preserved the symbolic figures of republican political culture to lend legitimacy to the power structures of managed, administered, modern liberalism.[117]

Though women—and, as I will explain below, African Americans—used the driver's seat as a sort of podium from which they staked their citizenship claims, the experience of driving supplied hegemonically appropriate metaphors for political agency, and served to draw potentially oppositional selves into the hegemonic fold. In other words, driving posed far more threat to human bodies than to bodies politic. Indeed, as dangerous as driving was (and remains), it has also served to produce "safe" subjects and citizens. The communications scholar Jeremy Packer has analyzed how the striated space of the American built environment and the subjects who move through that space have been organized by a logic of safety, understood as "a set of technical knowledges that prescribe human conduct." A 1936 driving manual Packer quotes affirms driving as training for citizenship: "*learning to drive must be closely connected with learning to live. . . .* You cannot teach people to be good drivers without teaching them the same kind of things that make them good citizens."[118]

As driving reformulated for the motor age the mix of obligation and autonomy that informed republican virtue, safety emerged as freedom's twin. As the historian Catherine Bertho Lavenir has argued regarding early automobility in France, the set of rules and norms that came to govern driving stood "in complete coherence with the values of the French republican bourgeoisie" by "link[ing] together the concepts of freedom and responsibility."[119] Safety as an organizing principle for the conduct of one's automobile and one's life could be read in articles such as "Motor Driving as a Fine Art" in a 1908 *Town & Country*:

> In one of Dan Leno's songs he used to tell us how, when hunting, his liberal spirit permitted the horse to take him through lonely gardens and the greenhouses thereof. So, there are men who do not drive motor-cars—they permit the car to take them, sometimes, as we know, through brick walls and at other times into

harboring ditches. These men owe their accidents to the fact that they never were drivers at all in the proper sense of the word.[120]

Here, "driver" in the honorific sense suggests a safe motorist, one whose performance behind the wheel expresses a politically significant amalgam of autonomy, submission, and potential transgression. By the end of the 1920s, the United States was a republic of drivers.[121]

## chapter three

# Crafting Autonomous Subjects: Automobility and the Cold War

Autonomous individuals are artefacts, made possible by the power of the modern state. —John Gray[1]

The free individual has been justified as his own master; the state as his servant. —Dwight D. Eisenhower[2]

### what are we for?

The world-historical conflict between capitalism and socialism that crystallized into the "cold war" in the 1940s was at bottom an ontological debate over "the status of the self and the authenticity of its experience of autonomy."[3] American rhetoricians characterized the conflict as a struggle between irreconcilable ideological systems; one in which the freedom of the individual prevailed, and one that bent the individual to the will of the collective. Because the representatives of both ideological systems had at their disposal the means to annihilate the planet as well as one another, this remained largely a war of ideology. The primary antagonists engaged one another, as they engaged their own populations, on the myriad fronts of culture.

As discussed above, the political culture of the United States evinced a "long-standing aversion to collectivism—of which the Soviet variety of communism appeared to be the most extreme example."[4] That political culture reacted to the cold war with a widespread preoccupation with individualism; or more specifically, with its erosion and resuscitation.

While the fear that the "autonomous self, long a linchpin of liberal culture, was being rendered unreal" was by no means a novel one, the cold war gave it a new immediacy.[5] The foreign policy architects of the Truman and Eisenhower administrations were convinced that the outcome of the cold war depended upon the vitality of American individualist virtue. Domestic prosperity and unprecedented global power, these elites feared, had debilitated and feminized the nation, sapping its martial resolve.

To the cold warriors, the current and future conflict presented "a test of will . . . a summons to Americans to pull themselves together and project their historic values."[6] Hence the assertion in the master document of American cold war strategy, the National Security Council's 1950 "United States Objectives and Programs for National Security" (better known as "NSC 68"), that despite the immensity of the collectivist threat, "the system of values which animates our society—the principles of freedom, tolerance, the importance of the individual, and the supremacy of reason over will—are valid and more vital than the ideology which is the fuel of Soviet dynamism." NSC 68 initiated a call for the "practical affirmation, abroad as well as at home, of our essential values," a call echoed in the same year by Foreign Affairs, which declared that "the Soviet Union is challenging the United States to renew and develop for our time the magnificent inheritance of western individualism."[7]

Yet that "individualism" was not its old self. As twentieth-century social science made a managerial turn, contributing its expertise to the enterprises of corporate capitalism and the state's management of populations in war and peace, the hegemonic discourse of political economy came to affirm the social matrices of selfhood even as it continued to speak worshipfully of individualism. By the era of the cold war, the individualism one found celebrated in the literature of business management and mainstream political thought named a centripetal ethic of teamwork and mechanistic "fit" within a bureaucratized community. Emphasizing both the autonomy of the individual and the latter's formation and fulfillment through social interaction, this refurbished subjectivity (articulated by social scientists as social and national "character") suited a political economy of corporate capitalism while "preserv[ing] the emotional sanctions of the ideal of individualism" so crucial to the ideological arsenal of the cold war.[8]

Over and above the reformulation of individualism, there remained questions of the form the renewal and affirmation of national values would assume. As U.S. propagandists sought "for our enemies, our allies, the uncommitted, and ourselves, a set of working principles, a definition of fundamental beliefs," they simultaneously sought to remove their finger-prints from the product.[9] Seeking to distance themselves from the trans-parently ideological political communication associated with totalitarian regimes, American experts theorized that nearly any cultural phenom-enon, properly positioned and interpreted, could assume a propaganda function.[10]

Compounding the propagandists' difficulties were the vagueness of the crucial term *freedom* and the fact that both of the belligerents claimed to embrace it. A prodigiously fertile signifier, "freedom" has always required clarification through material expression, "a fence," the sociologist Doro-thy Lee wrote, "around [its] formless idea."[11] A merely rhetorical affirma-tion of individual freedom, even one forcefully and consistently reiter-ated in official pronouncements, academic scholarship, and middlebrow media, would not suffice to summon the necessary martial energies. Ad-dressing the crucial question at the center of cold war America, "what are we for?," Eisenhower aide Arthur Larson asserted that "it is less important to stress that we are for freedom (since most uncommitted peoples accept freedom as an ideal) than to stress that *we are for the institutions that in fact create and advance freedom*" (italics his). "Freedom must find a purpose," echoed another Eisenhower staffer.[12] The defeat of collectivist ideology abroad and the liberation from "conformity" at home required a material infrastructure that would foreground the individual as the essential focus of American society. Thus by the 1950s, as Kim McQuaid observes, the cold war "began to be waged about everything."[13]

This chapter considers the Interstate Highway System as a component of the postwar "practical affirmation" of American values demanded by NSC 68 and other cold war rhetoric. It characterizes the interstates as a massive piece of propaganda expressing what one 1966 commentator called "the intense dedication of our age to motion."[14] In the years leading up to its authorization by the federal government in 1956, the proposed National System of Interstate and Defense Highways was portrayed by politicians, bureaucrats, engineers, military officials, business leaders, and the popular media as the fulfillment of middle-class Americans' de-sires for automotive safety, national security, economic prosperity, and expanded mobility. It was the largest public works project in human his-tory: from 1956 to 1975, over 42,500 miles of the continental U.S. would be paved; and a federal trust fund would raise and distribute an estimated $41 billion (in actuality, over $100 billion) in construction costs.

This chapter argues, then, that we look beyond what has become a standard explanation of the Interstate Highway System as a utilitarian product of postwar abundance and/or military exigency. We must pay attention instead to the ways in which the cold war organized the political and cultural conditions under which automobility took on a redoubled significatory power. The act of driving became, in this historical context, a sort of palliative ideological exercise that was seen to reverse, or at least to arrest, the postwar "decline of the individual" and the deterioration of the "American character" of a heroic and expansionist past. The figure of the driver, moreover, embodied the ideological gulf separating the United States from its communist antagonists, and proved—to those antagonists, to allied nations, to those cultures the United States sought to annex ideologically, and, most important, to Americans themselves—the continuing vitality of the essential individual freedom enjoyed under liberalism and capitalism.

The radical expansion of automobility that the Interstate Highway System enabled was catalyzed by at least five interrelated midcentury phenomena. The first is the revision of individualist ideology in mainstream political and business rhetoric to reflect more accurately and justify more effectively the contemporary corporate model of organization. Second is the elaboration of the social-scientific concept of "character" that, though it articulated selfhood as socially formed and culturally specific, nonetheless enabled the resurrection of the "autonomous individual"—as the heroic "American character." Third is the discourse of the *declining* American character and a corresponding reassertion of a heroic, archaic, and emphatically masculine individualism in cultural and scholarly production and state propaganda. Fourth is the related designation of mobility—automobility in particular—as a constituent element of the American character and therefore as an antidote to the latter's current decline. Fifth is the cold war state's *practical* acceptance of its role in creating and reinforcing specific subjects, even as that state, especially under the Eisenhower administration, disavowed such a role.

## the character compromise

The shattering of market triumphalism by the Great Depression occasioned what the historian Howard Brick has described as a "tropism toward collective social organization" and "vigorous arguments for a socialized conception of the individual" among intellectuals in the interwar years.[15] To commentators of various political stripes, the New Deal of the 1930s and the warfare-state socialism of the 1940s expressed collectivism in ascendancy, as the state acknowledged the limits of classical-liberal economic policy and expanded the authority of the federal government in steering economic (re)growth. The British political theorist Harold Laski, for example, saw in the New Deal "the completion of a continuous development of discontent with traditional individualism."[16] Yet critics of state stewardship of the economy, such as the economist Friedrich A. Hayek, wrote of a "road to serfdom" being paved over "the individualist tradition which has created Western civilization"; and others railed against collectivist infiltration of American education.[17]

Each of these social and political visions assumed a particular ideal of selfhood. Conservative thought, even as it affirmed a classical-liberal model of autonomy, was haunted by the social self: not the simultaneous constituent and effect of democratic life as envisioned by an earlier generation of pragmatists and feminists, but the easily manipulated denizen of the communist (or fascist) totalitarian state. Progressive political and economic thought was more affirmatively animated by the social sciences' vision of social selfhood, which itself found affinity with the historicist social critique leveled by socialism and Marxism—a claim noted by supporters and detractors alike.[18]

Yet American social science—sociology in particular—had begun to move in a more "engineering-reformatory-managerial" direction during the late nineteenth century, defining itself "primarily as empirical, quantitative, policy-related *method of inquiry* (not a system of beliefs)."[19] As they made this managerial turn, the social sciences gained greater legitimacy and entry into hegemonic institutions such as the state and business corporations. By the early twentieth century, social scientists had "arrived" in both industry and government in the capacities of organizationally specific technicians, diagnosticians, managers, and propagandists. Engaging in expert analysis rather than normative critique, many social scientists turned their attention to inefficiencies or "deviance" within an existing social system that they increasingly regarded as more or less sound.[20] Their partnership with the state solidified during and after World War II, as various agencies funded studies of troop morale, psychometric testing, and assays of psychological warfare. These social scientists under the patronage of the warfare state—characterized by the historian Ron Robin as "academic warriors"—tended to produce work of a distinctly pro-American and pro-capitalist cant, or in some cases openly used their research to craft more effective propaganda or techniques of control.[21]

The managerial turn sharpened in a postwar political climate in which deep prescriptive critique of American society was viewed as advancing a potentially treacherous agenda. Many right-leaning commentators and politicians continued to denounce what they considered social science's subversive foundations. A suspicious air clung to social science (if not to intellectualism more generally), despite its practitioners' avowals that their inquiries were informed by a "voluntaristic" theory of social action, which combined the liberal faith in individual autonomy and the assertion that human freedom was conditioned by environment, and not by Marxist determinism.[22] Still, a presumption of socialist axioms and aims justified 1952 and 1954 congressional investigations of the social sciences' purported tendencies "to weaken or discredit the capitalist system in the United States and to favor Marxist socialism."[23] Even the *Saturday Evening Post,* in a 1955 article titled "Human History Is Made By Men, Not 'Trends,'" noted with derision how "the southpaws among our intelligentsia" had scorned Disney's film portrayal of Davy Crockett as a rugged individualist, and reminded readers of "the enormous part played by strong individuals in making history."[24]

The practical dominance of the social self model particularly disturbed those crafters of cold war rhetoric, propaganda, and policy who sought to discredit Marxism by emphasizing its repudiation of the transcendent individual. "The communists," wrote Arthur Larson, "have struggled against the grain of human individuality"; the psychologist Robert Lindner described "militant socialism's *homo politicus*" as a figure denied "all title to individuality," for whom "abnegation of self [is] the core of his morality and the first article of his faith"; and the philosopher Abraham Kaplan averred that individual freedom was "of no consequence" to the communists, "because in the perspectives of their historical determinism liberty is an illusion: individual choice is bound by historical necessity."[25] At the same time, the American warfare state and its academic warrior partners responded quite positively to "behavioralism," which posited a decidedly deterministic selfhood, reducing the individual to a network of impulses, aversions, tendencies, and capacities. Despite the pervasive rhetorical defense of the individual, lingering reservations about theoretical bases were eclipsed by the social sciences' instrumental efficacy. From a hegemonic perspective, the vision of the self as emerging from social matrices and as manipulable grew less objectionable.

By the 1950s, a compromise had been forged: "character" emerged as an ideologically safe heuristic device that merged a conception of the self as contingent and constructed with the individualist rhetoric crucial to the prosecution of the cold war. National character, the historian David Potter wrote in *People of Plenty* (1954), was the "zone where history and the behavioral sciences meet."[26] The "American character" that appeared in so many postwar studies—over 150 books and articles (scholarly and quasi-scholarly) by one 1963 count—named what poststructuralists would call a subjectivity. But the American character was an appropriately martial and virile subjectivity, no less singular and worthy of emulation for his being created by cultural processes—especially if those processes themselves were characterized as singular and worthy of emulation.[27] Hence *People of Plenty,* for example, was boosterish in tone even as its ascension narrative emphasized environmental determinism: Potter looked to a god-given abundance, which had remained more or less static in American history, as a universal explanation for the vitality of American character and the culture it had produced, a culture characterized, in turn, by abundance.

Comparative studies in sociology, anthropology, political science, history, and humanities of this era tended to focus on strategically important Third World populations, seeking to determine why those cultures had failed at or rejected capitalist modernization. Diagnosing particular cultures' deficiencies in the individualistic and acquisitive worldviews sanctioned by American ideology, this work tended to recapitulate and put a scientific sheen on the standard claims of American exceptionalism. The psychologist David McClelland's *The Achieving Society* (1961), for example, attributed nations' economic success to an "achievement factor" in the personalities of their citizens. Since personality was formed in the mother-child relationship, changes in childrearing could potentially amplify the achievement factor in the population, enabling economic growth of the type found in populations in which that achievement factor was high. Not surprisingly, the United States, blessed with such a population, stood as the standard by which other nations were measured.[28] Viewed from the present, this focus on the "chaotic compound known as 'national character'" shows postwar academics' sympathy to the ideological agenda of the cold war state; but it also illustrates the incursion into many precincts of American society by the once-suspect conception of social selfhood.[29]

## the decline of the american character: conformity and feminization

Character, "the zone where history and the behavioral sciences meet," was a combat zone. Psychological and sociological analyses of the Soviet "New Man" or "Bolshevik ideal" reached into Russian history for the causes of the total "subjection" in which the Soviet citizen lived. Margaret Mead drew connections (and indicated points of discord) between the traditional Russian character, in whom self-control and individuation were "extremely underdeveloped" and "merging the individual in the group" was paramount, and the Bolshevik ideal, which "demands a complete subjection of the individual, by an act of individual will, to the control of the Party."[30] Other analysts observed that "American stress on autonomy, social approval, and personal achievement does not often appear in the Russian protocols," and that "Americans exhibit more inner conflict as to the dilemma of 'rebelling or submitting.'"[31] Nearly all Western accounts of the Soviet New Man noted the difficulty of transforming the traditional Russian character to suit the instrumental needs of the Party—the difficulty in remaking that character into a Taylorized machine part. This "poor fit" was due not so much to a rebellion against the collective, as the Russian character had a decidedly collectivist orientation, but rather involved the dominance in that character of sentimental, impulsive, and other irrational elements. Be he the dehumanized drone of the Soviet present or the overly emotional, romantic, superstitious peasant of the czarist past, the Russian character, American social scientists concurred, was an inferior creature, crippled by a too-powerful collective and a corresponding absence or atrophy of individual agency.[32]

Yet what is striking about a great deal of the scholarly and popular accounts of the American character in the postwar era is the *resemblance* that figure bears to its Soviet counterpart. The strategist elites of the cold war were not alone in their misgivings over the state of the American character. What the journal *Commentary* was perhaps first to diagnose in 1945 as the "crisis of the individual" drew the attention of an overwhelming number of social scientists, historians, economists, theologians, artists, and cultural critics.[33] This crisis shaped a postwar discourse of "invigorated commitment to the protection of the endangered self against the depredations of society" in which "expressions of support for liberal individualism . . . were frequent and endless."[34] Permeating this discourse was the dread of conformity.

A number of cultural critics diagnosed what Archibald MacLeish called "a massive, almost glacial, shift away from the passion for individual freedom and toward a desire for security of association, of belonging, of conformity." The novelist Wallace Stegner, for example, inveighed against the ascendant conformist sensibility "which reduces man to a unit and a cipher, ignoring his oneness and his unique and individual humanity," and which ultimately reveals a pervasive "contempt for individual man."

The literary critic R. W. B. Lewis registered with trepidation the near-disappearance of the "American Adam," a figure "going forth toward experience, the inventor of his own character and creator of his personal history." Harold W. Dodds, president of Princeton, urged the 1955 graduating class to resist the conformist impulse that gripped American society, to become the autonomous individuals that, if current trends continued, would soon go "the way of the buffalo." Internationalist intellectuals saw in the Marshall Plan the last, best hope for "the vital recognition that the integrity of society as a whole must rest on the respect for the dignity of the individual citizen." Even those writing from the margins of mainstream intellectual debate, such as Max Horkheimer, theorized the individual's decline against a culture of "adjustment" and conformity.[35]

Popular scholarly works, such as David Riesman's *The Lonely Crowd* (1950), C. Wright Mills's *White Collar* (1951), William Whyte's *The Organization Man* (1956), and Betty Friedan's *The Feminine Mystique* (1963), testified to the threat to individual autonomy posed by the postwar culture of abundance. These works focused on white middle-class men in their prime earning years (with the exception of Friedan's text, which plumbed the inner desolation endured by their wives), an ostensibly representative group for which "the most compelling dilemma [was] the waning of independent individualism as a life-style and as a social value, and the disappearance of social types and groups that made individualism a living reality."[36] Abundance, the scholars suggested, had enabled the growth of a species of "soft" totalitarianism, the control mechanisms of which were consumerism and the ethos of "belongingness" encouraged by bureaucratic organizations. There loomed something potentially authoritarian in the culture of the white middle class, with its patterns of social conformity, political quiescence, and susceptibility to the suasion of advertisers.[37] In these mostly liberal jeremiads one could nonetheless hear echoes of the claims of the cold warriors: the abject "lost individuals" who wandered their landscapes bore an uncomfortable likeness to the inhabitants of the Communist dystopia. Even Friedan's feminist critique reflected and contributed to a decidedly anti-collectivist cultural climate, and thus complemented the state's "narrative repetition of the Cold War message" of robust individualism.[38]

Cultural producers also militated against postwar conformity. As William Graebner has argued of the era, "The new fear (or, rather, anxiety, in a common distinction of the time) was that modern Americans—as well as Germans and Russians—had somehow fashioned for themselves a straitjacket of institutions and values that contained and thwarted the most basic desires for freedom of action and freedom of will."[39] Many visual artists, writers, filmmakers, and musicians identified their task as one of extricating themselves and their audiences from this straitjacket, and of reasserting the individual over the group. In literature, the radical egoism of Ayn Rand's "Objectivist" novels was perhaps the most exaggerated expression of an unease about collectivities that permeated the work of writers as stylistically disparate as Sloan Wilson, Grace Metalious, Norman Mailer, and J. D. Salinger. Noting the "various determinisms that ossify our wills," Stegner asserted literature's central function "has always been that of separating off individuals from the mass."[40] In the visual arts, abstract expressionism was hailed by critics as a celebration of individual will and agency over the formalistic—and therefore deterministic—rules of painting.[41] Even the more controversial popular culture of the 1950s—Nicholas Ray's *Rebel Without a Cause* and the rock and roll of Chuck Berry and Jerry Lee Lewis—registered with audiences as romanticized endorsements of the individual refusal and rebellion of the "juvenile delinquent."

Postwar anxiety over the "feminization" of American culture has been analyzed by scholars such as Elaine Tyler May, Suzanne Clark, Wendy Kozol, and K. A. Cuordileone. During the cold war, "gender issues were not separate from issues of national identity and were intertwined with the virulence of anticommunism."[42] Gender anxieties permeated two standard narratives plied by cold warriors, cultural producers, and social scientists alike. The first used gendered tropes of softness, frivolity, and vulnerability to emphasize the nation's weakness in the face of the communist threat. The second condemned American women and a coddling/suffocating culture of "Momism" for the erosion of individual (male) autonomy. These two narratives were mutually nurturing: the decline of "hard" male traits and the perceived transformation of American society into a "matriarchy in fact if not in declaration" had rendered the nation susceptible to "penetration" by communism (which was depicted as both feminized and feminizing).[43]

Cultural anxieties over feminization reflected, of course, deep unease over the state of masculinity; the fear was that, as Cuordileone writes, "American males had become the victims of a smothering, overpowering, suspiciously collectivist mass society—a society that had smashed the once-autonomous male self, elevated women to a position of power in the home, and doomed men to slavish conformity not wholly unlike that experienced by men living under Communist rule."[44] The reaffirmation of autonomous individuality, to which so many midcentury social critics, cultural producers, and representatives of the state directed their energies, doubled as a reaffirmation of masculinity.

## individualist propaganda and its discontents

Also beset and vexed by the "crisis of the individual" was the cold war state, the workings of which have been analyzed by scholars such as Aaron Friedberg, W. Scott Lucas, and Robert Griffith. Friedberg describes a set of "ideologically rooted, interest-driven, and institutionally amplified anti-statist influences [that] acted to constrict, constrain, and mold the federal government's efforts at power creation" during the cold war.[45] Lucas has argued that this thoroughgoing anti-statism limited the nation's propaganda capacities, as it mandated the perception "that the U.S. Government, unlike its evil Soviet counterpart, did not direct labor activity or academic research or journalistic endeavors; it was all the product of individuals freely making their own decisions and pursuing their own objectives."[46] Yet this highly individualistic view of society put the American warfare state at odds with itself, as Griffith has shown, as it simultaneously sought to marshal power as a collective entity in its policy acts and to deemphasize the importance of collectivities in its propaganda.[47]

Hence the Eisenhower administration crafted propaganda that not only emphasized individualistic themes, but that appeared itself to be the spontaneous creation of individual citizens or nonstate entities. These objectives, and indeed the nature of the Eisenhower administration's "policy culture" more generally, were embodied in the failed "People's Capitalism" campaign of 1956–57.[48] Assembled by members of the administration and the Advertising Council, and disseminated by the fledgling United States Information Agency (USIA), the campaign attempted to refute Soviet propagandists' portrayal of capitalism as an exploitative and immoral mode of production.[49] While it was intended to change international perceptions of the United States, it was also directed at domestic audiences, who, elites believed, also required "indoctrination in democracy" and "ideological rearmament" against incipient socialism. According to its creators, People's Capitalism would be "the greatest advertising and public relations campaign this country has ever known—a campaign with the single objective of reeducating the American people to our way of life."[50]

The campaign's fundamental claim was that, in the words of an Eisenhower advisor, the American economy was "an overall system of individual endeavor profitable to management, labor, and ownership, with vast numbers of labor among the stockholders and thus having ownership in their business."[51] This egalitarian capitalism differed substantively from the archaic "European" variety that, the propagandists allowed, Marx and his followers had been justified in condemning.[52] In an effort to secure credibility for the campaign's premises, a "People's Capitalism Round Table" was convened at Yale in 1956, with selected journalists and scholars endorsing the vision of American economic life as individualistic and egalitarian.[53] Similar efforts included the sponsorship and publication of a scholarly monograph, solicitation of an article by a prominent economist, film portrayals of life under People's Capitalism, and features in popular magazines such as *Reader's Digest* and *House Beautiful*.[54] However, few academics outside of the handpicked Yale group got on board. The *American Economic Review*, for example, disputed the claim of "an alleged qualitative change in structure" in the American economy, concluding that the assertion "that the rank and file of the population are becoming owners of the means of production in American industry is without foundation in fact."[55] *Reader's Digest, Newsweek, Collier's, Saturday Review*, and other middlebrow publications that tended to echo state propaganda cooperated, but others balked at the campaign's inflated claims; *Time*, for example, dismissed it simply as a repackaged conservatism.[56] Reflecting on the shelved campaign, co-creator George Allen remarked that "the more we protested, the more skeptical our listeners became."[57]

The failure of People's Capitalism—and of similar campaigns that aimed to show that the United States was "fighting enemy tyranny through the power of the individual"—epitomized the dilemma of the cold war state and its corporate partners-in-hegemony; namely, how to perpetuate an ideology of self-reliance and individual freedom in a corporate age.[58] The campaign's themes of increased individual agency ran counter to the dominant currents of postwar social and political thought, which, as discussed above, emphasized "the shrinkage of individual self-direction in the productive process" as it surveyed "the great and increasing proportion of our people [who] are no longer the independent, self-directing Americans of the old philosophy."[59]

People's Capitalism failed not only because its claims of individuals' participation in and "ownership" of the economy were not credible, but also because its mode of "re-education" was too abstract. Its narratives and images of employer-employee harmony and widespread stock ownership did not signify individual freedom or agency to the satisfaction of its audiences, and did little to convince those audiences that American society "allowed people to develop their identity in innumerable nonconformist ways."[60]

## (auto)mobility and the crisis of the individual

An America in which people are free, not in a rhetorical sense, but in the very real sense of being freed from congestion, waste, and blight—free to travel over routes whose very sight and feel give a lift to the heart—this is an America whose inner changes may far transcend the alterations on the surface. –Norman Bel Geddes[61]

If participation in a supposedly egalitarian economy failed to provide compelling evidence of Americans' freedom and agency, the question remained as to what practices might be shown, in the words of Arthur Larson, to "create and advance freedom" in the United States. Automobility's value to this end was suggested in the 1962 Warner Brothers/Department of Defense propaganda film *Red Nightmare*, a dystopian tale of small-town America under Soviet domination that concluded by cataloguing the social and political freedoms Americans enjoy. Over a series of wholesomely typical images of American life, the narrator, *Dragnet's* Jack Webb, gravely voices the film's moral:

> Freedom: no single word in all the languages of mankind has
> come to mean so much. Freedom to enjoy the simple things in life,
> in the circle of family and friends. Freedom to work in a vocation
> of our choosing. To vote, in open elections, for the candidate we
> believe best qualified. To come, to go, as we please.

*Red Nightmare* conveyed perhaps more than the filmmakers intended in its final appraisal of freedom: "no single word . . . has come to mean so much." Given the context of the film's fearful narrative, one assumes that the filmmakers were emphasizing freedom's preciousness to Americans; but parse the sentence differently, and it reveals the exhaustion "freedom" risked from oversignification. Yet as Webb intones *Red Nightmare's* last line, aerial footage of an urban highway, cars streaming in both directions, comes onscreen.[62] In *Red Nightmare*, as in so much postwar art and culture, automobility provided the crucial illustration of American freedom.

During the cold war, the literary scholar Suzanne Clark has argued, mobility invoked "a brand new configuration of cultural history," one that "called upon the old discourses of the West . . . to claim that there was and always had been one real American identity."[63] That identity was the frontier-ranging male individualist, whose heroic qualities derived from his constant movement. By most accounts, that subject was now all but extinguished. Could he be resuscitated? Or could his twentieth-century analogue arise from current conditions?

Many postwar scholars echoed Frederick Jackson Turner's 1893 celebration of mobility as essential to American dynamism and democracy. The historian George W. Pierson, for example, isolated the national genius in what he called the "M-Factor"—movement, migration, and mobility. Affirming that "movement has always been a major ligament in our culture, knit into the bone and sinew of that body of experience which we call our history. . . . [and] in the forging of an 'American' character," Pierson noted that American archetypes—pioneers, cowboys, rags-to-riches industrialists— had been shaped by experiences of migration.[64] Pierson argued that Americans were "in the process of reconstructing *the entire gamut of relations* for western (or mobile) man." Such a reconstruction could bring, he suggested, "new institutions patterned in part on free movement . . . new relations with the physical environment based on a view of nature different from the European . . . a new conception of human fellowship . . . and . . . even possibly a new attitude toward the self."[65]

Pierson made grand claims for mobility, but he was in eminent company: the historian Oscar Handlin credited the formation of a specifically American personality to the often traumatic practice of "uprooting"; the novelist John Steinbeck speculated that "Americans are a restless people, a mobile people"; even the urban theorist Lewis Mumford, no great proponent of the automobilized built environment, affirmed that movement had been the historical process by which "the social man could become an individual."[66] To sociologists such as David Riesman, who diagnosed anomie and conformity among the white professional-managerial class, "the overwhelming experience of American mobility" held promise as a therapeutic practice for the diminished selves of the age of organization.[67] The mobile individual was removed, if only temporarily, from a constricting social context, and thrown into situations both disorienting and liberating—what Pierson called "experiments in displacement." A great deal of postwar literature, too, celebrated the journey as a salutary trial by which the individual might locate the core of the authentic self. Jack Kerouac, for example, imagined the road as a maternal space (yet one free of women) that revivified those white men who took flight from the vitiating mediocrity of square society; *On the Road*'s Sal Paradise sought to leave "confusion and nonsense behind and [perform] our one and only noble function of the time, *move*."[68]

If the American road had traditionally been imagined as a sort of spartan retreat for the cultivation of the true self, that image complemented another, also implicit in Kerouac and others: the road as an emporium, stocked with an array of lifeways from which the individual could select. "Only in America," Riesman and Glazer wrote in *Faces in the Crowd* (1952),

> with all class and customary conventions nearly gone, does each geographical move imply a set of new and chancy human encounters—encounters with people who . . . compel and invite us to treat them to some degree as individuals. As tennis and golf players keep looking for those whose game is just a little better than theirs—but a game to which they can lift themselves by effort—so this mobility allows us to look for those whose life is in significant respects just a little better but whose "lifemanship" is still within our potential grasp.[69]

*Faces in the Crowd* and its predecessor, the highly influential *The Lonely Crowd*, rehearsed for the era of social psychology what had become a standard agon in American social criticism: reconciling the individualistic tenets of the culture's value system and the increasingly corporate nature of everyday life. Riesman and his collaborators asserted that "Americans"— implicitly defined as white, middle-class American men, and perhaps a few women—no longer possessed an individualistic orientation. Over the course of the twentieth century, "inner direction," the stuff of the rugged individualist, had given way to "other-direction," the code of the corporate man. Riesman's prescriptive, which I will discuss further in chapter 5, was "autonomy," which merged the best traits of both character types. Riesman envisioned "an organic development of autonomy out of other-direction," as the latter enabled "a sensitivity and rapidity of movement which under prevailing American institutions provide a large opportunity to explore the resources of character."[70]

Other social scientists, such as the sociologist Daniel Lerner, shared a view of the resourcefulness and mutability of the "mobile self" as indicative of nascent associational forms. Lerner affirmed the idea that mobility offered a wealth of resources for the construction of an authentic self; mobility had been both the cause of the shift in social character and the font of the best elements of other-direction—toleration, egalitarianism, facility for adaptation, and empathy. "The crucial word in the transformation of American lifeways," Lerner wrote, "is 'mobility.'"

> This nation was founded upon the mobility of the individual. . . . Mobile society required a mobile personality, a self-system so adaptive to change that rearrangement is its permanent mode. . . . The mobile person shows a high capacity for identifying himself with new and strange aspects of the environment. He is capable of handling unfamiliar demands upon himself outside his habitual experience. . . . Empathy is the psychic instrument which enables newly mobile persons to act effectively in the world. This is why the mobile personality is not to be regarded as mere psychic aberration or moral degeneration, but as a social phenomenon with a history. . . . The style of modern society is distinctive for its capacity to rearrange the "self-system" on short notice.[71]

Even among those social scientists somewhat sympathetic to other-direction, however, there remained suspicions that these best traits of the mobile personality ossified when the individual became ensconced in the "organization." Whatever their evaluations of other-direction, the proponents of therapeutic mobility acknowledge that the conditions of displacement and flux that had hewn the American character no longer governed the increasingly suburban, corporate present. Yet the American landscape remained one of potentially transformational mobility: automobility.

*Red Nightmare* was certainly not the only document to deploy the automobilized landscape as a definitive image of American freedom in the middle of the twentieth century. "One comes to perceive," wrote the historian Bernard DeVoto in *Freedom of the American Road,* a 1956 Ford highway-advocacy pamphlet, "that the American road represents a way of life."[72] That way of life had been forged in the mobile past. Eric Foner has observed that during the cold war, Americans "were constantly reminded in advertising, television shows, and popular songs" that, on the road, "they were truly 'free,' modern versions of western pioneers." Indeed, evoking the symbolically usable past of "the pioneers" was standard in the rhetoric of postwar automobility. Commenting that "'going somewhere' was becoming fun" through the use of the automobile, the novelist and critic Elizabeth Janeway noted that "Americans had 'gone somewhere' before—west across the country as pioneers." George Pierson quipped in 1962 that the archetypal pioneer in westward motion had been "the first auto-mobile." A 1957 *Time* article on roadbuilding asserted that the "panorama of road builders stringing highways across the land reflects a peculiarly American genius, one that lies deep in the traditional pioneering instincts of the nation." "America," two Soviet visitors archly noted in 1937, "is located on a large automobile highway." The author Bellamy Partridge declared in 1952 that, to the car owner,

> the family bus means a number of things, but above all it spells a freedom of movement undreamed of by his ancestors and known to all too few of his neighbors in other lands. Perhaps it is an unconscious realization of the deeper meaning of this freedom which puts added timbre in his voice as he drives up to the gasoline pump and calls out expansively, "Fill 'er up!"[73]

## the gender politics of cold war automobility

Promising a return to the mythologized past and heralding a limitless, abundant future, automobility seemed to offer the symbolic means to restore the American character—a character figured as masculine. As discussed above, driving "masculinized" as the automobile began to colonize the cultural, economic, and political landscape of the United States. The early years of the cold war show how the questioning of women's fitness to drive—an analogue of their capacity for self-governance and political agency—grew more pronounced during moments in which American masculinity was construed as threatened or enervated.

The image of the "woman driver," the focus of a body of disparaging humor since the 1920s, was revised somewhat during the Depression and World War II. During this time, economic and martial necessities shaped new representations in popular culture and state propaganda of women's fortitude and competence, and statistics compiled by insurance companies and others pointed to women as the more circumspect drivers.[74] The postwar era, however, resurrected the woman driver as clown and problem, and forcefully asserted gender as a prime indicator of driving aptitude. The 1946 CBS radio broadcast *Fifty Years on Wheels*, for example, featured the following conversation between two anachronistic Vaudeville comedians:

EDDIE: But Freddie—I'm not letting my wife drive my new car.
FREDDIE: But Eddie, I thought you said she drives like lightning.
EDDIE: So she does, Freddie, so she does. Always striking trees,
Freddie—always striking trees![75]

A compendium of accident data and cartoons published by the Travelers Insurance Company in 1954 showed women accounting for approximately 8 percent of fatal and 11 percent of nonfatal accidents in 1952–53; yet the majority of the cartoons poke fun at feminine illogic and carelessness.[76] Such japery reacted to the alleged feminization that had gripped a formerly virile American culture; it complemented the "compensating image" of postwar masculinity rooted in movement, mastery, and independence.[77]

If the journey is to fulfill its traditional goal of male individuation and distinction, it must be arduous, and take the subject far from the protective, familiar, and feminine spaces of domesticity. The political scientist Cynthia Enloe notes that "a principal difference between women and men in countless societies has been the licence to travel away from a place thought of as 'home'"; and the literary scholar Mary Gordon observes that male heroism in canonical American fiction is symbolized by centrifugal movement, with women representing an ominously, even morbidly, centripetal force.[78] Postwar social critics emphasized actual and metaphorical motion in their recommendations for the revitalization of American masculinity and society, as in the following passage by the psychologist Robert Lindner's *Prescription for Rebellion* (1952), the diction of which fairly radiates gender anxiety:

> Implicit throughout this discussion have been the methods for
> immunization against proletarianization. They comprise the
> creation and tending of a social climate which will give scope to
> the protestant proclivities of men, and the deliberate erection of
> such practical social preventives as may be required to oppose the
> trends—both natural (under certain circumstances) and artifi-
> cial—toward Mass Manhood. Of primary importance is the neces-
> sity to sustain, no matter what else may be done, the centrifugal
> movement of society. This . . . is that expansive, outthrusting
> motion of a culture that cleanses and keeps it vital. But for it to be
> everlasting, open frontiers have to be maintained as its dynamic
> condition.[79]

Not surprisingly, the postwar men's revolt against domesticity seemed to take its cue from Emerson's maxim, "everything good is on the highway." Yet the mobility practiced in the expansionist past and the automobility of contemporary motorists differed greatly. The archetypal experiences of American mobility had generally been those of immigration or migration across great distances (though what constituted a great distance had changed); automobility related more to circulation and shorter-distance movement for the purposes of commuting and consuming. Moreover, the controlled environments of modern highways, sumptuous, air-conditioned vehicle interiors, and plentiful roadside amenities made the vision of journey-as-trial increasingly difficult to sustain.[80] There was no question that contemporary automobiles were faster; but even speed, which had once promised "bigger living: quickened senses, aroused faculties, expanded powers of vision; acts of heroism, improvisation, and innovation; spectacular crashes and catastrophes; eruptions of laughter and glee," had been "routinized."[81] Hence George Pierson lamented the process of travel standardization as "the emasculation of the journey," movement in which "much of the excitement has been drained off"; M. M. Musselman complained that "cars have become as utilitarian as car openers and just about as thrilling"; and Daniel Boorstin inveighed against the "insulation" afforded by the automobile, and the standardized highway's degradation of once-ennobling travel to a "pseudo-event" and a "tautology."[82]

Nevertheless, the contemporary road journey could still yield what Sidonie Smith has characterized as "a masculinity whose trajectory is unplanned, undirected, unruly."[83] Kerouac's 1957 On the Road, for example, bears witness to the attempt to reintroduce contingency and risk into the male road experience, though the novel emphasizes that such pleasures are now exclusive to working-class outlaws, disaffected bohemians, and other such lumpen nomads. John Steinbeck's 1961 Travels With Charley opens with an affirmation of the author's working-class "fierceness"— "I've lifted, pulled, chopped, climbed, made love with joy and taken my hangovers as a consequence, not as a punishment"—as the explanation for his solo driving expedition. "I knew that ten or twelve thousand miles driving a truck, alone and unattended, would be hard work, but to me it represented the antidote for the poison of the professional sick man."[84]

As various postwar voices hailed the automobility of men, women were more discouraged from taking the wheel. The historian Roland Marchand notes that images of automobility in postwar popular magazines (both in advertisements and editorial content), film, television, and other popular cultural forms strongly suggest a re-gendering of the practice.[85] The characterization of women as maladroit drivers and untrustworthy custodians of automotive property could be read in popular texts like M. M. Musselman's 1950 Get a Horse!, which mused that "when it no longer took muscle to start a car the ladies quickly commandeered the family bus and the era of the accordion fender and the baffled traffic cop was at hand."[86]

Ironically, the popular reassertion of women's incapacity for driving proceeded even as suburbanization and the automobilization of residential areas after World War II necessitated that middle-class women drive more in order to fulfill their domestic duties, and as countless technical studies, newspapers, and magazines of popular science made what was on the surface a compelling case for women as superior drivers.[87] "Although often slandered by the male as being indecisive and hesitant in her driving," wrote the psychologist A. R. Lauer, director of the Driving Research Laboratory at Iowa State University, "she has a record for safe mobility that is enviable." Yet, in the context of the cold war, this praise was misleading; it simply marked women as insufficient subjects. Consider Lauer's evaluation of the female driver:

1. She is generally respectful of authority and if she violates it is usually due to some lack of information or lack of knowledge about the regulations.
2. She follows the rules of the game and is a good sport generally.
3. So far as automobiles are concerned she is not an exhibitionist. While she may like colored cars she does not go in for a lot of the frills that men quite often like.
4. She tends to lack confidence and is sometimes annoying in the work she does.
5. She is likely to be on the stable side; less likely to be delinquent in general, and less likely to get into traffic trouble.
6. At the wheel she is more conservative; follows at a greater distance and is more careful in passing.[88]

Women were, according to the studies and for the purposes of establishing auto insurers' risk, more effective at operating a car safely. Yet their automobility exemplified the wrong qualities: docility, tractability, other-direction. They were not *drivers* in the crucial sense of the term. Even as it issued recommendations for bringing violators to heel, highway safety literature cast "chronic traffic offenders" in a certain boys-will-be-boys light, as if to suggest that their deviance, like that of juvenile delinquents, might offer other-directed men a "prescription for rebellion."[89]

While they tended to pay lip service to women's driving proficiency, most mainstream media in the 1950s tended to affirm, directly or indirectly, that automotive mastery was to a large degree a matter of gender. Many articles implored women to submerge their femininity while on the road and assume the supposedly nongendered identity of the procedural driver. Tennis champion Alice Marble, for example, writing in the *New*

*York Times* in 1955, recommended that readers "try it on for size, being a driver rather than a woman"; and "stop being women when [they]'re behind the wheel."[90] Another *Times* article from 1956 (reprinted the same year in *Reader's Digest*) merits quoting at length:

> To put it bluntly, only the usual driver knows how to drive the car. It is only he who can glide easily in and out of traffic, who stays on his own side of the double white line, who adds no more than ten percent to the legal rate of speed. The others in the car simply lack ability. . . . especially . . . the one in the seat next to the driver's. . . . Naturally, the usual driver does most of the driving. This is only proper, since he alone drives well. On rare occasion, however, he changes places with the one sitting next to the driver. This is a searing experience. Where, before, that one had looked at nothing but the road, that one now looks at all else. . . . Someone must watch the road, and so the usual driver, in what should be his rest period, does so. He points out at once that the car is coming in this direction, and that the dog a bit ahead at the side of the road might decide to cross it. He points out that, while the marker displays a 35-mile speed zone, the speedometer says 50, and that the sign—apparently ignored—warns of a crossroad. He also jams his foot on the floor, just as though the brake were there. He suffers. He very soon will suggest a stop for coffee and, that pause over, will be back in the driver's seat. Where only he belongs.[91]

There is no mention of a "she" in this piece; the other driver's identity is clarified by reference to her usual position in the passenger seat: she is the wife of the "natural" driver. The current running through this and similar articles, as well as the postwar advertising that invariably depicted men driving family cars, was one of dissuasion.

## statist means to individualist ends

American culture has a deep affective stake in the historical connotations of individualism and will not lightly surrender it on the grounds of being responsible to some intellectual demand for historical accuracy and logical consistency. –John William Ward[92]

Automobility seemed to provide the means to resuscitate masculinity and individuality in a climate that, according to a myriad of voices, threatened to extinguish both. Nobody on the Senate floor rationalized its expansion in these terms, however; nobody needed to. That automobility had such salutary effects was occasionally articulated by works of social science, as I have tried to show; but more generally it manifested as common sense by the 1950s, if not earlier. Instead, automobility's expansion after World War II was justified as a matter of economic growth, technological progress, public health, national unity, and defense.

Historians have noted that the Eisenhower administration receives perhaps inordinate credit for implementing the Interstate Highway System, the original plan of which had been formulated by previous administrations.[93] However, as the historian Richard O. Davies has asserted, an examination of the Eisenhower administration does "provide an understanding of the temper of the times and the thinking of the administrative leaders that is essential for understanding the political climate that produced the Interstate system."[94] Eisenhower consistently admonished against "regimented statism" and dependence upon government to "'bring us happiness, security and opportunity'"; and he sought to "[arrest] the momentum of New Deal liberalism and [ensure] . . . that 'our economy . . . remain, to the greatest possible extent, in private hands.'"[95]

However, from his military experience Eisenhower gained a sense of the efficacy of bureaucratic entities in orchestrating massive projects and in enforcing harmony among a plurality of competing interests. His faith in centralized command organizations (of which the state and private corporations were both examples), coupled with his distrust of popular politics, led him to a politics that mediated between laissez-faire economics and state activism. This "middle of the road" sensibility, Eisenhower believed, safeguarded the freedom of the individual from all threats, whether they came from the operations of the private economy, from class conflict fueled by demagoguery, or from the tinge of socialism many saw in the most interventionist programs of the New Deal. Whatever its anxiety about statism, the Eisenhower administration demonstrated a willingness to channel state power to reinforce a "system that encourages individualism."[96]

Yet what type of individualism did Eisenhower mean? What was the state's genealogy of the self? Even as a chorus of postwar voices proclaimed that, in the words of cultural critic Philip Rieff, "the American character has been fatally damaged," the contours of a new hegemonic individualism were being delineated by the representatives of the cold war state and in the literature of business management.[97] Aware that in the middle of the twentieth century "the old values of individualism and self-help had been grievously discredited . . . and could never be resuscitated in their starkest form," Eisenhower and like-minded ideologues articulated an ethic that was not "rugged individualism in the old-fashioned Republican sense of the word," but merged "freedom and independence for the individual with its collateral responsibility for cooperation."[98] This revised individualism, which recognized that the self was socially formed and malleable, emerged as a key ideology by which the ostensibly anti-statist Eisenhower administration and its corporate allies justified the creation of the Interstate Highway System.

Yet even as the hegemonic institutions of American life made this environmental turn in regard to selfhood, they continued to trumpet a martial rhetoric of individualism and republican self-reliance. C. Wright Mills noted in 1956 the ubiquity of the "fetish of the American entrepreneur" despite that subject's near-disappearance from the landscape of modern capitalism.[99] The language and imagery of individualism, in other words, retained ideological force even as the concept shifted meaning. In their 1951 book *U.S.A.: The Permanent Revolution,* the editors of *Fortune* declaimed that individualism had "come of age" as an ethic of cooperation and fulfillment. This ethic reconciled the individual's desire for distinction and the corporate imperative for Taylorist regimentation through the concept of the *team.* As a member of a team, the editors wrote, the individual can "seek his self-expression, not along purely egoistic channels, but in a dynamic relationship to others, that is to say, mutually. A community is created, and through it the individual finds a higher expression of himself."[100] It was this individualism Eisenhower had in mind when he heralded "the age of the individual" in a 1949 commencement speech at Columbia: "there is no limit," he asserted, "to the temporal goals we set ourselves—as free individuals joined in a team with our fellows."[101]

In this "mature" individualism one could see remnants of earlier formulations that stressed fulfillment of the (social) self through association with various communities. Here were shards, for example, of Croly's "constructive individualism," or of Dewey's "new individualism." Yet the robust and hopeful prescriptions for the realization of selfhood articulated by pragmatists had been emptied of their radically democratic notions, and appropriated to reflect and serve the interests of corporate capital and the warfare state.

The idealized American subject of the cold war was an analogue, ironically, of what Soviet psychologists heralded as the New Man. By the 1930s Soviet theorists had largely abandoned the extreme environmentalism of "vulgar" Marxist conceptions of the individual, and reevaluated the degree to which individuals could be "conscious, purposeful actors" in society.

The revised model of subjectivity, known as the New Man, informed Party-sanctioned literature, history, and economic policy under Stalin. Whatever the American image of Soviet citizen as degraded "mass man" and automaton, the New Man model ascribed greater agency to the individual; one Soviet psychologist lauded the state's attempt to produce "a socially 'open' man who is easily collectivized and quickly and profoundly transformed in behaviour—a man capable of being a steady, conscious and independent person, politically and ideologically well trained."[102] However, as the American social psychologist Raymond A. Bauer insisted, the independence of the New Man relied on his total internalization of Party doctrine; the individual was thus "free to act only within the limits circumscribed by the regime, free to act only in the pursuit of socially-accepted goals."[103]

Soviet psychology held only passing interest to American political elites, except as an egregious example of the way in which social science played handmaiden to the Soviet state. More crucial to their critique was the condemnation of the state's belief that it could and should—through structured environments, education, propaganda, coercion, or reward—manufacture the types of citizens it desired.[104] In the official stance of the cold warriors, the idea that individuals were shaped by the state, and existed only by its imprimatur, exposed the monstrous nature of the Soviet system. Yet as the Soviet Union engineered its New Man—"politically and ideologically well-trained"—so did the United States require a representative countersubject, the salient quality of which was *manifest* individual autonomy.

What was an individual, after all? Gabriel Hauge, Eisenhower's special assistant for economic affairs, asserted that

> the individual is neither Athene sprung full-blown from the brow of Zeus nor a shapeless lump of clay to be molded this way and that by an autonomous environment. He comes into this world a bundle of unrealized potentials with a capacity for growth. Our concept of the interaction between the individual and his environment is that his capacities must be exercised to attain their full potential and must be developed in order to be effectively exercised.[105]

Sharing Hauge's assessment was a historian of Russia and Rockefeller Foundation consultant, Geroid Tanquary Robinson, who in a 1949 *Foreign Affairs* pondered the role of the state in cultivating the individuals required for the "ideological combat" of the cold war:

The end and aim of society and the state ought to be the nurture and propagation of a certain kind of man—the independent and self-directing individual. . . . Today there is hardly a man in the United States who does not believe that within recent decades it has become necessary for the Government to do more for the people than it did a hundred years ago. Yet there still persists . . . much more vigorously here than in any other great country, a vigorous individualism and a strong and wholesome fear of all great concentrations of power, whether in private or public hands. If the fundamental objective were agreed upon, and kept steadily in mind—the nurture of a certain kind of man—might there not be hope of at least a partial reconciliation of the old individualism with the new stateism of today? Could not the beginnings of a reconciliation be made by recognizing as fundamental the difference between government action which is designed to build up the independence and self-sufficiency of the individual citizen, and government action which tends to establish permanent discipline and dependence?[106]

For this conflict, Eisenhower and other hegemonic actors would have to use, to paraphrase Herbert Croly, "statist means to individualist ends"; that is, they would have to craft policies and institutions conducive to a particular artifactual subjectivity, even as they disavowed the legitimacy of this role for the state.[107]

With the end of the Korean War in 1953, the Eisenhower administration devoted more attention to highway matters. In a speech to the annual Governor's Conference at Lake George, New York, in July 1954, Vice President Nixon (Eisenhower was at a funeral) stunned an audience acclimated to the administration's usual fiscal conservatism by announcing a $50 billion highway plan. This speech provides a sense of the political gymnastics required for Eisenhower to undertake such a massive public works project and still retain his credibility as a conservative. More illuminating for this analysis than the particulars of the plan itself, however, is the opening apologia with which Nixon primed his audience of state governors and officials. "Where is the United States going," he asked, "and by what road?"

The road we should take is outlined by the American philosophy of government . . . rooted in individual rights and obligations— expressed in maximum opportunity for every individual to use rights and to discharge obligations—maintained by keeping close to the individual his control over his government—it is sparked by local initiative, encouraged and furthered by the Federal government. Financed traditionally by demanding of visible, tangible and profitable return on every dollar spent. A tax economy of enterprises, directly or indirectly, which are self-liquidating. Now, that philosophy, applied to public affairs, is the middle road between chaos on the one side, and regimentation on the other. It is significant that in the United States we talk of individual rights, we talk of States' rights, but not of Federal rights, because the Federal Government is normally considered a depository of certain well-defined and limited obligations: for national security, for foreign affairs, for leadership within the community of 48 States. Now, in that light, what are the domestic jobs that must be done to further the purposes of America? What is the prospect before us?[108]

Eisenhower was clearly anxious to differentiate its initiative from the Democratic endeavors of the recent past. His intention was to make the project appear less statist than it inevitably was, and thereby to avoid what critics in his own party would condemn as "another ascent into the stratosphere of New Deal jitterbug economics."[109] He was unsympathetic to the utopian plans of social planners such as Robert Moses and Norman Bel Geddes, which while sharing Eisenhower's enthusiasm for automobility evinced too much of a "planning" sensibility.[110] Instead of proposing the highway system as a form of progressive social engineering, Eisenhower and his allies emphasized the former as a *response to a crisis*.

First named and approved as a public works priority in 1944, the National System of Interstate Highways had been promoted forcefully over the previous three decades by a constellation of interests identified collectively as the highway lobby. This group, also known as the "Road Gang," consisted of the oil, cement, rubber, automobile, insurance, trucking, chemical, and construction industries, consumer and political groups, financial institutions, and media. Military leaders—Eisenhower's erstwhile comrades—also backed the project. Having seen Germany's *Reichsautobahn* at the end of the war, they envisioned a network of efficient and durable highways for the rapid movement of troops and materiel (though most of the Third Reich's troops and equipment had been moved by rail).

The *Reichsautobahn* system, the first sections of which opened in 1935, stood as the exemplar of a modern state's commitment to automobility. The splendor of the Third Reich's "national auto road" prompted the 1938 House Roads Committee chairman, Wilburn Cartwright, to state that "we must give Fuerhrer [sic] Hitler credit for building a system of superhighways in his country [that would provide the German people with] innumerable peacetime commercial, industrial, social and cultural benefits."[111] Though it was not the first limited-access highway—that distinction belonged to the 1923 Italian *autostrada* that connected Milan and Varese—the *Autobahn* inspired the first such highways constructed in the United States in the 1930s: the Pennsylvania Turnpike, Connecticut's Merritt Parkway, and Los Angeles's Arroyo Seco Parkway.

However technically and aesthetically inspiring, in political-philosophical terms, for Eisenhower and many other cold warriors, the *Reichsautobahn* was anathema; its American doppelgänger would have to be justified "within the ideological and institutional strictures of the weak state."[112] To this end, midcentury analysts of transportation—especially those affiliated with the automotive industry—claimed the distinguishing feature of American automobility to be its organic, democratic, "grassroots" evolution, emphasizing that it had achieved its dominance through incremental change and the public's increasingly enthusiastic stance toward an automobilized everyday life. Industrial public relations offices, automotive historians, representatives of government, and commentators in the mainstream media all explained the narrowing of alternatives to increased roadbuilding and automobile use as the outcome of a sort of plebiscite in which Americans had given automobility "an overwhelming public mandate," in the words of Henry Ford II.[113] Moreover, the democratic nature of the development of the road infrastructure in the United States could be read in its haphazardness. The current highway system, Vice President Nixon declared, "is obsolete because it just happened"; in the development of automobility, "government raised no controlling hand," wrote two 1951 commentators; and American Motors executive George Romney asserted that the modern highway was "like the vehicles that created it . . . the product of the people, a thing made by the people for the people."[114]

Such voices argued that, while American roadbuilding had never been exactly private enterprise, neither had it been a component of an imperial social plan designed and implemented in a top-down manner. Instead, the aggregate will of millions of individuals had caused roads to proliferate; and it would be the cooperation of "individual citizens" that would, according to the Ford Motor Company, "solve many of [the] highway, traffic, and safe driving problems."[115] Eisenhower's anti-statism and national self-representation during the cold war required that the highway project be framed within an individualist imaginary. Consider the anti-collectivist polemics in Romney's 1950 discussion of German automobility, which had "sedulously imitated" American roadbuilding and auto manufacturing models:

> After careful study of American production and construction methods, the master-planners of Germany's National Socialist Government drew up elaborate plans both for production of the *Volkswagen*, or "People's Car," and for construction of the *Autobahnen*, an elaborate network of the most modern kind of motor-highways. Widely advertised in the late 1930s as means for motorizing the masses of Germany, these devices were the result of deliberate bureaucratic planning, rather than the end-products of that interplay of related forces which . . . govern the natural evolution of the vehicle and the road. The irony of such master-planning obtrudes from the fact that, when the real test came, the *Volkswagen*, though revealed to have been actually designed as a military vehicle, failed in contest with the military adaptations of automotive vehicles which the American people turned out; and the *Autobahnen*, though carefully built by *Organization Todt* as a device to implement the speedy conquest of neighboring nations, became the ideal means for the quick dismemberment of the German military machine in 1945.[116]

Romney's distinction characterized the thought of many advocates of automobility who were also staunch anti-statists; these advocates, of whom President Eisenhower was one, insisted on a fundamental ideological difference between planning that transformed society, and planning that resolved a crisis, and enabled society to continue along its already chosen path. According to Romney and like-minded thinkers, the *Reichsautobahn*, however expertly built and ordered, remained a monument to the political imaginary of socialism.

Such ideological gymnastics obscured the fact that in implementing its interstate plan, the American federal government and its industrial partners had done more than "accelerate a shift that was already under way" and give "added impetus to the rising dominance of the auto"; they had adopted an activist role in promoting automobility.[117] Beneath the justifying rhetoric of economic prosperity and national unity lay a subtext stressing highway driving as an eminently worthwhile practice, one constitutive of the right kind of American subjects. In other words, there was more than one reason that highways were, as David Riesman noted, "aside from schools, the only collective product not to be condemned as creeping socialism."[118]

## something to want: the interstate highway system

[The] performance of freedom, its virtuosity, needs to *appear,* to be witnessed, in order for it to be political. —Vikki Bell[119]

The efforts of Eisenhower and the "Road Gang" came to fruition in the
Federal-Aid Highway Act of 1956, the battles over and passage of which
have been amply documented by Mark Rose, Tom Lewis, Richard Weingroff, and others, and which "foreclosed most of the options in American
road politics."[120] Given the number of Road Gang alumni on the committee
assembled by Eisenhower in 1954 to spearhead the planning and financing of
the highway system (known as the Clay Committee after its chair, retired
general and executive Lucius D. Clay), and the nature of the testimony
the committee solicited, it was not surprising that its 1955 report recommended that the system be 90 percent subsidized by federal money rather
than tax levies or tolls on road users. Also not surprisingly, various opposed
groups criticized the Clay plan as a massive state subsidy for the automobile, gasoline, oil, tire, cement, construction, and trucking industries.[121]

The mainstream press was largely sympathetic to the Clay plan—
indeed, to highway building in general, not least because of the windfall
its advertisers would receive. Herbert Brean, writing in *Life,* heralded
the plan as a bold vision of the future, and lamented its stormy recep-
tion by cowardly legislators.[122] Similarly boosterish was a January 1955
New York *Daily News* editorial cartoon that depicted Uncle Sam driving a
steamroller bearing the inscription "$100 Billion U.S. Good Roads Proj-
ect" toward the gravel-and-tar pile upon which a Hearst newspaperman
stands; written on the soon-to-be asphalt below the newspaperman's feet
is "Spade Work." Despite favorable exposure in the press, the Clay plan
did not make it far in Congress, where Democratic legislators demanded
that industry bear a portion of the costs. To Eisenhower's dismay, 1955
passed without the dramatic new highway legislation. In 1956, however,
the Road Gang, perhaps sensing the potential profits lost by another year
of inaction, was willing to acquiesce on user taxes. A bill sponsored by
Representative George Fallon, which called for $24.8 billion in federal
funds, was merged with Representative Hale Boggs's Highway Revenue
Act, which established a "pay-as-you-go" scheme of gas and other taxes.
Combined, these two acts became the Federal-Aid Highway Act of 1956,
which Eisenhower signed into law in June.

It has been speculated that the military and nuclear threat the cold
war presented was the key factor in enabling the Road Gang to defeat its

rivals—the railroad, pipeline, and nautical shipping industries, and politicians averse to tax-funded infrastructural projects. This latter alliance, H. W. Brands writes, "had been holding off the road gangs for years. The Cold War was the new element in the situation, and it provided just the additional argument needed to bulldoze the opposition and get the graders going."[123] I see the national-security angle played by Eisenhower and congressional highway supporters as simply another selling point for the project, and one deployed rather late in the day. Indeed, Fallon has been credited with making the defense aspects of the highway explicit by adding "Defense" to the system's name in 1956.[124]

The assertion of the highways' military and civil defense utility is perhaps best understood as an element of a more general rhetoric of crisis. The early 1950s saw the Road Gang embark upon a major new public relations offensive, the theme of which was "the highway crisis." As noted above, advertising and editorial content in diverse media articulated a crisis of mobility brought on by the paucity, poor quality, and unsafe condition of American roads, while simultaneously asserting automobility's dominance to be the consequence of individual Americans overwhelmingly "voting" for it. Mainstream publications stressed the vexing and dangerous nature of driving under current conditions. *Life* warned in 1955 that "we are actually building cars faster than we are pouring the concrete on which to park them. Barring a world war or a five-year strike in the auto business, the United States in the next decade faces highway congestion and general traffic paralysis that will be simply incredible"; *Reader's Digest* shared with its readers "Why Motorists Blow Their Tops"; *Time* profiled "Neurotics at the Wheel"; and *Collier's* caricatured the various types of "Highwaymen."[125]

Such pieces complemented the advertisements for decidedly pro-highway concerns such as Portland Cement, Caterpillar ("The World's no. 1 Road Building Equipment"), and the Asphalt Institute ("Ribbons of Velvet Smoothness"), that similarly lamented subpar and perilous highway conditions, and encouraged drivers to lobby their elected officials. In 1951, the trucking industry, complaining of revenue lost through delays and expensive tolls, launched "Project Adequate Roads," a lobbying initiative dedicated to making the interstate highway program politically visible and viable. "The crux of the problem," R. W. Litchfield of Goodyear Tire declared, "is not the number of cars or the size of trucks—*it is too few modern roads!*"[126] Promotional films such as those produced in the early 1950s by General Motors (*Anatomy of a Road* and *Give Yourself the Green Light*) and Ford (*Freedom of the American Road*) featured scenes of drivers languishing in traffic jams, negotiating bottlenecks, dodging potholes, and crawling through ubiquitous construction zones.

Nearly all invocations of the highway crisis attempted to stir nationalistic feelings and instill in their audiences a sense of civic obligation. For example, 1954 saw the White House Conference on Highway Safety, at which representatives of industry, highway associations, government, labor, media, and women's groups used the language of public health to elicit support for the highway plan. The 1956 Ford pamphlet *Freedom of the American Road* (the centerpiece of multifaceted public relations campaign) opened with Henry Ford II bemoaning the seeming intractability of "our highway situation." The opposite page featured a dramatic photograph of the Los Angeles freeway, its caption calling it "a standard for highway planning" and further rhapsodizing that "unlike any other country, America takes gigantic works of man in stride to produce its wealth and better life." To garner citizens' support for the project, Ford deployed a rhetoric of self-interest merging seamlessly with service to others and to the republic. The citizen, the company emphasized, "has to stop thinking of his personal payment for highways, such as taxes, tolls, or property, as contributions to a vague someone else, and back the necessary measures as an investment of permanent value to his nation and himself."[127]

In highway engineers, the Road Gang had a credible "scientific" proxy speaking in favor of their interests. Roadbuilding agencies continued to describe their own roles as merely apolitical executors of the public's automobility imperative and as facilitators of safety.[128] Virtually nowhere was the interstate project put forth as an inducement to further automobility, though of course it was. *Life's* 1956 profile of Bertram D. Tallamy, Eisenhower's federal highway administrator appointee, observed that "though the interstate system is designed to relieve the worsening traffic jam, Tallamy predicts it will actually increase traffic by at least 50 percent."[129] Convincing citizens to spend more time behind the wheel was an endeavor most justifiably undertaken by the industries that increased driving would enrich: a series of 1950s advertising campaigns funded by the Ethyl Corporation, the American Petroleum Institute, and others encouraged drivers to "Drive More . . . it gets cheaper by the mile!" and touted the low price of gasoline compared to other commodities.

But automobility did not merely require expansion, it *merited* it. The industrial designer Norman Bel Geddes's "Futurama" exhibit at the 1939 World's Fair in New York, which conveyed fairgoers through a future America (the world of 1960) in which automotive traffic flowed effortlessly through urban areas and scenic, landscaped, high-speed highways traversed the countryside, linked automobility with *progress* and the material abundance, freedom, and social harmony that term signified. Writing in support of his urban and suburban plan, Bel Geddes explicitly tethered his proposed "magic motorways" to a modern vision of the good life:

> Already the automobile has done great things for people. It has taken man out beyond the small confines of the world in which he used to live. Distant communities have been brought closer together. Throughout all recorded history, man has made repeated efforts to reach out farther and farther and to communicate with other men more easily and quickly, and these efforts have reached the climax of their success in the twentieth century. This increasing freedom of movement makes possible a magnificently full, rich life for the people of our time. A free-flowing movement of people and goods across our nation is a requirement of modern living and prosperity.[130]

Bel Geddes's 1940 paean to automobility would be echoed over the next two decades by a growing chorus of industrial interests and representatives of the state (who often were one and the same). Like Frederick Jackson Turner, George Romney was confident that the American tradition of mobility would compel further and grander roadbuilding. "For we Americans," he wrote in 1950, "are inherently the most restless of peoples; and, as long as this trait is dominant in us, our land shall doubtless continue to provide the ideal climate for the vehicle's road-creative proclivity." "America lives on wheels," Eisenhower's Treasury Secretary George Humphrey proclaimed, "and we have to provide the highways to keep America living on wheels and keep the kind and form of life we want." A participant at the 1950 "Highways in Our National Life" symposium at Princeton University similarly stated that "the dynamic character of American society owes much to the first rude highways over which toiled the pioneers on horseback, on foot, in wagons, and in prairie schooners. It owes even more to the hard-surfaced highway which today links the country in a huge and mobile network."[131]

The full promise of the interstate system was intimated by a 1955 advertisement for Republic Steel—a major highway contractor—which asked *Saturday Evening Post* readers, "Do you ever dream of an *open* road?" The ad depicted a young white couple out for a leisurely drive on a modern highway, the sleek overpasses in the distance confirming that it is one of the limited-access highways currently being deliberated by Congress. The man wears a suit and tie and a pleasantly surprised smile; he's also the only thing in color. The woman smiles broadly, her face angled toward him. They are likely married, suburban, middle-class: the intended beneficiaries of the postwar economic boom. "To whirl along with all the joy your car has to offer," the copy gushed, "that's something to want" (fig. 6).[132]

As stated above, the equation of driving with freedom was generally implicit in "highway crisis" advocacy; but occasionally it was made explicit. Ford's *Freedom of the American Road* and its supporting materials were emphatic on the point: a "Notes for a Talk" transcript, for example, urged its hypothetical audiences to read this "very remarkable book,"

> which I have here in my hand. . . . It's an eye-opener, right from
> the title on through to the last page. Why?—because it says that
> our ability to travel around this country in our own cars, any-
> where we want, is a special kind of freedom, a unique freedom
> people have here in America, not quite like travel anywhere else in
> the world.

The transcript later quotes Henry Ford II on the provenance of the title (sounding suspiciously like Jack Webb in *Red Nightmare*): "[Ford] says: 'This book is called *Freedom of the American Road* simply because we American always have liked plenty of elbowroom—freedom to come and go as we please in this big country of ours.'"[133]

Such rhetoric aimed, like People's Capitalism, at the reeducation of the American public as to the animating merits of the American way of life. On at least two occasions the connection between the highway project and the propaganda campaign was made plain: "'People's Capitalism' has, besides a bold ring, the great virtue of truth," began an editorial in the January 1956 *Collier's*. After enumerating the tenets of the campaign, the piece concluded with, simply, "We agree." The inset of the page featured a sidebar paragraph, "Your Highways," which encouraged readers to "speak up" for the interstate program. That program was described later in the issue in an article, "Where Are Those New Roads?," that resonated with the claims of People's Capitalism:

> Each new overpass, each new split-lane seems to have added
> dimension to our power and imagination as individuals. . . . It is
> the automobile, more than any single phenomenon, that sets our
> way of life apart from the rest of the world. Everywhere else, com-
> mon people have always been separated from their betters by the
> simple distinction of whether they walked or rode. In times past,

**figure 6.** The automotive utopia, circa 1955. Reprinted courtesy of Republic Engineered Products.

# *of an open road?*

are safer and smoother to drive on and they resist longer the destructive power of ice.

Ready for the new highways are the sinews of steel built by Republic—over 40 tons for each mile of average road, tremendously more for each mile of super turnpike.

Road building is an investment in and for the future. Roads benefit every one. They stimulate commerce and create employment. The construction of the highway is only the beginning. The buildings which will follow the highways call for millions of man hours and millions of tons of materials. Republic is ready with the steel.

## STEEL
OHIO

*Standard Steels and Steel Products*

**WHAT HAPPENS TO STREAMS** that want to cross a road? They flow under it through drainage structures by Republic. Sectional plate arches and pipe carry the heaviest trucks, burdened with the heaviest loads without crushing or cracking, without weather damage. Corrugated metal pipe protects taxpayers because it saves on installation costs and lasts and lasts and lasts.

**EVERY NEW ROAD OPENS PIONEER COUNTRY.** New service stations are forerunners of light, bright restaurants windowed in glass and steel by Republic's Truscon Division. Ever-lustrous, easy-to-clean food preparation and serving equipment, counters and interior wall panels are made of Republic ENDURO Stainless Steel.

**MANY OF TODAY'S SAFE, ROOMY AUTO BODIES,** as well as hoods and fenders, are made of Republic sheet steel from the world's widest continuous strip mill. Many have shiny trim inside and out that simple cleaning keeps new looking for the life of the car—that does not chip or peel—because it's solid Republic ENDURO Stainless Steel. Remember: There's a BIG difference in BRIGHT trim.

people who rode were "cavaliers," hence aristocrats. In America today, every man is a cavalier.[134]

We have seen this conferral of a blithe, regal identity on the driver before (the columnist George Will has more recently rehearsed that "in the land of the automobile, every man's a king").[135] Later in 1956, *Collier's* again affirmed the People's Capitalism campaign in the evocatively titled article "Every Man a Capitalist"; also once again, the same page featured an endorsement of the Interstate Highway System.[136]

We need not identify cold war anxieties over the American character as the exclusive *cause* of the Interstate Highway System to understand their effect as a key *catalyst*. By fulfilling imperatives that "freedom must find a purpose" as a reliable exemplar, automobility performed crucial ideological work at this time. First, the interstate highways, in addition to their commercial and military benefits, also made for effective cold war propaganda, as they literally made concrete the individual freedom of which, *The New Republic* wrote in 1948, "Americans hunger for tangible evidence."[137] The accomplishment of these "vast and beautiful works of engineering," as a 1966 commentator explained, was their expression of "a new attitude in which high-speed motion and the qualities of change are not mere abstract conceptions but a vital part of our everyday experiences."[138] Second, the highways' appearance as mute features of the built environment, democratically mandated by a driving public, obscured their function as *disciplinary structures* through which the cold war state, to return to the political philosopher John Gray's quote above, "made possible" the autonomous individuals it required.

For this anxious liberal state, "the goal of governing [was] not to simply guard against too much freedom, but to produce the type of freedom that accord[ed] with the expansive demands of culture and economy."[139] Like the Soviet New Man, the idealized subject of American liberalism was free to act and to choose, but only "within the limits circumscribed by the regime." Automobility—in particular that of the elevated, limited-access highway of the postwar era—provided a quotidian performance of both autonomous self-direction *and* acquiescence to systemic parameters. To drive, in other words, was to live motion without change.

## chapter four

# "So That We as a Race Might Have Something Authentic to Travel By": African American Automobility and Midcentury Liberalism

Merging his Ford Model T with the traffic stream of E. L. Doctorow's peripatetic 1974 novel *Ragtime,* the African American pianist Coalhouse Walker is involved in a collision of sorts, one that will eventually prove fatal. En route to New York City after a visit with his fiancée on Long Island, Walker is humiliated by the Irish American firemen of the Emerald Isle Engine brigade, to whom the sight of an urbane black man at the wheel of a new car is an intolerable affront. After denying Walker passage on the public road in front of the firehouse, the firemen vandalize and destroy his Model T. When his appeals for redress are dismissed by local authorities, and when his fiancée is killed while attempting to elicit aid from a politician, Walker responds with what we call, then as now, terrorism: he kills members of the brigade, bombs several firehouses, and later occupies and threatens to destroy Manhattan's Morgan Library. Throughout the conflict, Walker's demand remains the same: that the fire chief restore the Model T ("black, with the custom pantasote top") to its prior condition. The police accede, but then gun Walker down on 36th Street as he gives up his siege. The car, however, spirits away Walker's comrades-in-arms, one of whom is a white man, a young bourgeois-turned-revolutionary identified only as Younger Brother. Leaving the other members of Walker's gang in Harlem, he drives unmolested across the nation to the Mexican border, his whiteness licensing his flight. Walker's failed crusade will soon fade from official memory, just like the evanescent "trail of dust in the sky" kicked up by the southbound Model T.[1]

I recount the fictional tragedy of Coalhouse Walker, which takes place around 1915, as a compelling illustration of the limited access that has governed the American road and, by extension, the political culture the road reflects and constructs. Joining conversations among cultural historians and literary scholars (not to mention artists and musicians) on the high stakes, pleasures, and perils of African Americans' driving and car ownership, claims to the public space of the road, and general participation in an expanding culture of automobility, this chapter focuses on the midcentury guidebooks *Travelguide (Vacation & Recreation Without Humiliation)* and *The Negro Motorist Green Book*.[2] These texts, which directed black drivers to hospitable roadside lodging, restaurants, and mechanical assistance, did more than offer helpful information. Through their images and editorial copy, they also provided a multifaceted, often contradictory rhetoric of communal racial uplift and liberal individualism figured around driving. Racial attitudes and policies shifted during these guidebooks' years of publication, 1936 to 1957, as World War II and the cold war made the national doctrine of white supremacy a global political liability. It was in this historical context that African Americans' desire and fitness for citizenship were tethered to and divined in their participation in automobility, a practice that fused self-determination and self-representation, mobility, consumption, and social encounter. The rhetorical strategies of these guidebooks complemented a particular strain of liberal antiracism necessitated by the cold war, facilitated by the nationalization of postwar politics and economics, and performed in increasingly standardized public spaces, such as the interstate highways.

## driving while black

The literary scholar Philip Fisher has described vectors of movement such as the American road as democratic social space, "a universal and everywhere similar medium in which rights and opportunities are identical, a space in which the right and even the ability to move from place to place is assured." This space, the essential characteristics of which are "mobility [and] the right to enter or exit," provides a stage for the enactment of democratic, egalitarian citizenship.[3] The film scholar Barbara Klinger has similarly noted the ways in which the road constitutes "a space by definition democratic since in theory no class systems or unfair hierarchies exist there; a space then where individual renewal, property relations, and industry can be achieved within a democratic framework."[4] The road is thus the representation and product of what the political theorist Charles W. Mills has called the "ideal nonracial polity," in which "one's personhood is guaranteed, independent of race, and as such is stable, not subject to loss or gain."[5]

These authors take various positions toward this idealized conception, but let mine be clear: the space of the American road, like the contours of citizenship, was established under specific regimes of racialized inequality and limited access whose codes it reproduces. The predicament of African American drivers in the middle of the twentieth century (and beyond) illustrates the correlation between the politics of individualism and the structures and protocols of driving. By the circumscription of these drivers' movements through public space we glimpse the formula by which some people are accorded personhood and others—"those persons with bodies marked as nonwhite, nonmale, and/or economically dependent"—are not.[6] Just as the ideology of individualism "encouraged an insular self-assertion that prevented the individual from recognizing the selfhood of others," so is it that "*mobility relies on immobility*; it is precisely because certain subjects and objects are immobilized that others can travel."[7] Not surprisingly, then, as Kathleen Franz asserts, "although white travelers constructed the open road as a technological democracy, open to anyone who owned a car, they simultaneously limited access to automobility through a system of discrimination and representation that positioned nonwhites outside the new motor culture."[8]

Because spatial mobility has often been a means to or evidence of the social mobility of racial others, regimes of white supremacy have sought to control or curtail those forms and moments of nonwhite mobility that they could not instrumentalize for their own purposes. For example, in addition to imposing the Black Codes and Jim Crow in the decades between Emancipation and World War I, southern legislatures attempted to limit the mobility of African Americans, though such measures were generally piecemeal and unable to prevent the migrations to the north during and after Reconstruction. According to William Cohen, these years marked "a time when southern blacks lived at freedom's edge, suspended between the world of slavery that had once been theirs and a world of freedom that still belonged mostly to whites. The extent of black freedom varied with time and place, but always the right to move without hindrance was one of its most important features."[9] A chief effect of Jim Crow in the twentieth century was "a geography of thwarted action, of arrested motion" for African Americans.[10] The cold war offered a cruel new dimension to black immobility in the age of white flight, as shown in the civil-defense map of the fictional River City in Philip Wylie's 1954 doomsday novel *Tomorrow!*, which places the "Negro District" at ground zero.[11] This legislated and de facto immobility of African Americans in a culture obsessed with mobility was yet another instance of what Saidiya Hartman has called liberalism's "double bind of freedom," a liminal state of "being freed from slavery and free of resources, emancipated and subordinated, self-possessed and indebted, equal and inferior, liberated and encumbered, sovereign and dominated, citizen and subject."[12]

Spatial forms, the urban theorist Manuel Castells has written, provide a "fundamental material dimension" of any given society, and will therefore express that society's relationships of dominance and subordination. Yet "spatial forms will also be marked by resistance from exploited classes [and] oppressed subjects. And the work of this contradictory historical process on space will be accomplished on an already inherited spatial form, the product of history and support of new interests, projects, protests, and dreams."[13] Ideal figurations of the transformative road disintegrate when one contrasts Coalhouse Walker's capacities for self-determination and convenient self-erasure with those of Younger Brother. As the literary scholar Sharon Willis has noted, when women, gays, and people of color embark on automobile journeys, "the central point and problem that define the journey reside in embodiment and visibility, as all meanings tend to be organized by race, gender, and sexuality. . . . The meaning of the trip is inevitably understood through the meanings the witnesses assign to the bodies of the travelers."[14]

Yet African Americans in the twentieth century, subject to whites' "extraordinary efforts to limit their freedom to occupy, use, or even move through space," nonetheless affirmed idealized spaces and moments of freedom. Consequently, the iconic road they crafted through imagery and narrative was both democratic social space and racial minefield.[15] Automobility's promise was one of escape from Jim Crow: upward through socioeconomic strata and outward across geographical space. Yet Coalhouse Walker's story synthesizes—and rewrites as revenge tragedy—countless stories of trouble on the road that have informed a black "highway consciousness" distinct from that of white drivers. From the earliest days of automobility, overlapping and mutually sustaining racist laws, social codes, governmental regulation, and commercial practices have attenuated the mobility of the black driver: segregated roadside mechanical and medical aid, food, and shelter; the discriminatory membership policies of motoring organizations such as the American Automobile Association (AAA); profiling of minority drivers by law enforcement and regulatory agencies; the racial-spatial politics of highway planning and placement, especially in urban areas; the racebound economics of auto financing and insurance underwriting; and the venerable practice of general police harassment for "driving while black."[16]

Moreover, since the advent of mass automobility in the 1920s, participation in the automotive market served to delineate the boundaries of republican personhood. As we have seen, driving and car ownership were anchored by themes of competence and self-determination; the figures of the driver and the citizen were regularly conflated, as they were established in racialized (and gendered) terms. A 1923 auto trade journal, for example, defined "illiterate, immigrant, Negro and other families" as aliens in the auto consumer's polity.[17] Myriad representations of nonwhites and immigrants as physically graceless, technologically inept, and deservedly indigent served as reminders of the incapacity of racial others to fulfill the obligations of citizenship in a modern and complex republic. Even the masterful prizefighter Jack Johnson was not immune from the stereotype of black driving incompetence. Johnson's unsuccessful 1910 challenge of the white driving champion Barney Oldfield led another white racer, "Wild Bob" Burman, to assert, "Just because Johnson has succeeded in reaching the top in pugilism, it does not alter the fact that he is a Negro and is not entitled to prestige in the cleaner and better sport of automobile racing."[18] The historian Daniel M. Albert notes that early traffic safety officials "correlate[d] their definitions of the good and bad driver with existing socially constructed categories. . . . As a result, African Americans were disproportionately labeled as 'primitive' and barred or removed from that inner circle of citizenship, the driver's seat."[19]

African Americans challenged these representations and proscriptions, supplying counterimages and counternarratives emphasizing mastery, elegance, self-possession, and decorum. The social theorist Paul Gilroy has recently observed that blacks' "histories of confinement and coerced labour must have given them additional receptivity to the pleasures of auto-autonomy as a means of escape, transcendence and even resistance."[20] In 1922, the *Chicago Defender* chronicled A. L. Headen's journey from Chicago to Kansas City, celebrating "both the superior design of the car and Headen's technological expertise and physical prowess."[21] Charlie Wiggins, "The Negro Speed King," was held up as a model of guts and wits for his exploits on the segregated racing circuit.[22] Arna Bontemps's grim 1932 short story "A Summer Tragedy" features an elderly black couple, worn down by years of sharecropping, using "the little rattletrap car [that] had been regarded as a peculiar treasure" as their implement of suicide. Like their decrepit Model T, the couple is "used up," no longer useful to the regime of production; yet their suicide—dressed in their Sunday best, they drive into a rushing river—testifies to self-possession and dignity even in despair.[23] "It's mighty good to be the skipper for a change," wrote Washington, DC, schoolteacher Alfred Edgar Smith, "and pilot our craft whither and when we will. . . . it's good for the spirit to give the old railroad Jim Crow the laugh."[24] (Smith's farewell wave to Jim Crow in the rearview mirror was, in 1933, a year that saw at least twenty-four lynchings, a premature gesture.) In Robert MacNeill's 1938 WPA photograph "New Car," a proud driver-owner stands with one foot on the running board, smiling cavalierly and surrounded by admirers.[25] Seven years later, Chester Himes's novel *If He Hollers Let Him Go* featured a protagonist to whom the roadscapes of Los Angeles offer a space for racial combat. The character, Bob Jones, avers that his Buick Roadmaster is "proof of something to me, a symbol"; the car is also his instrument in a score-settling campaign wherein he doles out "stare for stare, hate for hate" to whites in his peregrinations around the city. While the white drivers he challenges and overtakes may well enjoy their morning commute, Jones tells us, "to me it was racial. . . . All I wanted in the world was to push my Buick Roadmaster over some white peckerwood's face."[26] Whatever Jones's personal satisfactions, Jim Crow is diminished not in the slightest.

A disproportionate number of black road narratives impress upon the reader the traveler's near-constant anxiety on unfamiliar roads. The journalist Courtland Milloy recalled from his childhood a menacing environment in which "so many black travelers were just not making it to their destinations." More recently, the writer Eddy Harris has recounted his motorcycle journey through a southern landscape where he is "glared at, threatened, turned away, called names, and made afraid."[27] Given the racist harassment and violence the automobile's signification of affluence and "a kind of mystically perceived total freedom" could prompt, it is unsurprising that, unlike their white-authored counterparts, black road narratives "do not concern the pursuit of the ideal self"; rather, they "reveal the fraudulence of space viewed as an essence, transcending class and color" and "resist all utopian fantasies predicated on the virtues of elsewhere."[28] And yet those narratives, such as the guidebooks examined here, engaged nonetheless with a utopian fantasy peculiar to and animated by the political imaginary of corporate liberalism; that fantasy, glimpsed by bell hooks as a young girl, conjures a place "beyond the sign of race" just behind the horizon.[29]

## black automobility as cold war imperative

The first in a long series of incidents on Route 40 on the way to Washington occurred when a dark-skinned man, refused service at a Howard Johnson restaurant at Dover, Delaware, in 1957, turned out to be the Finance Minister of Ghana. —Harold Isaacs[30]

*Travelguide* and *The Negro Motorist Green Book* refract a historical moment of the early cold war, when the political costs of racial discrimination compelled American institutions to confront it as a social problem of priority, and when automobility, as I have tried to show, was called upon to signify an important range of martial values and ideals. "The conflict with Communist power from time to time throws a harsh light on our own society," J. Robert Oppenheimer observed at the American Style conference at MIT in 1957. "As this conflict continues, and its obduracy, scope, and deadliness become increasingly manifest, we begin to see traits in American society of which we were barely aware, and which in this context appear as grievous disabilities."[31] "Few would debate," remarked the editors of *Fortune* in 1951, "the assertion that the greatest failure of American democracy has been its failure to achieve a real emancipation of the Negro." Such acknowledgments of the racial situation were commonplace in the middlebrow media and in the official transmissions of the Truman and Eisenhower administrations; they were almost inevitably followed by avowals of the problem's imminent resolution, as in George Schuyler's claim, reprinted in a 1951 *Reader's Digest*, that "the progressive improvement of race relations and the economic rise of the Negro in the United States is a flattering example of democracy in action. The most 'exploited' Negroes in Mississippi are better off than the citizens of Russia or her satellites."[32] Such comparisons, also typical of the era, indicated that racial equality—or at least its appearance—was a matter of cold war expediency.[33] A 1955 *Reader's Digest* article titled "The Negroes Among Us," made explicit to a middlebrow audience the potential bitter harvest of racial discrimination:

> Throughout much of the world, and especially in the Asian
> countries that have but recently emerged from colonial rule, the

greatest single obstacle to friendship and cooperation is ignorance of great changes that have taken place in the status of the Negro. Typical is the question which Prime Minister Nehru of India says he is repeatedly asked: "What guarantee do we have that, if we side with the Western World instead of with Russia, that we won't eventually be treated as Negroes are in the United States?"[34]

By the early 1950s, Soviet propagandists were emphasizing racial injustice in the United States in nearly half of their global output.

Though the 1954 *Brown* decision marked the beginning of genuine structural change to official hierarchies of race, political elites of the era saw as paramount to actual melioration the dissemination of images and accounts of the "model Negro" moving forward in a racially enlightened nation.[35] The exigencies of the cold war put a broad range of images and narratives of African Americans as first-class citizens into circulation, however atypical these representations might have been.[36] Declarations of opportunity, equality, and color-blindness (though few endorsements of integration) became standard components of the cold war ethic developed in the middlebrow press and state propaganda. For example, Adam Clayton Powell affirmed his and other black leaders' "delighted astonishment" at Eisenhower's feeble desegregation policy in *Reader's Digest*, citing the advances made in the most internationally visible and officially representative of cities, Washington, DC.[37] The *Saturday Evening Post* happily noted in 1955 that "Negroes Have Their Own Wall Street Firm," a development that posed "a challenge to many a preconception." "They Always Ask Me About Negroes," a *Post* article from the following year, related the experiences of a black cultural attaché in Italy as "a living refutation" of the charges of racism leveled by communists, charges that nonwhite foreign nationals were inclined to believe. Activist Max Yergan's speech to Nigerian audiences occasioned a USIA press release that announced, "Yergan Says Trend In U.S. Race Relations is Toward Full Civil Rights for Negroes."[38]

Given cold war policy architects' antipathy toward collective and structural modes of social therapy, many of these images of the model Negro reflected the abiding liberal faith in a naturally egalitarian capitalist market, and in the notion that "freed individual achievement, and it alone, would dissolve caste."[39] Essential to the "vital center" consensus crystallizing in the postwar period was the belief that "the American free-enterprise system . . . has a revolutionary potential for social justice."[40] An expanding, soberly regulated consumer economy, the rhetoric maintained, spurred progressive social change even in the most recalcitrant areas of American life, such as race relations. Such rhetoric echoed Booker T. Washington's 1895 assertion that "no race that has anything to contribute to the markets of the world is long in any degree ostracized," but updated it for a cold war audience.[41] Indeed, this rosy vision of naturally improving race relations was intended to flatter domestic audiences—who could "be counted on to follow decent instincts without legislation"—and to assuage international ones.[42]

The approach of full citizenship for African Americans could be divined, then, from the "vast new market with a purchasing power of over 16 billion dollars a year—more than the annual value of all our exports" announced by *Reader's Digest* in 1955.[43] One index of this purchasing power was the increasing rate of car ownership among African Americans over the previous few decades. The car, as both commodity and symbol, affected the American economy, landscape, and social structure more than any other consumer product; and a given group's level of automobile use and ownership could be taken as an index of its participation in the "American way of life." In 1949, an *Ebony* editorial explained "Why Negroes Buy Cadillacs"; the editors' predictable conclusion, observed a skeptical sociologist, Franklin Frazier, was that "the Cadillac is a worthy symbol of their aspiration to be a genuinely first-class American."[44] Two years later, a piece in the same magazine on an upscale African American neighborhood in Queens, New York, noted with enthusiasm the number of two-car households and the frequency, moreover, of Cadillacs.[45] Chuck Berry's 1950s "motorvatin'" rock and roll songs, which expressed "a strong faith in mobility as a guarantee of dignity, democracy, pastoralism, and equal opportunity," and which also featured Cadillacs, staked his and other African Americans' claim to citizenship in the republic of drivers.[46]

As Paul Gilroy notes, "It is difficult to resist the idea that the special seductions of car culture have become an important part of what binds the black populations of the overdeveloped countries to the most mainstream of dreams. . . . Cars seem to have conferred or rather suggested dimensions of citizenship and status that were blocked by formal politics and violently inhibited by informal codes."[47] The power of the automobile to signify national membership was apparent to Herbert Hoover, writing in a 1955 article titled "Saying Something Good About Ourselves." "Much as I feel deeply the lag in giving a full equal chance to our Negro population," he wrote, "yet I cannot refrain from mentioning that our 14 million American Negroes own more automobiles than all the 200 million Russians and the 300 million Negroes in Africa put together."[48] African American automobility, considered in Hoover's terms, demonstrated a pair of triumphalist truths: first, that the American market of consumer goods had properly provided the natural fulcrum for the evolutionary movement of American society toward universal citizenship; and second, that the ownership and operation of an automobile bespoke membership in a fully modern and elite order of humanity housed exclusively in the "free world."

## responding to "negro motoring conditions": *travelguide* and *the negro motorist green book*

So far as travel is concerned, Negroes are America's last pioneers.
—Lester B. Granger, National Urban League, 1947[49]

Would a Negro like to pursue a little happiness at a theatre, a beach, pool, hotel, restaurant, on a train, plane, or ship, a golf course, summer or winter resort? Would he like to stop overnight in a tourist camp while he motors about his native land "Seeing America First"? Well, just let him try!
—*The Crisis*, 1947[50]

Rising (though still low) rates of car ownership among African Americans in the postwar era, as well as the plentiful images of joyous and footloose drivers in black publications and popular culture, suggested that automobility had ceased to be an exclusively white prerogative. As discussed above, these phenomena were held up by apologists as signs of African Americans' ascent into the middle class and of racism's decline. Automobility expressed a forward-looking, individualistic, and emphatically modern sensibility; it provided practical and visible models of the social, political, and economic freedom of all Americans. Its promise to African Americans, as bell hooks notes, lay in its perceived ability to enable escape from the racialized structures of American society and "find a world where there is no black or white."[51] Yet it was precisely in the act of driving through unfamiliar territory that the inescapability of race became, for so many African Americans, so apparent. To be sure, the kindness the rural Michigan farmers showed an out-of-gas Charles Horton Cooley in 1923, as discussed in chapter 2, was in no small measure due to his whiteness. Whites' responses to black drivers generally ranged from the merely contemptuous—as in one writer's recalling of a policemen's plans for jailing an "uppity nigra" thwarted by her Cadillac-driving cousin's quick payment of an unjust fine—to the lethal, as in the 1948 case of Robert Mallard, attacked in his car by a Georgia mob (allegedly for being "too prosperous" and "not the right kind of negro") and murdered in front of his wife and child. Occasionally, too, whites could be solicitous, as in Charles Chesnutt's account of having his tire changed by a group of white men after he demonstrates his own ineptitude at the task. For black drivers, the road's only constant was uncertainty.[52]

Poised between the Jim Crow and civil rights eras, *Travelguide* and *The Negro Motorist Green Book* simultaneously protested the discrimination that confronted black motorists on American roads and proffered the hegemonic image of American freedom through driving. They articulated a collectivist racial politics, mobilizing their midcentury audiences for social change; yet they also rehearsed the individualistic, market-oriented strategies of black capitalism and the vital-center consensus, where, as Lizabeth Cohen notes, "the individual's access to the free market was a sacred concept."[53] This dualism was not so novel; many progressive publications by and for African Americans, from *The Crisis* to *Ebony*, deployed rhetorics affirming black communal struggle in a society that "spoke individualism" to the exclusion of other social philosophies. The salient and novel element of *Travelguide* and *The Negro Motorist Green Book* was their focus on automobility as the practice through which African Americans could reconcile, both in symbolic and practical terms, the competing values of individual agency and collective uplift.[54] Like other black business enterprises catering to black consumers in an era of eroding yet still-compelled deference, these guidebooks were rarely radical in their challenge to the legal segregation that circumscribed the mobility of touring black entertainers and athletes, business travelers, and other motorists; instead, they mounted a decorous campaign for racial reform informed by liberal principles of market agency, cross-racial "understanding," the prerogative of free mobility, and the assumption of human goodwill.

As the guidebooks rehabilitated automobility as something in which all who possessed the necessary means should and could take part, they simultaneously made claims about the republican "fitness" of their readership. From the first, then, these guidebooks emphasized the proximity, in matters of temperament and class, of black and white drivers. In the teeth of Jim Crow, they sounded a tone of aggrieved entitlement, mildly articulated, as when *The Negro Motorist Green Book* (see fig. 7) reports that most of the better conveyances, hotels, resorts, and restaurants are "not available." In 1936, New York travel agent Victor H. Green, the guide's founder and namesake, began soliciting for his fledgling publication manuscripts describing road experiences comparable to those of white drivers. Green paid a dollar (by 1941, five dollars) to the writer for each accepted account

**figure 7.** Representing the black driver—the *Green Book,* 1948. Courtesy of Schomburg Center for Research in Black Culture, New York Public Library.

"based on the Negro motoring conditions, scenic wonders in your travels, places visited of interest and short stories on one's motoring experience."

In subsequent years, Green included letters of testimonial and thanks from the guidebook's ideal subscribers. These letters functioned almost as a sort of ventriloquism by Green, who was silent in his editorial capacity, in terms of articulating the *Green Book's* purpose. In the 1938 edition, a letter from William Smith of Hackensack, New Jersey, declared,

It is a great pleasure for me to give credit where credit is due. Many of my friends have joined me in admitting *The Negro Motorist Green Book* is a credit to the Negro Race. It is a book badly needed among our Race since the advance of the motor age. Realizing the only way we knew where and how to reach our pleasure resorts was in a way of speaking, by word of mouth, until the publication of *The Negro Motorist Green Book.* . . . We earnestly believe that [the guidebook] will mean as much if not more to us as the A.A.A. means to the white race.

In 1941, a similar letter from William H. Denkins, Jr., of Trenton read,

I am proud of your *Green Book,* and consider it a great little motorist guide. After receiving a copy I only wished that I had one with me on a recent trip I had made, as I am sure it would have made the entire vacation perfect. The *Green Book* not only serves the Negro motorist well, but does a splendid job for its advertisers.

When the publisher did speak, it was to thank the publication's sponsors and influential supporters, among them the Cleveland *Call and Post,* the Louisville *Leader,* and James "Billboard" Jackson, the pioneering black marketing representative for Standard Oil. In 1940, Green made it clear that by sponsoring the guidebook these organizations and individuals were doing work of tremendous necessity and value.

The Publishers of this guide wish to publically [sic] thank the following people and newspapers who have contributed and worked to bring this travel guide before the public and up to date, so that we as a race might have something authentic to travel by and to make traveling better for the Negro.[55]

*Travelguide,* which began publication in 1947, updated Green's tactics and language for an era informed by the official, if superficial, antiracist stance of the nation emerging out of World War II and into the cold war, and awakening to the integrationist sensibilities of the nascent civil rights movement. The guidebook's founder and publisher, William H. "Billy" Butler (1903–1981), had been a jazz musician and bandleader in the 1930s and 1940s, and had borne his share of indignity and privation while on tour. At Butler's funeral in 1981, a friend eulogized him with a telling anecdote:

I am reminded of the time back in the early days, when racial differences still kept many Americans apart. And Billy was traveling with his fellow musicians in the South. They were tired and hungry. But there was no place in this town that would let them all eat together. So, Billy got the idea to go to the wardrobe mistress to get some capes and turbans. Newly attired, they entered the restaurant of their choice, and had a most enjoyable evening as visiting foreign dignitaries.[56]

The Pittsburgh *Courier* heralded *Travelguide's* arrival in 1947, and, in subsequent years, ran columns and articles by Butler, including a six-part 1954 series titled "Travel Vs. Discrimination." The *Crisis* routinely ran advertisements for Butler's publication, and sold it through the Crisis Book Shop in midtown Manhattan. The New York *Post* profiled Butler in 1947, describing him as "Musician and Guide to His Bedeviled Race."[57] *Travelguide's* usefulness to itinerant black entertainers and athletes was emphasized in a back-cover testimonial by Mabel A. Roane, administrative secretary of the Negro Actors Guild, who stated,

> TRAVELGUIDE should create confidence for the traveler in the acting profession as well as those in the entire field of entertainment. Its orderly and authentic information covers necessary news and eventually should eliminate sitting-up-all-night in railroad stations, hotel lobbies, and lunchrooms. Often unemployment of Negroes results because placement while traveling is such a problem.[58]

Though this audience remained an important one, *Travelguide,* like its predecessor, was more ambitious. These guides depicted, even in the context of Jim Crow's all-too-evident circumscription of mobility, African Americans as upwardly and outwardly vacationers, habitually mobile business travelers, and blithely gallivanting consumers: indeed, the guidebook's subtitle promised "vacation and recreation without humiliation." And however pernicious and widespread the discrimination black drivers met on the American road, it was crucial that the *Green Book* and *Travelguide* aver their continuing faith in the equalizing mechanisms of American democracy and consumer capitalism.

According to classical free-market doctrine, all who possessed the appropriate values and engaged in the right practices could compete in an arena in which they were rewarded or penalized for their assiduity as individuals and not for their categorical status. Black intellectuals in the early twentieth century, intent on countering the myriad and increasingly vicious stereotypes that saturated all manner of media, fashioned positive and even heroic images of "a new class of colored people, the 'New Negro,' . . . who have arisen since the [Civil] war, with education, refinement, and money."[59] By midcentury, this "black bourgeoisie" had expanded sufficiently to make possible publications such as *Travelguide* and the *Green Book*, which offered images of the good life through consumption to African Americans living under Jim Crow.[60] The 1937 issue of the *Green Book* featured, in addition to national listings for lodgings hospitable to black travelers, advertisements for top-shelf liquor and New York–area auto repair shops, beauty salons, restaurants, nightclubs, and country clubs, including the Harris Tea Room, "Westchester's sepia rendezvous," and Harlem-on-the-Hudson, "featuring a talented cast of sepia beauties."[61] *Travelguide* also featured profiles of prominent African American personages (i.e., Jackie Robinson, George Schuyler, and Langston Hughes) and racially progressive companies.[62] These features complemented the publication's attribution of racism to whites' ignorance of black achievement, respectability, and economic vitality.

In their depictions of mobile, affluent, benign, and generally quiescent black travelers, the *Green Book* and *Travelguide* implied the economic, if not the moral, costs of discrimination. Deploying a rhetoric of antidiscrimination increasingly common in what Cohen has called the postwar "consumer's republic," the guidebooks asserted that, however one evaluated the ethics of segregation, in the long run it was bad for white-owned businesses.[63] As one of *Travelguide*'s editors, Marguerite Cartwright, wrote in the inaugural 1947 edition,

> hundreds of millions of dollars are spent annually by discerning members of minority groups in the course of their travels throughout the U.S. Many worthy enterprises, unaware of the tremendous potentialities, deny themselves of this revenue. It is the purpose of TRAVELGUIDE to assist in bringing these two groups together for the benefit of ALL.

The increasingly affluent, numerous, and mobile members of the black middle class, the guidebook editors suggested, were more identifiable by their status as consumers than by their race.[64] Hotels, restaurants, nightclubs, service stations, and other enterprises that discriminated on the basis of race would be won over by the purchasing power of these travelers of color. The guidebooks' covers accented the gentility of their readership. *Travelguide* depicted no men on its covers; these were usually graced by well-dressed and light-skinned women, who almost always carried golf clubs with them (figs. 8, 9, and 10).[65] These seemingly trivial but highly symbolic objects were the exclamation points on *Travelguide*'s declaration of African American arrival into the middle class, at a time when the overwhelming majority of golf courses remained barred to black players. If the links to which these visibly affluent golfers were heading did not discriminate, *Travelguide* implied, how could any business not follow their example? The placement of Mark Twain's dictum "Travel is fatal to prejudice" on the cover of the 1949 *Green Book* shifted its usual meaning: here it was the visited, rather than the visitors, who would find themselves enriched by the encounter.

Yet vital-center liberalism conceded that the market alone would not resolve social problems; rather, an institutionally cultivated will to humanitarianism (in this case, antiracism) *expressed* through market transactions would produce conditions of equality. The admixture of consumer and political sensibilities in *Travelguide* and *The Negro Motorist Green Book*—their simultaneous pitches for the NAACP and, say, *Field & Stream*—typified the vital-center strategy for racial harmony. Organizations such as the NAACP were conducive to the proliferation of the antiracist sensibility, as was the cold war propaganda of the United States Information Agency, *Life,* and *Reader's Digest*. But much of the real advance in civil rights and national unity, the guidebooks and like publications intimated, would be made through the quasi-intimate realm of transactional encounter. "I should like to urge Negroes to visit North Dakota," wrote an ostensibly white *Green Book* reader in the small town of Dickinson, "not only for the tourist attractions, not only because of the friendliness of her people, but also because of [*sic*] these visitations would enable North Dakotans to better know and understand a great part of our national citizenry."[66]

The guidebooks articulated their own role as sacrificial. "It is perhaps a significant barometer of the progress we have made in our democracy that such a listing is even required," Cartwright mordantly noted.

> However, we have faith that the day is not long distant when such a booklet will be outmoded and considered unnecessary. Racial distinctions and creedal "restrictions" (or "church nearby"), whether through openly cruel barriers or hypocritical evasions, are contrary to the American ideal and repugnant to people of good-will. We think that such persons will show their displeasure in the manner in which it hurts most—through economic boycott—and TRAVELGUIDE will in this way hasten the day

**Travelguide**

"Vacation & Recreation Without Humiliation"

50!

**figure 9.**
*Travelguide*, 1952.
Courtesy of Schomburg Center for Research in Black Culture, New York Public Library.

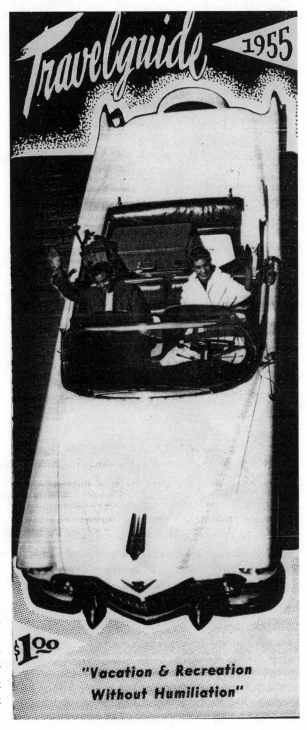

**figure 10.**
*Travelguide,* 1955.
Courtesy of Schomburg Center for Research in Black Culture, New York Public Library.

when considerations such as these artificial and subject distinctions will be a thing of the past. We pledge to do all in our power to hasten the day when we "can put ourselves out of business."[67]

The Green Book editors expressed their hope in nearly identical language:

> There will be a day sometime in the near future when this guide will not have to be published. That is when we as a race will have equal opportunities and privileges in the United States. It will be a great day for us to suspend this publication for then we can go wherever we please, and without embarrassment.[68]

One would be hard-pressed to hear such a wish for self-annihilation coming from, say, a handgun manufacturer, or another commercial enterprise dependent upon fear and sadism. Yet perhaps such rhetoric did not indicate a martyr sensibility among the editors of the guidebooks; perhaps they anticipated the evolution of their publications with the onset of integration, and with it a jump in circulation. In 1955, Travelguide declared,

> The time is rapidly approaching when TRAVELGUIDE will cease to be a "specialized" publication, but as long as racial prejudice exists, we will continue to cope with the news of a changing situation, working toward the day when all established directories will serve EVERYONE.[69]

This rhetoric paid lip service to, even as it undercut, the gradualist language of the state and most institutions: given the current glacial pace of racial reform in the United States, the guidebooks were under no immediate threat of losing their utility. Recalling his 1955 move from Chicago to California with the aid of the Green Book, Earl Hutchinson Sr. writes in his autobiography that "you literally didn't leave home without it."[70]

Anyway, there would be no place for these publications after their specialization was no longer necessary. Though African American guidebooks exist today, directing travelers to sites of significance in black history, Travelguide and the Green Book would suffer the fate of Negro League baseball and other Jim Crow institutions—absorption by larger, richer, white-controlled entities. They would be crippled, ironically, by the successes of a civil rights movement "premised on claiming the power to move, and in so doing to remap space."[71] Although the power to move with the heedlessness of whites remains an ideal for African Americans, aggrieved black drivers of the present era have at their disposal a formal set of legal and political tools for the redress of grievance of which the readers and editors of the Jim Crow guidebooks could only dream. *Travelguide* closed up shop in 1957; the *Green Book* would drop the *Negro* from its title and limp along until 1964. These publications had articulated a link between a driving subjectivity and a national identity, and had pressed that deeply problematic ideal into worthy service.

## limited-access highways and the decline of jim crow

There was some truth to automobility's promise for African Americans. Despite the violence and intimidation directed toward black drivers, the road even in its earlier iteration had to some degree provided a space where the everyday discrimination and coercion African Americans faced in other public spaces—in stores, theaters, public buildings, and restaurants, for example, or on sidewalks and public transportation—could be blunted, circumvented, and even avenged. "Only in automobiles on public roads," one commentator wrote in 1936, "do landlords and tenants and white people and Negroes of the Black Belt meet on a basis of equality." Another noted the procedural equality mandated by the "rules of the road" even in the rural South of the early 1900s. "The geographic mobility and equality on the road of automobile travel," the historian Cory Lesseig writes of the early twentieth century, "helped usher in a new age of political, social, and economic opportunity for Mississippi."[72] "I wasn't particularly happy about driving in the South," Chester Himes wrote in his autobiography, *The Quality of Hurt*. "I had a bad temper and wanted to avoid trouble. But it was like driving anywhere else—priorities were controlled by the traffic laws. They don't discriminate against cars, just people."[73] Most recently, *Washington Post* columnist Warren Brown, remembering his New Orleans childhood, recalls that "freedom of mind, spirit, and movement came with my family's acquisition of personal cars. We in fact called them 'freedom machines.'"[74]

Instances of formal equality on the road no doubt multiplied after 1956, with the coming of the National System of Interstate and Defense Highways. In what we might call their high-modernist moment, the highways of the postwar era were more than simply better roads. Fundamental to the interstate project was the extraction of the highways out of their geographical and social context; this elevation minimized their contact with the surrounding countryside or cityscape and created an enclosed and standardized zone to which access could be limited. The interstate highways and their ancillary built environments enervated what we would call "place" by traumatically reconfiguring a range of landscapes and communities. Nowhere was the obliteration of local spaces of value and the disruption of patterns of everyday life more apparent than in the nation's urban centers, where highway planners sought to facilitate (white) suburban commuters' blithe mobility over the defunded and deteriorating (black and brown) city. The destruction of the main African American commercial and residential districts of Miami, Detroit, Nashville, and Birmingham are particularly stark examples of a more wholesale "negro removal" component to the postwar schemes of "urban renewal" to which expressway construction was imperative.[75]

At the same time, the interstate highway as a new, temporarily inhabitable *space* enabled an emancipatory leveling of the status-oriented social relations that characterized premodernity. Driving on—or, more accurately, within—the more totalized space of the interstates diminished the risk of humiliation of and violence against "marked" drivers, especially when compared to the state roads, which, passing through every town and accessible at myriad crossroads, exposed those drivers to the casual racism of white citizens and the various prejudices and predilections of local businesses and law enforcement. It was the limited-access, high-speed interstate, rather than the automobile, that effected the anonymity of the driving subject.

"Once you were on the Interstate," Tom Lewis observes, "you could be anywhere; an Interstate in the Deep South felt much like an Interstate in the North." Lewis's claim that "at last, African Americans enjoyed the right to move where and when they wanted" is egregious; but it is certain that the neutral space of the interstate and its standardized gas-food-lodging environs afforded black motorists "a measure of protection . . . however thin a veneer as that protection might be."[76] The interstate highway, set apart from and above the landscape and local culture through which it cut, provided the spatial opportunity for the obscuring of one's identity from the scrutiny of others. As I will argue in the next chapter, the self-obscuring speed and procedural regulation of highway driving provides a metaphor for the abstraction of the subject in the liberal public sphere.

It is important to see the deterritorialized and standardized space of the Interstate Highway System in the context of a more overarching federal presence—and with it a progressive enervation of parochialism—effected by World War II and its aftermath, the cold war. Virginia Scharff notes that postwar America saw "new political and economic connections [that] penetrated and disrupted settled patterns of locale and of region, offering unprecedented opportunities and risks. People and places often suffered in the change, but the breaching of local isolation by national-

Spring 1957 $1.25

The Negro Travelers'

# Green Book

**THE GUIDE FOR TRAVEL AND VACATIONS**
*20 Years of Service to the Negro Traveler*

Carry your GREEN BOOK with you—you may need it.

**figure 11.** The road, deracinated. *The Negro Travelers' Green Book*, 1957. Courtesy of Library of Congress.

izing forces also carried the power to upset local tyrannies and offer open horizons."[77] Certainly, Miami's black Overtown neighborhood, decimated by the building of I-395 in the mid-1960s, was one of these places that suffered in the change; but so too was rural Florida rendered less menacing to African American drivers, velocitized by the highway and sustained by increasingly national "McDonaldized" amenity businesses at the interchanges.[78]

This new national public space of which the interstate system was but one example would be the ground on which the civil rights movement would expand, and in which Jim Crow would be buried. It was this space of and from which Chuck Berry sang in "Maybellene" (1955) and "No Particular Place to Go" (1956) as he seized the independence promised by the automobile and hurtled down the highway, bound only by the gas gauge and the limits of the pavement. And this space would also render superfluous the guidebooks that had served the black drivers of the previous decades. The cover of the 1957 edition of the *Green Book* reminded readers of its "20 Years of Service to the Negro Traveler." But the cover depicted no black travelers, no golf clubs, no Cadillacs, just an overhead view of the sleek, deracinated space of the interstate highway (fig. 11), in which "disassociated, encased in speed, you ha[d] nowhere to go but forward."[79]

Yet highway automobility did not, and does not, inspire a genuinely democratic political imaginary beyond liberalism. Rather, the new interstate highway enabled the African American driver to *pass* as the blank liberal subject, and to effect, under certain circumstances, the privatist withdrawal that has been such an extravagant and problematic characteristic of American citizenship. "Liberalism," the literary scholar Christopher Newfield has written, "is a transitional ideology, midway between authoritarian and democratic structures."[80] The limits of highway automobility as an emancipatory practice are coterminous with those of liberalism as a democratic political sensibility: both obscure or negate, in order to manage, racial difference; both offer their subjects only procedural participation in already established regimes. Whatever citizenship under the democratic structures of the future will look like, it won't look like driving. But the assumption of the figure of the driver by the readers of *Travelguide* and *The Negro Motorist Green Book* corresponded to Martin Luther King's invocation of the Declaration of Independence and various foundational myths in his rhetoric: both explicitly tethered the quest for civil rights to a national narrative of exceptionalism, progress, and individual freedom.

## chapter five

# "How Can the Driver Be Remodeled?": Automobility and the Liberal Subject

It seems at first sight as if all the minds of the Americans were formed upon one model, so accurately do they follow the same route.
  —Alexis de Tocqueville[1]

We call "subject" that which results from the relation between living things and *"dispositifs"* [apparatuses]. —Giorgio Agamben[2]

As with African Americans and other people of color, the expansion of automobility in the 1950s increased women's capacity to perform freedom in the twentieth century. That is to say, highways and enhanced automotive technology provided a means for women to blunt the disempowering spectacle of their physical particularity. Speeding down the detached limited-access highways, one could assume anonymity, disappear. Tom Lewis offers as proof of automobility's empowering effect on marginalized groups a poem by the writer Barbara Smith. The poem, "I–80," places the reader with a female protagonist as she drives across Nevada, the car and the driver moving in a way "so different from 1954." Lewis concludes his analysis with the approving observation that "Smith is alone."[3] No longer suffering the indignity of "limited access" to public space, women and racially marginalized people can now enact the individualist practice *nonpareil:* traveling alone.

I am suspicious of the tone of congratulation in such claims. Moreover, it is unclear to whom and/or what specifically we owe thanks: is it to white men, for "extending" the prerogatives of citizenship to women and people of color (as though it was not the result of bitter struggle); the interstate highways and their builders, for delivering this freedom; or women and people of color themselves, for successfully appropriating the subjectivity of the driver-citizen and the faith that "everything good is on the highway"?[4] Rather than join the chorus singing of the concurrent expansion of automobility and freedom, here I would like to ask, What kind of republic is composed of drivers?

Piloting his rented car down the freeways of 1980s Los Angeles, the enthralled French philosopher Jean Baudrillard mused that "the point is not to write the sociology or psychology of the car, the point is to drive. . . . All you need to know about American society can be gleaned from an anthropology of its driving behavior."[5] Taking Baudrillard's words as they should perhaps never be taken—at face value—I will consider in this chapter the highway, with its engineered and delimited environments, and highway driving, with its sensations of freedom and anonymity and its procedural regulation, as integral to the American liberal imaginary in the twentieth century (and beyond). Just as the spectacle of the lone driver provides a visual representation of selfhood, the image of the highway traffic stream represents the dominant conception of sociality and public space. The scene of Smith alone in her car, for example, calls to mind the individualism John Dewey and others sought to overthrow, one expressed "merely externally."[6]

The past chapters have all asked, in one way or another, *what driving does*; and we have seen it described as liberating, individuating, revivifying, equalizing. Here I once again consider this question in the context of the postwar highway automobility that extended the reach of systems of governmentality. In this light I argue that we consider contemporary driving as reconciling "competing claims and attractions of subjection and independence."[7] To do this we must recognize the performative freedom of the driver as an effect of a "multiplicity of interventions concerned with the promotion of a specific 'form of life'" in the twentieth century.[8] It is that form of life and its environments that I attempt to sketch in the final section of this chapter.

## autonomy: the power to live as you will

I have tried to show that the legitimacy of modern liberal societies depends to a large degree on their capacity not merely to tolerate but to enable performances of self-determination in all those individuals identified as citizens. It is imperative that those citizens be described as moving and choosing agents, not automatons or "subjects" of a dictatorial power. For this reason the state and other hegemonic institutions must provide occasions and spaces for the symbolic and spectacular performance of individual will and choice—such as voting, consumption, and mobility, all practices that are unlikely to transform established arrangements of power. As I have argued above, postwar American society, beset by ideological rivalry, self-doubt, and a narrowing of the viable spectrum of political discourse, saw a range of hegemonic institutions work to construct and affirm an idealized subject. That subject would demonstrate and affirm "freedom" even as it adhered to well-trodden paths of thought and behavior; it would be, in other words, autonomous.

Derived from the ancient Greek term for "self-governance," "autonomy" obtained much of its modern meaning through the work of Immanuel Kant. Kant affirmed the freedom of individuals to self-determination, but insisted that the condition of true autonomy consisted in adhering, through one's own choosing, to universal laws of reason and justice.[9] Autonomy in this sense described the reconciliation of one's own desires with the necessity for the harmonious and moral functioning of a community. In the 1950s, David Riesman offered, in works such as the bestselling *The Lonely Crowd* (1950), as well as *Faces in the Crowd* (1952) and *Individualism Reconsidered* (1954), a compelling and timely revision of the concept.

As discussed in chapter 3, at this time the American character was judged to have lost its individualistic orientation, or "inner-direction," substituting for it a disposition of "other-direction," in which the self derived its identity and governed its actions by following the directives of others. Whatever Riesman's sympathy to the shift, his readers tended to characterize this new American self as a lesser being, an embodiment of the loss and betrayal of the individualistic and masculine ideals that had "made America." Widespread condemnation of the other-directed self signaled not only anxieties about the feminization of postwar America, but also a fear that the representative white middle-class bore an uncomfortable resemblance to the collectivist subjects of communist societies. Even Riesman himself found the threat of "groupism" no less evident in American society than in the "grisly present of the Soviet Union."[10]

Riesman's formulation of autonomy, for which he borrowed from the psychologist and social theorist Erich Fromm as well as Kant, merged the best traits of social character past and present.[11] It joined the forceful inner discipline that had characterized the archaic inner-direction to the life-enhancing potentials of the consumer market, leisure culture, and corporate "teamwork" apparent in the contemporary world of other-direction. The first condition of Riesmanian autonomy was "self-awareness about the fact of choice, about possible ways of living." Those ways of living, however, were finite, bounded by particular historical conditions; these limitations the autonomous individual, which Riesman sketched as a heroic prototype, accepted without resentment and even with concord. Nor did the autonomous individual see the need to rebel simply for rebellion's sake, like Marlon Brando's delinquent Johnny in *The Wild One*. Rather, as Riesman asserted, "an autonomous person has no compulsive need to follow the other-direction of his culture and milieu—and no compulsive need to flout it either."[12]

Autonomy was the condition of the self acting freely, which is to say, rationally, morally, and normatively. "For what is freedom?" wrote Cicero, another of Riesman's philosophical forebears: "The power to live *as you will*. Who then lives as he will except one who follows the things that are *right*?"[13] To live autonomously entailed "self-governance," as a antidote both to the influence of others (along a continuum starting with other-direction and ending with totalitarian domination) and to a potentially atomizing and dangerous freedom. To the degree that Riesman's autonomous individual rebelled, that rebellion expressed itself through the appropriate channels of liberal dissent and distinctive consumption. For a depiction of autonomy in practice, *Time* magazine looked no further than Riesman himself: a personal-profile sidebar identified the author as "An Autonomous Man," a polite maverick who "plays vigorous, year-round tennis [and] drinks orange juice mixed with soda."[14] Riesman crafted and performed his own autonomy within a social and political order that narrowed the range of substantive political choices as it multiplied the opportunities for demonstrating one's distinction and mastery.[15]

The autonomous character was free, in other words, to behave in an appropriate and "safe" manner. As many progressive intellectuals, politicians, and activists discovered, appropriate ways of living, thinking, writing, and speaking narrowed during the cold war to identification with a rigidly policed set of "American" practices and beliefs. Freedom, everywhere proclaimed as the genius of the nation, could wreck, so to speak, those who practiced it "irresponsibly." Riesman's formulation thus recalled the type of human freedom Kant idealized, that of willed submission to authority.

## if you leave me you are lost:
## the highway engineers' utopia

Once on a superhighway, you are a kind of captive.
   —*Good Housekeeping*, 1955[16]

Something akin to this midcentury formulation of autonomy—both emphatic performance of self-directed agency and amenability to regulation—informed the era's technical literature of automobility, such as driving manuals and highway engineering publications. The rhetoric of these forms generally oscillates between the two dimensions of liberalism—that of *doctrine* and that of *mode of government*.[17] Driving education materials, which date from the 1930s, generally were produced or underwritten by entities with a vested interest in the promotion of expanded automobility, such as automobile, oil, or insurance companies, or advocacy groups such as the AAA. Not surprisingly, they tended to emphasize the ways in which driving amplifies the individual's natural agency. "Most individuals have more power at their direct disposal in driving than in any of their daily activities," as the manual *Man and the Motor Car* put it in 1954.[18] Though these texts stressed the weighty responsibility of automobility, their overwhelming theme was faith in those empowered individuals' better angels directing them to drive and to live the autonomy sketched above.

The belief that educated, rational individuals will behave properly anchors the doctrine of liberalism; this approach to constructing what Jeremy Packer has referred to as "safe subjects" has not, however, been the only one.[19] Other rhetorical strategies in driver education manuals and especially highway engineering literature reflect liberalism as a mode of government; that is, as a rationale and a set of instruments for imposing a particular type of order. This approach is far more skeptical about the capacities of the citizen-driver to govern himself; rather, it emphasizes that he must be made to behave through various disciplinary mechanisms. This dimension of liberalism is reflected in, for example, the AAA manual *Sportsmanlike Driving*'s 1955 call for "*the training of every individual for modern traffic conditions*" or the somewhat contemptuous recommendation in a 1931 *Motor* for "education and more education to convince man that he must live up to his car."[20] It is still more apparent in the discourse of midcentury highway engineering.

As we have seen, the "open road" has always been an oxymoron. Not only has taking to the road voluntarily been a prerogative only of those ascribed full personhood; the road itself is a device by which territories and subjects can be measured and surveilled. James Clifford has pointed out the mythic nature of the figure of the "free" traveler, noting that "most bourgeois, commercial, aesthetic travelers moved within highly determined circuits."[21] These circuits have structured patterns of power, exchange, and selfhood since long before the interstates; even since long before Whitman plumbed such effects in his 1856 "Song of the Open Road":

> O highway I travel, do you say to me *Do not leave me?*
> Do you not say *Venture not—if you leave me you are lost?*
> Do you say *I am already prepared, I am well-beaten and undenied,*
>     *adhere to me?*
>
> O public road, I say back I am not afraid to leave you, yet I love you
> You express me better than I can express myself.[22]

In offering its "well beaten and undenied" surface to Whitman, the road voices (it actually *speaks!*) the hegemonic anxieties about the uncontrolled mobility and illegibility of subjects that motivated various public works (i.e., roadbuilding), urban planning, and census projects in the nineteenth century.

As we have also seen, from the earliest years of automobility, driving has been described as epitomizing a salutary agency and self-determination, even when its sensations were characterized as potentially transgressive. As the apparatus of automobility developed, however, more and more commentators on the "open road" noted the imperatives in which the road speaks, its propensity to draw drivers and passengers into the ambit of governmentality where they can be known, protected, and improved. John Steinbeck, for example, at the wheel of his truck Rocinante in 1960, for example, described feeling both regimented and batted around by I–90, "a wide gash of a super-highway. . . ."

> Instructions screamed at me from the road once: "Do not stop! No stopping. Maintain speed." Trucks and freighters went roaring by, delivering a wind like the blow of a fist. These great roads are wonderful for moving goods but not for the inspection of a countryside. You are bound to the wheel and your eyes to the car ahead and to the rear-view mirror for the car behind and the side mirror for the car or truck about to pass, and at the same time you must read all the signs for fear you may miss some instructions or orders.[23]

Twenty years after Steinbeck's cross-country ramble, Baudrillard, on his own journey, observed that despite automobility's much-hailed individuating function, "the freeway is a place of integration," its codes constantly organizing "a total collective act":

> To the person who knows the American freeways, their signs read like a litany. "Right lane must exit." This "must exit" has always struck me as a sign of destiny. I have got to go, to expel myself from this paradise, leave this providential highway which leads nowhere, but keeps me in touch with everyone. This is the only real society or warmth here, this collective propulsion, this compulsion—a compulsion of lemmings plunging suicidally together. Why should I tear myself away to revert to an individual trajectory, a vain sense of responsibility? "Must exit": you are being sentenced. You are a player being exiled from the only—useless and glorious—form of collective existence.[24]

To drive on the highway, these authors assert, is to be subject to what John Urry calls a "peculiar combination of flexibility and coercion."[25] Being on the road promises freedom, but a freedom the "freeway" itself structures and delimits. *I am already prepared*, the road promises; *if you leave me you are lost*, it warns.

Twentieth-century highway engineers, with their ever more sophisticated structural achievements (from two-lane roads to scenic parkways to multilane superhighways), have been the creators of this modern version of Whitman's "well beaten and undenied" open road. In accordance with the liberal mode of government's instrumentalization of freedom and safety, these engineers envisioned and built highways that would restrict and regulate the driver even as they facilitated speed and expanded the choice of vectors. The ideal highway was to be, in other words, a sort of Möbius strip on which "despite the thrill of acceleration, escape is illusory, and the drive into the sunset takes you right back where you started."[26] As I have suggested above, the limited-access highway that communicated freedom as it limited the possibility of deviation provided a spatial metaphor for the narrowed political culture of the cold war. Though human fallibility—"bad human judgment, human carelessness and human stupidity"—had been a general complaint of technicians for many years, the postwar discourse of highway engineering positively clamored for removing the human factor from driving, through rationally engineered roads, cars, and ancillary safety devices.[27]

"The man at the wheel," declared a speaker at a postwar highway conference, "is in many ways the most complex and baffling element in the trafficway-driver-vehicle system."[28] In contrast to those who celebrated the freedom and power of the driver, technicians generally lamented the habit of motorized cavaliers—to borrow the language of the 1955 *Collier's* article discussed above—of becoming too cavalier. A 1949 highway-safety text, for example, warned that "at the wheel, many an American tends to transform himself into a god"; and 1955's *Sportsmanlike Driving* caricatured "The Egotist," "The Show-Off," "Mr. Milktoast," and "Baby Blow-Horn" in its rogues' gallery of drivers.[29] Drivers' bad behavior could be attributed to social and psychological conditions, even sympathized with, according to a 1958 article on road safety: "In each of us is a desire for calculated risks of excitement. Our daily activities may provide little of that excitement and indeed may represent a series of minor frustrations . . . so that, consciously or not, we sometimes enjoy taking a little risk, such as speeding and cutting in and out of traffic."[30] But all this meant was that each and every citizen of the republic of drivers was a potential subversive.

Indeed, the experts' low estimation of the nation's drivers paralleled many of the cold warriors' opinions of its citizens. Occasionally the political character of bad or profligate driving was made clear, as in the psychologist and traffic expert A. R. Lauer's comment that "conservatism usually is associated with carefulness at the wheel" or George Kennan's disdain for the motorization of contemporary life.[31] However, where some cold warriors saw terminal decline, highway engineers saw a problem to be solved: through study, planning, and regulation, the "baffling" man at the wheel would be made knowable and corrigible, and the license afforded by driving would be transformed into autonomy in the Riesmanian sense (see fig. 12).

As with their disappointment with drivers, the experts' optimism was not new to the postwar era; indeed, the preceding two decades had seen their share of technocratic utopianism, as transportation and consumer technology became more advanced and inexpensive, and as the federal, state, and local governments, in partnership with industry, funded a variety of visionary public-works projects. Epitomizing both the optimism and the impatience of the engineers, Norman Bel Geddes observed in 1940 that the contemporary driver's "car has been entirely remodeled" and that "his highway is being remodeled." Looking ahead to the "magic motorways" of 1960, Bel Geddes asked, "How can the driver be remodeled?" He predicted that

> these cars of 1960 and the highways on which they drive will have in them devices which will correct the faults of human beings as drivers. They will prevent the driver from committing errors. They

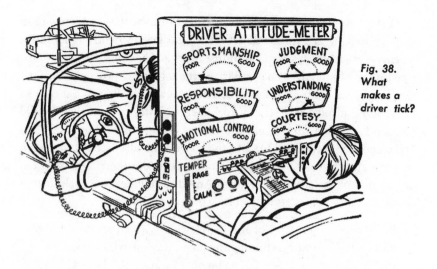

Fig. 38.
What
makes a
driver tick?

**figure 12.** Analyzing the incorrigible driver. American Automobile Association,
*Sportsmanlike Driving* (Washington, DC: AAA, 1955), 74.

will prevent him from turning out into traffic except when he
should. They will aid him in passing through intersections without
slowing down or causing anyone else to do so and without en-
dangering himself or others. Many present beginnings give hints
of the kind of over-all planning on which the near future could
realize. Everything will be designed by engineering, not by legislation, not in piecemeal fashion, but as a complete job. The two, the
car and the road, are both essential to the realization of automatic
safety . . . . In 1960 [all drivers] stay out of the ditch. It is not done
by law, but through the very nature of the car and the highway.[32]

This sort of fantasy of control proliferated after 1950, when Bel Geddes's
magic motorways had begun to be realized. In its 1956 profile of newly
appointed Federal Highway Administrator Bertram D. Tallamy, *Life* asserted that this prescient engineer

knows that the existing highway network is but a sample of what
is to come and he does not believe that the Thruway will be the
last word in road-building. He can visualize technological developments that will necessitate new forms of highways and introduce
new concepts. One of these, he thinks, just might be a system of
traffic and vehicular controls whereby the motorist can relinquish
the wheel and his car speeds along in perfect automatic safety.[33]

There were, however, strict parameters to this fantasy, which we can map by looking at a proposal submitted to, and evidently ignored by, Eisenhower's advisory Clay Committee in 1954. The proposal, titled "Surface for the Mounted," also emphasized the regulatory possibilities of the new roads, but with a critical difference. Its author, Roy E. Babcock of Pittsburgh, advocated a strictly regulated highway system that "would just about exclude whimsical, or arbitrary, automobile riding. . . . Time and money cannot be saved, nor traffic congestions alleviated, unless such controls are exercised that would tend to regiment the riding practices on the part of the automobile-riding American public." Babcock further advised that

> Those important factors of automobile riding which are concerned with "getting to work, running the farm, staying in business, bringing home the groceries, going on a vacation . . . " would be considered opportune to the scheduling plan. Those instances, however, where "getting the milk, the mail, the morning paper, a package of cigarettes, or a ride just for the fun of it," where such excursions would adversely merge into a scheduled and regulated traffic flow—these practices would have to be considered inopportune, and hence, excluded.

There is little evidence that the thirty-four-page plan received much attention from the Clay Committee (except its retention in the committee's records)—its prescriptions and aspirations likely rang damnably socialistic: "A new world had been opened up for Mr. Average Motorist and his family," Babcock concluded. "There were no driving problems in his life now. He had given up only a few of his unnecessary driving habits to join the millions of other happy motorists who were enthralled over the new Utopia—America's adequate highway system!"[34]

In attempting to *curtail* highway driving, Babcock's proposal failed to recognize American automobility's crucial function as a performance of freedom. Moreover, it did not understand the highway as an instrument for maintaining what Mark Simpson calls "disciplinary pace," which "marshals the technologics of motion to achieve a productive *regulation* of velocity that . . . aims to make bodies in motion the objects, not agents of their velocity."[35] By contrast, Tallamy's and Bel Geddes's desire to relieve the driver of the wheel (which finds contemporary echoes in cutting-edge "smart car" plans) did not necessarily vitiate that function. Tallamy, Bel Geddes, and other highway engineers did not really expect to "remodel" the driver. Rather, they saw their task, as Frederick Taylor had seen his, as that of bringing *inexorably* unruly human bodies into line.[36] The superbly engineered limited-access-and-egress highways constructed in the post-war era were the means by which people's dissidence could be restrained as their forward motion was accelerated.

## driving as disappearing: submission and self-abstraction

The climactic act that asserts the full possession of the individual is the act of disappearing. −Philip Fisher[37]

I have argued above that to drive is to be made visible—to be monitored, recognized, and apprehended by expanding regimes of surveillance and legibility. Now I want to assert what might seem a contradictory point; namely, that to drive is to disappear—to be divested of one's particularities and, having assumed the blank identity of the liberal subject, to flow anonymously in the traffic stream.

Highway driving has been described by a number of late twentieth-century commentators as inducing narcosis and invisibility, and obliterating one's sense of time, space, and corporeality. "Being alone in a car," the novelist Larry McMurtry writes, "is . . . like being in one's own time machine, in which the mind can rove ahead to the future or scan the past"; the French philosopher Simone de Beauvoir drove herself into a "happy stupor" on the American highway (admittedly, rest-stop martinis aided in her stupefaction); Baudrillard puzzled at, but relished, "the truly profound pleasure . . . of keeping on the move"; Steinbeck wrote of his reduction to a "machine-like unconscious" behind the wheel; Kerouac's characters in *On the Road* spent many of their waking hours in a driving-induced trance; the country music artist Merle Haggard sings of the "white line fever" that effaces distance and time; and the literary scholar Catherine Stimpson, feeling swallowed by the mesmerizing flow of the New Jersey Turnpike, writes, "I began to wonder if my Toyota and I were invisible."[38]

Whence this annihilation of self, so different from the testaments to automobility's quickening and empowering qualities made earlier in the century? The media scholar Margaret Morse has described the "virtual" practice of highway driving as enabling the "derealisation" of the subject: the driver sits "in a realm of passage, both over the outside world and from inside an idyllic, intensely private, steel-enclosed world of relative safety."[39] The driver's seat becomes a vantage from which one apprehends both the contours of the dominant social formation and one's place in it.

As we have seen, the driver is, ideally, able to abstract herself—to divest of her particularity and enter on a par with the other individuals on the public road, all of whom are similarly veiled by their machines and following the uniform protocols of driving. In this vein Joan Didion has explored highway driving as a "secular communion" that inducts one into a particular form of sociality. "Mere driving on the freeway," she writes,

> is in no way the same as participating in it. Anyone can "drive" on the freeway, and many people with no vocation for it do, hesitating here and resisting there, losing the rhythm of the lane change, thinking about where they came from and where they are going. Actual participants think only about where they are.

Becoming an adept in this communal ritual of motion requires "a total surrender, a concentration so intense as to seem a kind of narcosis, a rapture-of-the-freeway." For the protagonist of Didion's 1970 novel *Play It as It Lays*, driving the freeways—which she does "as a riverman runs a river . . . in the lull between sleeping and waking"—provides both a semblance of agency and a singularly effective tranquilizer.[40] Complementing, not negating, driving's sensations of agency, feelings of self-abstraction, anonymity, isolation, and *submission* to determining structures are central to the American fascination with automobility.

Yet driving's efficacy as a forge of subjects depends on the crucial fact that the driver feels anything but submissive or circumscribed. As Raymond Williams observed,

> Looked at from right outside, the traffic flows and their regulation are clearly a social order of a determined kind, yet what is experienced inside them—in the conditioned atmosphere and internal music of this windowed shell—is movement, choice of direction, the pursuit of self-determined private purposes. All the other shells . . . are not so much other people, in any full sense, but other units that signal and are signalled to . . . . And if this is seen from the outside as in deep ways determined, or in some sweeping glance as dehumanised, that is not at all how if feels inside the shell.[41]

The essence of the empowering feeling of driving consists in the way in which the practice seems—in "enabling people and objects to congregate and mix without meeting"—to *extrude* the driver from the claims of society.[42]

The ethos of the speeding, supplicating highway driver finds roots in

Emerson's social and political thought, which encourages an "individualism so radical it [is] functionally inconsequential," and whose renaissance in American intellectual culture coincided with the midcentury "crisis of the individual."[43] Christopher Newfield has argued that Emersonian individualism provides philosophical justification for citizens' abdication of political agency under twentieth-century liberalism. According to Newfield, the linguistic blandishments of individualism, self-reliance, and independence that surround the liberal subject disguise its actual orientation of accommodation and obedience through which "nondemocratic modes of democratic governance continue to actualize themselves." Newfield sees ample evidence of this "Emerson effect" in current liberal rhetoric about the global market, the federal government, and other seemingly unassailable institutional powers, under the thrall of which "the autonomous individual has disappeared, but so has democratic sovereignty." The possessive individualism that animated republican political culture *and* the "new individualism" upon which pragmatists and feminists sought to build democracy have given way to a make-believe autonomy, "the seeing of freedom as an uncontrollable system's flexibility."[44]

Newfield's aversion to the social and political effects of Emersonian individualism recalls the nineteenth-century critique leveled by Alexis de Tocqueville in *Democracy in America*. As Tocqueville envisioned it, individualism, with its emphasis on private gratification and the spectacle of independence, was essentially a practice of withdrawal. It turns political nonparticipation into a sort of virtue, and leaves to an abstract "majority" the power to govern. As the historian Richard Sennett describes the scenario, "Since supposedly the majority is making decisions in his interests, the individual enshrines himself in his private anxieties because political participation would seem to threaten the very value of 'self-directed" experience.'[45] This "democratic" withdrawal into privatism threatened to bring about the conditions for the rise of what Tocqueville called an "immense and tutelary power." This power would require little of its citizens beyond adherence to a minimal social contract; its role would be

> to secure [citizens'] gratifications and watch over their fate. That power is absolute, minute, provident, and mild. . . . [I]t tries to keep them in perpetual childhood . . . [;] it daily makes the exercise of free choice less useful and rarer, restricts the activity of free will within a narrower compass, and little by little robs each citizen of the proper use of his own faculties. . . . I have always thought that this brand of orderly, gentle, peaceful slavery which I

have just described could be combined, more easily than is generally supposed, with some of the external forms of freedom.[46]

The irony is striking: the individualist ethos ultimately produces an apathetic and infantile citizenry that willingly abdicates its authority to a paternalistic power; in return that power maximizes the opportunities for the spectacular expression of freedom and autonomy so affirming to the individualist. The individualist thus withdraws further from the political, consoling himself with a life increasingly oriented toward "a display of energy"—movement and consumption in lieu of democratic entanglement.[47]

Even a celebrant of American mobility such as George W. Pierson could see its unforeseen, disappointing effect as presaged by Tocqueville. "Looked at in the large," he wrote, "our empty continent was supposed to foster individualism of action and belief . . . . But in the long run mobility overruns space, and the circulation and recirculation of peoples induces conformity."[48] Automobility, which radically expanded the proclivity and "capacity to disengage, withdraw, and move away," and which perpetually announced itself (in advertising and other representations) as "all that remains of adventure in everyday life," only made the individualist's symptoms more pronounced.[49]

Tocqueville found no appropriate name for the type of regime he saw approaching on the American horizon (perhaps he had only one good neologism, individualisme, in him). "Our contemporaries," he wrote, "will find no prototype of it in their memories . . . . The thing is new."[50] In this power, which enabled a myriad of freedoms and paths to personal transformation and salvation, Tocqueville presaged what more recent analysts have called "soft totalitarian" or "pastoral" power, forms distinguished by their capacity to produce and equip, as opposed to proscribe and immobilize, subjects. Tocqueville's scenario finds affinity with, for example, Foucault's theory of the "productive" rather than repressive operation of modern subjection, and the descriptions of "totalitarian democracy" and "repressive tolerance" in the work of the Frankfurt School.[51]

Indeed, the almost zombified drivers that populate the work of Didion and others would have been depressingly familiar to another erstwhile Angeleno, Theodor Adorno, who pondered the contemporary "liquidation of the individual" while sojourning in that capital of automobility in the 1940s. Adorno theorized that practices intended to control the subject and reproduce dominant ideology are never, under liberalism and capitalism, articulated as such; instead, such practices—which for Adorno included

**figure 13.** Policing onself. American Automobile Association, *Society's Responsibilities* (Washington, DC: American Automobile Association, 1937), 99.

the consumption of the products of the "culture industry"—would be characterized as the maximization of individual agency. He assailed the ersatz individualism that "may ultimately become a mere ideological veil in a society which actually *is* inhuman and whose intrinsic tendency [is] toward the 'subsumption' of everything." This society would be characterized by "standardized, opaque, and overpowering social processes which leave to the 'individual' but little freedom for action and true individuation."[52] In automobility—need it be said that by all evidence Adorno refused to learn to drive?—Adorno saw another pseudoindividualistic social process that promised the subject freedom and transformation but effected only "successful adaptation to the inevitable."[53] As with popular music, particularly the jazz Adorno so loathed, the automobile's signification of centrifugal energy was precisely what enabled it to function as such an effective tool for the centripetal regulation of the subject.

Adorno and other analysts stressed that, unlike previous forms of power, whose demands for their subjects' submission tended also to be demands for their sessility, liberal-capitalist hegemony requires that its subjects submit by being *free* and *in motion.* Jeremy Packer has described Foucault's understanding of power as consisting in "enabling and activating 'men and things' in a manner that allows them to and in fact demands that they move outside of confined and continuously surveyed arenas."[54] Subjects' desire for and competence at autonomous mobility (that is, automobility) serves as an index of their internalization of hegemonic ways of being in the world, to such a degree that the threat of coercion recedes to the edge of perception. As the 1937 AAA publication *Society's Responsibilities* asked, "Is not *self-discipline* to be preferred to discipline by force[?]"[55] (see fig. 13). Driving, then, becomes a performance of energy and speed whereby one affirms one's disciplined subjectivity; it expresses, in other words, the liberal freedom that Newfield has described as the individual's "power to adapt to the uncontrollable flux."[56]

Perhaps it is no longer even "discipline" that characterizes highway automobility. Gilles Deleuze, after William S. Burroughs, described how what he called a "control society" was enacted through "freedom" just as the *disciplinary* societies elaborated by Foucault were organized by spaces of confinement. Under this model, hegemonic institutions provide technologies of "freedom"—the Internet, credit and ATM cards, air travel, and widespread automobility—all of which facilitate a putatively limitless mobility. In turn, this mobility, as it allows for more precise and bountiful data on individuals "captured" by ever more expansive systems of surveillance and tracking, achieves a compulsory character. "Control," Deleuze writes,

> is not discipline. You do not control people with a highway. But by making highways, you multiply the means of control. I am not saying this is the only aim of highways, but people can travel indefinitely and "freely" without being confined while being perfectly controlled. That is our future.[57]

## landscapes of compulsory automobility

Americans are broad-minded people. They'll accept the fact that a person can be an alcoholic, a dope fiend, a wife beater, and even a newspaperman, but if a man doesn't drive, there is something wrong with him.
  −Art Buchwald, 1966[58]

Driving, as I have argued, enables an affirmative performance of energy, speed, and motion even as it emplaces the subject in social relations and environments not of her making and decreasingly malleable by democratic, collective will. The environment of automobility expanded middle-class consumer and residential "choice" and provided the sensory experience of freedom as it simultaneously shut down the possibilities for alternative spatial, economic, social, and political configurations. Here I want to decipher the spatial hieroglyphs of automobility—the patterns of highways and feeder roads, the commercial and residential built environment, the protocols of driving, and the traffic stream—as representations of what we have come to understand as public space, individual agency, and "the social" itself.

"The American Road," asserted the Ford Motor Company in 1956, "is now more than 3,500,000 miles long and always growing. It typifies the striding pace and prosperity of a vital nation still young, still free, still reaching for frontiers."[59] Nearly every commentary on automobility (this one included) concurs with Ford's claim that the spaces of American automobility offer, in the words of the geographer Karl Raitz, "a trope for social and economic life in the United States."[60] More recent commentators have put forth, implicitly or explicitly, a corollary claim that the Interstate Highway System made automobility a more or less mandatory practice: the apparatus of automobility that surrounds us and within which we conduct our daily lives deters us from imagining and especially undertaking other forms of association. This is an *ideological* accomplishment that some applaud and others condemn.

Sudhir Chella Rajan, for example, argues that "the automobilized world that we inhabit spawns an entire set of dominant beliefs and codes about such wide-ranging sentiments as the 'nature' of social relations and individual desires."[61] It is to this automobilized world, in which the car "emotionally remains . . . a symbol of freedom" that we are "indenture[d]," avers the urban planner Marvin Adelson.[62] The journalist Stephen Moore's recent claim that "the automobile is one of the two most liberating inventions of the past century" epitomizes this conditioning of national value and narrative, not to mention policy, by the cultural dominant of automobility. "The car," Moore continues, in a familiar vein, "allowed even the common working man total freedom of mobility—the means to go anywhere, anytime, for any reason. In many ways, the automobile is the most egalitarian invention in history, dramatically bridging the quality-of-life gap between rich and poor. The car stands for individualism; mass transit for collectivism."[63]

I agree with Moore that automobility provides an individualist social imaginary. But what is that imaginary, precisely? It is, in a word, traffic. Noting that "underlying social relations often manifest themselves in . . . habitual and conventional ways," Raymond Williams argues that

> traffic is not only a technique; it is a form of consciousness and a
> form of social relations . . . . It is impossible to read the early de-
> scriptions of crowded metropolitan streets—the people as isolated
> atoms, flowing this way and that; a common stream of separated
> identities and directions—without seeing, past them, this mode
> of relationship embodied in the modern car: private, enclosed,
> an individual vehicle in a pressing and merely aggregated com-
> mon flow; certain underlying conventions of external control but

within them the passing of rapid signals of warning, avoidance, concession, irritation, as we pursue our ultimately separate ways but in a common mode.[64]

Traffic is the signal social form of the modern tendency distinguished by Williams as "mobile privatization," in which public space is increasingly an agglomeration of privately inhabited spaces, mediated by technologies of transportation and communication.[65]

As we have seen, contemporary driving's sociality is one in which identity is effaced for both the driver and her fellow inhabitants of the road.[66] Didion refers to this abstracting process as approximating narcosis; Henri Lefebvre downgrades the condition to a "psychosis" in which each person dons an armoring shell (a term used also by Williams) and engages in automobility's facsimile of social interaction and its fostering of hierarchies.[67] The pleasures of this form of sociality are those of disconnection and civil indifference—this latter phenomenon on one end of a continuum that progresses to competition and then to aggression. Hence André Gorz's observation that "mass motoring effects an absolute triumph of bourgeois ideology on the level of daily life. It gives and supports in everyone the illusion that each individual can seek his or her own benefit at the expense of everyone else. Take the cruel and aggressive selfishness of the driver who at any moment is figuratively killing the 'others,' who appear merely as physical obstacles to his or her own speed."[68]

If liberal sociality is traffic, the built environment of the road is both its substrate and representation. John Steinbeck characterized the "empty, eventless" (yet frenetic) highway and its orderly environment of efficient service stations and immaculate automated restaurants as "life at a peak of some kind of civilization." Its highways—"great wide traffic slashes which promote the self by fostering daydreams"—privilege speed, contest, and combat, thereby frustrating Steinbeck's romantic desire for connection to (and observation of) his fellow citizens.[69] John Updike sees the impress of Emersonian individualism, which, like Newfield, he characterizes as "a curious counsel of fatalism couched in the accents of activism," not only in the inner lives of Americans and in the institutions of liberalism, but also in the built environment. Emerson's "encouragements," Updike writes, "have their trace elements in the magnificent sprawl we see on all sides—the parking lots and skyscrapers, the voracious tracts of single-family homes, the heaped supermarket aisles and crowded ribbons of highway: the architectural manifestations of a nation of individuals, of wagons each hitched, in his famous phrase, to its own star."[70]

The political theorist John Dunn has written that "the modern demo-cratic capitalist state is . . . the natural political expression of a form of society irritably but rationally aware of its own internal contradictions, but also irritably but rationally unconvinced of the possibility of trans-forming itself into a less contradictory form."[71] As I write this, I look out over Interstate 70 where it rises over the Missouri River and the railroad switchyard in the bottoms and cleaves through downtown Kansas City. It is two o'clock on a clear autumn afternoon, and so what I see in my window is the republic of drivers in a moment of plenitude: the drivers move freely in their sociality of "simultaneity without exchange"; and the landscape through which they pass orders and enables their movements.[72] I am not driving; but I will be soon.

## epilogue
# Automobility's Futures

This study has offered a genealogical account of "the ways in which what we take to be freedom has been historically put together, the practices which support it, and the techniques, strategies and relations of power that go to make up what we term a free society," in the words of the sociologist Nikolas Rose. To be sure, automobility, an effect of "our organizing our relations with ourselves in terms of freedom," has provided Americans the means to tremendous economic growth, ease of life, and, in some cases, formal political equality for marginalized groups.[1] Yet automobility is an instantiation of freedom that, having once appeared as a sort of tonic for the beleaguered republican self, has over the twentieth century taken on the character of cultural neurosis.

The history of driving as I have narrated it involves a compulsive rehearsal of the individualistic claims of the American past even as the claimants move within "settings . . . thoroughly permeated by expert knowledge" and organized to produce their submission.[2] The subjects produced by the apparatus of automobility pronounce and feel themselves free with an intensity that asserts motion to be the epitome, and not simply one possible dimension, of freedom.

The past two decades have witnessed, with the development of the infrastructures and products of information technology, a profusion of the sort of enthusiastic rhetoric that attached to early automobility. Of course, there was an interstate before there was an Internet: certainly the term "information superhighway" suggests a latter-day conjunction of reading and highway driving. One can hear, moreover, in the promises of unlimited mobility and endless opportunities for the individual to re-define himself that imbue the internet with utopian power, echoes of the champions of the automobile circa 1910 and 1955.

As we have seen, periods of transformation—of regimes of accumula-tion and/or moments of political and cultural threat—tend in the United States to cause individualist rhetoric and imagery to "spike"—to be as-serted forcefully and ubiquitously—even as the meaning of individualism is revised to render it consonant with new conditions. In our current era, which marks its newness with the bet-hedging prefix "post-," increasingly global networks of power and capital pull the foundation out from un-der the formerly crucial abstraction of "nation" and, more importantly, transform the nature of work for the majority of working- and middle-class people. As what we might call Taylorization's first phase foisted upon workers a certain type of immobility—as with the assembly line's moving the objects of labor past their static bodies—so does our current "infor-mation economy" phase achieve capital's objectives by emplacing workers behind screens on which data travels.

As work deskills and the workplace becomes even less hospitable to the demonstration of autonomy, technologies of the self—fostering virtual rather than physical mobility—once again provide a "fix" for subjectiv-ity and other solid things that melt into air. It is in this context that the Microsoft Corporation asks its customer/subjects, "Where do you want to go today?" This and other invitations to navigate the digital networks for fun and transformation model themselves on car advertising and the rhetoric of automobility more generally: indeed, web "surfing" suggests a more distracted, yet exciting, analogue of driving.

Of course, this incitement to blithe virtual mobility finds its negative twin in the cultural dread of physical mobility after September 11, 2001. In the wake of that crime, hegemonic institutions charged with promot-ing the mobility of people, goods, and money have been working through a dilemma. On the one hand, the public desire for mobility (especially business and leisure air travel) have had to be reanimated; on the other, fear of terrorism must also pervade the traveler's consciousness to autho-rize the expanded governmentality over a wider array of experiences of mobility—automobility included. The increase in levels and vantages of surveillance (i.e., the E-Z Pass, face recognition technology, and "aggressive driver imaging") in public space and the suspension of various rights to mobile privacy (i.e., vehicle searches) are symptoms, perhaps, of the republic of drivers' evolution.

Yet as the wholesale borrowing of driving's rhetoric and imagery in the marketing of digital technology suggests, automobility as a structural paradigm and an ideological prop will be with us in the United States for some time, well after the exhaustion of the petroleum supply makes its twentieth-century manifestation impossible. The recent expansion of automobility in China and India, which will accelerate the depletion of petroleum, will transform those societies. Especially in China, which makes no pretense to liberalism and therefore has no ideological tradition of "freedom," automobility will likely have a liberalizing effect; which is to say, it will—along with the rise of a driving middle class—force that society to inflect its authoritarian mode of governmentality with greater and more efficient automobility—the approximation of freedom—for its citizens. Thus the recent and rapid construction of highway infrastructure in China is hailed by hegemonic American institutions as evidence of the successful deployment of a Trojan horse—the American subjectivity of freedom—which will subvert the Chinese state. "It's a great feeling speeding through beautiful scenery," declares a Beijing driver quoted in *USA Today.* "I feel so free on the road."[3]

Whether China will become a republic of drivers is a less pressing question than that of the United States remaining one. I hope the reader will consider this social and political vision and the subjectivity of the driver—and indeed, the ideology of individualism itself—as somewhat cheap consolations for the absence of those things that enable a more robust democratic politics: a historically nourished sense of community, a more-than-superficial awareness of the conditions of others, and the imaginative faculties to put oneself in their shoes. A republic of drivers will never sustain these.

# abbreviations

**BFRC:** Benson Ford Research Center, the Henry Ford, Dearborn, MI

**Butler Papers:** William H. Butler Papers, Schomburg Center for Research in Black Culture, New York Public Library

**Clay Committee Records:** U.S. President's Advisory Committee on a National Highway System, records, DDEL

**DDEL:** Dwight D. Eisenhower Library, Abilene, KS

**Lambie Files:** Staff Files: Files of the Special Assistant Relating to the Office of Coordinator of Government Public Service Advertising (James M. Lambie, Jr.), DDEL

**NMAH:** Warshaw Collection of Business Americana, National Museum of American History, Smithsonian Institution, Washington, DC

# notes

## introduction

1. Walt Whitman, "Song of the Open Road," *Leaves of Grass* (New York: Library of America, 1996), 298.

2. Tom Lewis, *Divided Highways: Building the Interstate Highways, Transforming American Life* (New York: Penguin Books, 1997), xiv.

3. Jane Holtz Kay, for example, condemns "the maiming of America" after 1956, while James A. Dunn extols the interstates for the freedom and prosperity they've brought; Mike Bryan finds the "real America" along the West Texas interstates, while William Least Heat-Moon indicts the highways for the disappearance of that same "real America." See Kay, *Asphalt Nation: How the Automobile Took Over America and How We Can Take It Back* (New York: Crown Publishers, 1997); Dunn, *Driving Forces: The Automobile, Its Enemies, and the Politics of Mobility* (Washington, DC: Brookings Institution Press, 1998); Bryan, *Uneasy Rider: The Interstate Way of Knowledge* (New York: Vintage, 1998); and Heat-Moon, *Blue Highways: A Journey Into America* (Boston: Back Bay Books, 1999). Other examples include William Kascynski, *The American Highway: The History and Culture of Roads in the United States* (Jefferson, NC: McFarland Publishers, 2000); James Howard Kunstler, *The Geography of Nowhere: The Rise and Decline*

*of America's Man-Made Landscape* (New York: Free Press, 1994); John Burby, *The Great American Motion Sickness, or, Why You Can't Get There from Here* (Boston: Little, Brown, 1971); K. T. Berger, *Where the Road and the Sky Collide: America Through the Eyes of Its Drivers* (New York: Henry Holt & Co. 1993); Mark S. Foster, *A Nation on Wheels: The Automobile Culture in America Since 1945* (Belmont, CA: Wadsworth/Thomson, 2003); Randal O'Toole, *The Vanishing Automobile and Other Myths* (Bandon, OR: Thoreau Institute, 2001); Leon Mandel, *Driven: The American Four-Wheeled Love Affair* (New York: Stein and Day, 1977); John Keats, *The Insolent Chariots* (Philadelphia: J. B. Lippincott, 1958); Katie Alvord, *Divorce Your Car!: Ending the Love Affair with the Automobile* (Gabriola, BC: New Society Publishers, 2000); Ben Kelley, *The Pavers and the Paved* (New York: Donald W. Brown Inc., 1971); Helen Leavitt, *Superhighway—Superhoax* (Garden City, NY: Doubleday & Company, 1970); B. Bruce-Briggs, *The War Against the Automobile* (New York: Dutton, 1977); Dan McNichol, *The Roads that Built America: The Incredible Story of the U.S. Interstate System* (New York: Sterling Publishers, 2005); A. Q. Mowbray, *Road to Ruin* (Philadelphia: Lippincott, 1969); Ronald A. Buel, *Dead End: The Automobile in Mass Transportation* (Englewood Cliffs, NJ: Prentice-Hall, 1972); and Kenneth R. Schneider, *Autokind vs. Mankind* (New York: W. W. Norton & Company, 1971). I do not include here examples of the staggering volume of literature on automobility produced by government agencies, engineers, and corporate entities over the past half-century.

4. My selection of 1895 as American automobility's inaugural year follows directly from James J. Flink's rich account, *America Adopts the Automobile, 1895–1910* (Cambridge: MIT Press, 1970). Pioneering auto engineer Hiram Percy Maxim noted in his autobiography, *Horseless Carriage Days*, that "we waited until 1895" to develop the automobile. Quoted in John B. Rae, *The American Automobile: A Brief History* (Chicago: University of Chicago Press, 1965), 6. The historian Tom McCarthy has written that "the automobile decisively and irreversibly entered the American national consciousness in October 1895, as a result of newspaper publicity given to an automobile race from Paris to Bordeaux and back." McCarthy, "The Coming Wonder? Foresight and Early Concerns about the Automobile," *Environmental History* 6.1 (December 2001):46. On the adoption of the language of automobility in the United States, see Albert H. Marckwardt, *American English* (New York: Oxford University Press, 1958); Theodore Hornberger, "The Automobile and American English," *American Speech* 5.4 (April 1930): 271–278; and Patricia W. Lipski, "The Introduction of 'Automobile' into American English," *American Speech* 39.3 (October 1964): 178–179.

5. This study pursues a project similar to that accomplished by Wolfgang Schivelbusch in his compelling *The Railway Journey: The Industrialization of Time and Space in the 19th Century* (Berkeley: University of California Press, 1986). As Alan Trachtenberg writes in his foreword, Schivelbusch sought "to recover the subjective experience of the railway journey at the very moment of its newness,

its pure particularity: to construct from a magnificent display of documents written and graphic what can be called the industrial *subject*" (xv).

6. In the United States, a rhetoric of the beset and unfree individual has been deployed routinely and with great success across the liberal spectrum to advance or counter various claims, institutions, and agendas—from civil rights reform (the individual bound by racism) to early feminism (the individual bound by sexism) to free-market orthodoxy (the individual bound by state regulation of the economy).

7. The historian Nan Enstad observes that subjectivity "is based on the premise that *who one is* is neither essential nor fixed, but is continually shaped and reshaped in human social exchange." Enstad, *Ladies of Labor, Girls of Adventure: Working Women, Popular Culture, and Labor Politics at the Turn of the Twentieth Century* (New York: Columbia University Press, 1999), 13. "The subject," writes Paul Smith, "is determined—the object of determinant forces; whereas 'the individual' is assumed to be determining." Smith, *Discerning the Subject* (Minneapolis: University of Minnesota Press, 1988), xxxiv.

8. Indeed, we can speak and act *only* through these discourses. As Judith Butler writes, "The constituted character of the subject is the very precondition of its agency." Butler, "Contingent Foundations," *Feminists Theorize the Political*, eds. Judith Butler and Joan W. Scott (New York: Routledge, 1995), 12. See also Butler, *The Psychic Life of Power: Theories in Subjection* (Stanford: Stanford University Press, 1997).

9. See Susie Dent, *The Language Report* (Oxford: Oxford University Press, 2004), 6–7.

10. John C. Burnham, "The Gasoline Tax and the Automobile Revolution," *Mississippi Valley Historical Review* 48.3 (December 1961): 435.

11. Mark Rose, *Interstate: Express Highway Politics 1939–1989* (Knoxville: University of Tennessee Press, 1990), 93.

12. Flink, "The Three Stages of American Automobile Consciousness," *American Quarterly* 24.4 (1972): 451.

13. John Urry, "The System of Automobility," *Theory, Culture, and Society* 21.4/5 (2004): 27; Sidonie Smith, *Moving Lives: Twentieth-Century Women's Travel Writing* (Minneapolis: University of Minnesota Press, 2001), 185; and Jörg Beckmann, "Automobility—a Social Problem and Theoretical Concept," *Environment and Planning D: Society and Space* 19 (2001): 597.

14. Sudhir Chella Rajan, *The Enigma of Automobility: Democratic Politics and Pollution Control* (Pittsburgh: University of Pittsburgh Press, 1996), 18.

15. Michel Foucault, *Power/Knowledge: Selected Interviews and Other Writings*, ed. Colin Gordon (New York: Pantheon Books, 1980), 194–195. See also Foucault's description of the *dispositifs* (apparatuses) of carcerality and sexuality in, respectively, *Discipline and Punish: The Birth of the Prison* (New York: Pantheon Books, 1977), and *The History of Sexuality*, vol. 1: introduction (New York: Vintage Books, 1990).

16. Gilles Deleuze, "What Is a Dispositif?" *Michel Foucault: Philosopher*, translated and edited by Timothy J. Armstrong (New York: Routledge, 1992), 159.

17. Giorgio Agamben, *Che Cos'è un Dispositivo?* (Rome: Nottetempo, 2006), 18. I am greatly indebted to John Ransom for his translation of and helpful commentary on Agamben's essay.

18. John B. Rae opened his 1965 study with the assertion that "the automobile is European by birth, American by adoption. . . . the transformation of the automobile from a luxury for the few to a convenience for the many was definitely an American achievement . . . American life is organized predominantly on the basis of the universal availability of motor transportation." Rae, *The American Automobile*, 1.

19. "Especially in America," write Thomas C. Heller and David E. Wellbery, "the poststructuralist critique of individuality has had only a feeble impact on the persistently individualist imagery of our institutions and popular culture." Heller and Wellbery, introduction to *Reconstructing Individualism: Autonomy, Individuality, and the Self in Western Thought*, ed. Heller et al. (Stanford: Stanford University Press, 1986), 12.

20. *History and American Society: Essays of David M. Potter* (Oxford: Oxford University Press, 1973), 236.

21. Hector St. John de Crevecoeur, *Letters from an American Farmer*, ed. Albert E. Stone (New York: Penguin, 1981), 69.

22. I borrow this phrase from Andrew Barry, Thomas Osborne, and Nikolas Rose in their introduction to *Foucault and Political Reason*, ed. Barry, Osborne, and Rose (London: UCL Press, 1996), 8.

23. Indeed, Mandel writes, "mobility for the sake of mobility seems to be more important than getting to wherever it is we think we're going." Mandel, *Driven*, 76.

24. Mark Simpson, *Trafficking Subjects: The Politics of Mobility in Nineteenth-Century America* (Minneapolis: University of Minnesota Press, 2005), xxvi. See also Mark Seltzer's discussion of "the idea of the American *as* the typical—of Americans as typical, general, and reproducible" in *Bodies and Machines* (New York: Routledge, 1992), 55.

25. Jean Baudrillard, *America*, trans. Chris Turner (London: Verso, 1988), 10.

26. On legibility, see James Scott, *Seeing Like a State: Why Certain Schemes to Improve the Human Condition Have Failed* (New Haven: Yale University Press, 1998).

27. Brenda Bright, "'Heart like a Car': Hispano/Chicano Culture in Northern New Mexico," *American Ethnologist* 25.4 (November 1998): 585. See also Soo Ah Kwon, "Autoexoticizing: Asian American Youth and the Import Car Scene," *Journal of Asian American Studies* 7.1 (2004): 1–26.

28. See John B. Rae, *The Road and the Car in American Life* (Cambridge, MA: MIT Press, 1971), and *The American Automobile*; Flink, *The Automobile Age* (Cambridge: MIT Press, 2001), *America Adopts the Automobile*, and "The Three Stages

of American Automobile Consciousness"; Rose, *Interstate;* Bruce Seely, *Building the American Highway System: Engineers as Policy Makers* (Philadelphia: Temple University Press, 1987); Lewis, *Divided Highways;* Frank Donovan, *Wheels for a Nation* (New York: Thomas Y. Cromwell Company, 1965); and Phil Patton, *Open Road: A Celebration of the American Highway* (New York: Simon & Schuster, 1986).

29. See James Livingston, *Pragmatism and the Political Economy of Cultural Revolution, 1850–1940* (Chapel Hill: University of North Carolina Press, 1997); Livingston, *Pragmatism, Feminism and Democracy* (New York: Routledge, 2001); T. J. Jackson Lears, *No Place of Grace: Antimodernism and the Transformation of American Culture, 1880–1920* (Chicago: University of Chicago Press, 1994); Gail Bederman, *Manliness and Civilization: A Cultural History of Gender and Race in the United States, 1880–1917* (Chicago: University of Chicago Press, 1996); Alan Trachtenberg, *The Incorporation of America: Culture and Society in the Gilded Age* (New York: Hill & Wang, 1982); Barry Shank, *A Token of My Affection: Greeting Cards and American Business Culture* (New York: Columbia University Press, 2004); Charles McGovern, *Sold American: Consumption and Citizenship, 1890–1945* (Chapel Hill: University of North Carolina Press, 2006); Christopher Newfield, *The Emerson Effect: Individualism and Submission in American Life* (Chicago: University of Chicago Press, 1996); R. Jeffrey Lustig, *Corporate Liberalism: The Origins of Modern American Political Theory* (Berkeley: University of California Press, 1982); Jeffrey Sklansky, *The Soul's Economy: Market Society and Selfhood in American Thought, 1820–1920* (Chapel Hill: University of North Carolina Press, 2002); Ellen Gruber Garvey, *The Adman in the Parlor: Magazines and the Gendering of Consumer Culture, 1880s–1910s* (Oxford: Oxford University Press, 1996); Seltzer, *Bodies and Machines;* Wilfred M. McClay, *The Masterless: Self & Society in Modern America* (Chapel Hill & London: University of North Carolina Press, 1994), 224; Martin J. Sklar, *The Corporate Reconstruction of American Capitalism, 1890–1916* (Cambridge: Cambridge University Press, 1988); James T. Kloppenberg, *Uncertain Victory: Social Democracy and Progressivism in European and American Thought, 1870–1920* (New York and Oxford: Oxford University Press, 1986); and Charlene Haddock Seigfried, *Pragmatism and Feminism: Reweaving the Social Fabric* (Chicago: University of Chicago Press, 1996).

30. See Virginia Scharff, *Taking the Wheel: Women and the Coming of the Motor Age* (New York: Free Press, 1991), and *Twenty Thousand Roads: Women, Movement, and the West* (Berkeley: University of California Press, 2003); Clay McShane, *Down the Asphalt Path: The Automobile and the American City* (New York: Columbia University Press, 1994), and *The Automobile: A Chronology of its Antecedents, Development, and Impact* (Westport, Conn.: Greenwood Press, 1997; David Gartman, *Auto-Opium: A Social History of American Automobile Design* (New York: Routledge, 1994); Peter J. Ling, *America and the Automobile: Technology, Reform, and Social Change* (Manchester: Manchester University Press); Judy Wajcman, *Feminism Confronts Technology* (Cambridge: Polity Press, 1991); Kathleen Franz, "'The Open Road': Automobility and Racial Uplift in the

Interwar Years," in Daniel Miller, ed., *Technology and the African-American Experience* (Cambridge: MIT Press, 2004), 131–154, and *Tinkering: Early Consumers Reinvent the Automobile* (Philadelphia: University of Pennsylvania Press, 2005); Michael L. Berger, *The Automobile in American History and Culture; A Reference Guide* (Westport, Conn.: Greenwood Press, 2001), and *The Devil Wagon in God's Country: The Automobile and Social Change in Rural America, 1893–1929* (Hamden, CT: Archon Books, 1979); Wolfgang Sachs, *For the Love of the Automobile: Looking Back into the History of Our Desires* (Berkeley: University of California Press, 1992); Sean O'Connell, *The Car in British Society: Class, Gender, and Motoring, 1896–1939* (Manchester: Manchester University Press, 1998); and Gijs Mom, *The Electric Vehicle: Technology and Expectations in the Automobile Age* (Baltimore: Johns Hopkins University Press, 2004).

31. See Simpson, *Trafficking Subjects*. The "politics of mobility" Simpson interrogates was briefly sketched by the geographer Doreen Massey in *Space, Place, and Gender* (Cambridge: Polity Press, 1994). See also James Clifford, *Routes: Travel and Translation in the Late Twentieth Century* (Cambridge, MA: Harvard University Press, 1997); Seltzer, *Bodies and Machines*; Patricia Fumerton, *Unsettled: The Culture of Mobility and the Working Poor in Early Modern England* (Chicago: University of Chicago Press, 2006); Sarah Jain, "'Dangerous Instrumentality': The Bystander as Subject in Automobility," *Cultural Anthropology* 19.1 (February 2004): 61–94, and "Violent Submission: Gendered Automobility," *Cultural Critique* 61 (Fall 2005): 186–214; Paul Gilroy, "Driving While Black," in Daniel Miller, ed., *Car Cultures* (Oxford: Berg, 2001), 81–104; Jeffrey T. Schnapp, "Crash: Speed as Engine of Individuation," *Modernism/Modernity* 6.1 (1999): 1–49; Kristin Ross, *Fast Cars, Clean Bodies: Decolonization and the Reordering of French Culture* (Cambridge, Mass.: MIT Press, 1995); Kris Lackey, *RoadFrames: The American Highway Narrative* (Lincoln: University of Nebraska Press, 1997); Smith, *Moving Lives*; Schivelbusch, *The Railway Journey*; and Eric Leed, *The Mind of the Traveler: From Gilgamesh to Global Tourism* (New York: Basic Books, 1991).

32. See Beckmann, "Automobility," and "Mobility and Safety," *Theory, Culture, and Society* 21.4/5 (2000); Rajan, *The Enigma of Automobility*; Jeremy Packer, "Disciplining Mobility," in *Foucault, Cultural Studies, and Governmentality*, ed. Jack Z. Bratich, Jeremy Packer, and Cameron McCarthy (Albany: State University of New York Press, 2003), 135–161; Mimi Sheller and John Urry, "The City and the Car," *International Journal of Urban and Regional Research* 24 (2000): 737–757; Urry, "The System of Automobility"; and Sheller, "Automotive Emotions: Feeling the Car," *Theory, Culture, and Society* 21.4/5 (2004): 221–242. (This issue of *Theory, Culture, and Society* is devoted to automobility.) See also Martin Dodge and Rob Kitchin, "Code, Vehicle, and Governmentality: The Automatic Production of Driving Spaces," *National Institute for Regional and Spatial Analysis (Ireland) Working Paper Series*, no. 29 (March 2006).

33. See Foucault, *Security, Territory, Population: Lectures at the College de France, 1977–1978* (London: Palgrave MacMillan, 2007).

34. Ralph Waldo Emerson, *Essays and Lectures* (New York: Library of America, 1983), 480.

## chapter one

1. Mark Bahnisch, "Embodied Work, Divided Labour: Subjectivity and the Scientific Management of the Body in Frederick W. Taylor's 1907 'Lecture on Management,'" *Body & Society* 6.1 (2000): 54.

2. C. B. Macpherson, *The Political Theory of Possessive Individualism: Hobbes to Locke* (Oxford: Oxford University Press, 1962), 3.

3. J. G. A. Pocock, *Virtue, Commerce, and History: Essays on Political Thought and History, Chiefly in the Eighteenth Century* (Cambridge: Cambridge University Press, 1985), 60.

4. Republicanism mitigated the threat of atomism indwelling in capital-ism by merging the imperatives of self-possession and self-interest with those of "disinterested" civic duty, positing a crucial space and subjectivity outside of market culture. See Joyce Appleby, *Capitalism and a New Social Order: The Republican Vision of the 1790s* (New York: New York University Press, 1984), and *Liberalism and Republicanism in the Historical Imagination* (Cambridge, MA: Harvard University Press, 1992); Isaac Kramnick, *Republicanism and Bourgeois Radicalism: Political Ideology in Late Eighteenth-Century England and America* (Ithaca: Cornell University Press, 1990). See also Daniel T. Rodgers's evaluation of the republican historiographic paradigm, "Republicanism: The Career of a Concept," *Journal of American History* 79.1 (June 1992): 11–38.

5. For a more traditional view, see Daniel Walker Howe, *Making the American Self: From Jonathan Edwards to Abraham Lincoln* (Cambridge: Harvard University Press, 1997). Howe posits the model of autonomous selfhood as a rather unproblematic normative ideal, with little attention paid to how, as Charles Ponce de Leon put it in his review of Howe's study, "normative ideals . . . serve hegemonic functions." Ponce de Leon, "Is There an American Self?" *Reviews in American History* 26.3 (September 1998): 493.

6. As Saidiya Hartman notes, "The universality or unencumbered individual-ity of liberalism relies on tacit exclusions and norms that preclude substantive equality; all do not equally partake of the resplendent, plenipotent, indivisible, and steely singularity that it proffers." *Scenes of Subjection: Terror, Slavery, and Self-Making in Nineteenth-Century America* (New York and Oxford: Oxford University Press, 1997), 122. See also, for example, Stephanie McCurry, *Masters of Small Worlds: Yeoman Households, Gender Relations, and the Political Culture of the Antebellum South Carolina Low Country* (Oxford: Oxford University Press, 1997); Michael Warner, *The Letters of the Republic: Publication and the Public Sphere in*

*Eighteenth-Century America* (Cambridge, MA: Harvard University Press, 1990); Carole Pateman, *The Disorder of Women: Democracy, Feminism, and Political Theory* (Stanford: Stanford University Press, 1990); Mark E. Kann, *On the Man Question: Gender and Civic Virtue in America* (Philadelphia: Temple University Press, 1991); Bruce Burgett, *Sentimental Bodies: Sex, Gender, and Citizenship in the Early Republic* (Princeton: Princeton University Press, 1998); and Joyce W. Warren, *The American Narcissus: Individualism and Women in Nineteenth-Century American Fiction* (New Brunswick: Rutgers University Press, 1984).

7. Jefferson cited in Eric Foner, "Free Labor and Nineteenth-Century Political Ideology," *The Market Revolution in America: Social, Political, and Religious Expressions, 1800–1880,* Melvin Stokes and Stephen Conway, eds. (Charlottesville: University Press of Virginia, 1996), 101.

8. Bernard Bailyn, *Faces of Revolution: Personalities and Themes in the Struggle for American Independence* (New York: Vintage, 1992), 234. John Adams declared that "there are but two sorts of men in the world, freemen and slaves." Quoted in Joyce Appleby, *Liberalism and Republicanism in the Historical Imagination* (Cambridge, MA: Harvard University Press, 1992), 158.

9. Linda K. Kerber, "The Republican Mother: Women and the Enlightenment—An American Perspective," *American Quarterly* 28.2 (1976): 187–205. See also, for example, Kerber, *No Constitutional Right to Be Ladies: Women and the Obligations of Citizenship* (New York: Hill and Wang, 1998); Nancy Isenberg, *Sex and Citizenship in Antebellum America* (Chapel Hill: University of North Carolina Press, 1998); and Caroline Winterer, "Venus on the Sofa: Women, Neoclassicism, and the Early American Republic," *Modern Intellectual History* 2.1 (2005): 29–60.

10. "The political culture of a country," write the political scientists Gabriel A. Almond and Sidney Verba, "is the for that country characteristic distribution of patterns of orientation on political objects." Almond and Verba, *The Civic Culture* (Princeton: Princeton University Press, 1963), 14–15.

11. Alexis de Tocqueville, *Democracy in America,* trans. George Lawrence, 2 vols. (New York: Harper & Row, 1966), vol. 2, 506. Entering into usage in the lexicon of the nascent social sciences in France in the 1830s, "*l'odieux individualisme*" described a pathological ethic of disassociation and selfishness enabled by the democratizing tendencies in postrevolutionary French society and the practices of the capitalist market. Koenraad W. Swart, "'Individualism' in the Mid-Nineteenth Century (1826–1860)," *Journal of the History of Ideas* 23.1 (January 1962): 79. Yehoshua Arieli has noted individualism's shift "from a term of abuse (as used by Tocqueville) to one of approval, from a remote sociological notion to one which more than any other defined Americanism." Arieli, "Individualism and National Identity," *American Chameleon: Individualism in Trans-National Context,* eds. Richard O. Curry and Laurence B. Goodheart (Kent, OH: Kent State University Press, 1991), 167.

12. Emerson continues to exert a compelling influence over the ways in which Americans, however different their origins and experiences, imagine individual freedom as well as the shape and character of the social. As Joel Porte has remarked, "To the extent which the sentiments of power, self-reliance, subjectivity, and independence attract to themselves a distinctly American nuance, its source is Emerson." Porte, *Representative Man: Ralph Waldo Emerson in His Time*, 2nd ed. (New York: Columbia University Press, 1988), x.

13. Quentin Anderson, *Making Americans: An Essay on Individualism and Money* (New York: Harcourt Brace Jovanovich, 1992), 29.

14. See Thomas Haskell and Richard F. Teichgraeber III, "Introduction: The Culture of the Market," *The Culture of the Market: Historical Essays*, eds. Haskell and Teichgraeber (Cambridge: Cambridge University Press, 1993), 1–42.

15. Emerson, *Essays and Lectures*, 263, 261.

16. Cyrus R. K. Patell, "Emersonian Strategies: Negative Liberty, Self-Reliance, and Democratic Individuality," *Nineteenth-Century Literature* 48.4 (March 1994): 441.

17. If an individual held a distinctive and powerful position in society (or conversely, an abject one), so the social-Darwinist mythos held, it was the result of his own exertions alone: as one commentator averred of railroad baron Cornelius Vanderbilt, "He was not the creation of luck nor chance nor circumstances." Chauncey M. Depew, quoted in John William Ward, *Red, White, and Blue: Men, Books, and Ideas in American Culture* (New York: Oxford University Press, 1969), 240–241. The mystical component of social Darwinism could be seen in farm-machinery magnate Cyrus McCormick's declaration, in a letter to the editor of the *American Sociological Review*, that there existed something very like a great chain of being in American society, one that found him and his fellow tycoons at the top by divine fiat. McCormick to Albion Small, February 3, 1915, cited in Olivier Zunz, *Making America Corporate, 1870–1920* (Chicago: University of Chicago Press, 1990), 199.

18. Frederick Jackson Turner, *The Frontier in American History* (New York: Henry Holt and Company, 1947), 37. Alan Trachtenberg has noted that, despite its tragic overtones, the Turner thesis "distilled" the American character as it would come to be known. "To be sure, [Turner] argued, the story of the frontier had reached its end, but the product of that experience remains. It remains in the predominant *character*, the traits of selfhood, with which the frontier experience has endowed Americans, that 'dominant individualism' which now must learn to cope with novel demands." Trachtenberg, *The Incorporation of America*, 15.

19. Leed also describes an English ritual, dating back to the time of Henry II, by which a manorial lord pronounced one of his serfs free. That lord, after publicly announcing the serf's status as a freeman and giving him a lance, brought the serf "to a crossroads to show him that 'all ways lie open to his feet.'"

These two features—arms and the right of free departure—long remained the distinguishing marks of the 'free' man. Their opposites—the forbidding of arms or of travel—were the marks of unfreedom." Leed, *The Mind of the Traveler*, 13.

20. I am referring here to the famous passage from *The Communist Manifesto* in which Marx and Engels describe modernity as a maelstrom in which "all that is solid melts into air"; Blackstone quoted in Frederick G. Whelan, "Citizenship and the Right to Leave," *American Political Science Review* 75.3 (September 1981): 644; Whitman, "Song of the Open Road," 299.

21. Leslie Dale Feldman, *Freedom as Motion* (Lanham, MD: University Press of America, 2001); James Oliver Robertson, *American Myth, American Reality* (New York: Hill & Wang, 1980), 128; Gerald L. Houseman, *The Right of Mobility* (Port Washington, NY: Kennikat Press, 1979), 9.

22. Raymond Williams, *Television,* ed. Ederyn Williams (London: Routledge, 2003), 20.

23. *Changing Directions: The Report of the Independent Commission on Transport* (London: Coronet, 1974), 106, quoted in Houseman, *The Right of Mobility,* 19.

24. Mark Simpson, *Trafficking Subjects,* xxvii. See also Beverly Skeggs, *Class, Self, Culture* (New York: Routledge, 2003), esp. chap. 3.

25. Clifford, *Routes,* 35–36; Fumerton, *Unsettled.* James Scott has noted that "nomads and pastoralists (such as Berbers and Bedouins), hunter-gatherers, Gypsies, vagrants, homeless people, itinerants, runaway slaves, and serfs have always been a thorn in the side of states. Efforts to permanently settle these mobile peoples (sedentarization) seemed to be a perennial state project— perennial, in part, because it so *seldom* succeeded." James Scott, *Seeing Like a State,* 1.

26. Leed, *The Mind of the Traveler*, 113. "In the history of patriarchal civiliza- tions," Leed further notes, "—and, as yet, there are no other kinds—humanity has worn the mask of masculinity, and travel has been a performance of this persona" (220).

27. Sidonie Smith, *Moving Lives,* 10, 20. James Clifford has similarly argued that narratives of mobility have tended to privilege "specific, largely male, experiences of worldliness." "Women," he writes, "have their own histories of labor migration, pilgrimage, emigration, exploration, tourism, and even military travel—histories linked with and distinct from those of men. For example, the everyday practice of driving a car [has been] a potent symbol, a contested experience. . . . specific histories of freedom and danger in movement need to be articulated along gender lines." Clifford, *Routes,* 4–6. See also Doreen Massey, *Space, Place, and Gender;* Janet Wolff, "On the Road Again: Metaphors of Travel in Cultural Criticism," *Cultural Studies* (1993): 224–239; and Annette Kolodny, *The Lay of the Land: Metaphors of Experience and History in American Life and Let- ters* (Chapel Hill: University of North Carolina Press, 1975).

28. Evander Bradley McGilvary, "Society and the Individual," *Philosophical Review* 9.2 (1900): 132.

29. The phrase is from Thomas L. Haskell's illuminating case study of a determinist challenge to liberal theory, "Persons as Uncaused Causes: John Stuart Mill, the Spirit of Capitalism, and the 'Invention' of Formalism," in Haskell and Teichgraeber, eds., *The Culture of the Market*, 441–502. See also James B. Gilbert, *Work Without Salvation: America's Intellectuals and Industrial Alienation, 1880–1910* (Baltimore: Johns Hopkins University Press, 1977).

30. Robert Owen, *A New View of Society and Report to the County of Lanark* (Baltimore: Penguin Books, 1969 [1813]), 140.

31. Karl Marx and Friedrich Engels, "Economic and Philosophic Manuscripts of 1844," "The *Grundrisse*," and "Manifesto of the Communist Party," *The Marx-Engels Reader*, 2nd ed. (New York: W. W. Norton and Company, 1978), 86, 222, 486.

32. See, for example, Leon Fink, *Workingmen's Democracy: The Knights of Labor and American Politics* (Urbana: University of Illinois Press, 1983); and Sean Wilentz, "Against Exceptionalism: Class Consciousness and the American Labor Movement, 1790–1920," *International Labor and Working Class History* 26 (Fall 1984): 1–24. Michael Kazin characterizes so-called working-class republicanism as "simply a species of populist rhetoric." Kazin, "The Agony and Romance of the American Left," *American Historical Review* 100.5 (December 1995): 1501.

33. John P. Davis, "The Nature of Corporations," *Political Science Quarterly* 12.2 (1897): 292. It appeared, moreover, that corporations had replaced the human individual as the primary social unit. In their behavior—rational, self-seeking, competitive—they embodied the autonomous individuals of the "state of nature" imagined by Enlightenment thinkers. Jurists codified their status as the private persons represented in the Fourteenth Amendment and protected their rapidly growing property from "undue" encroachment and redistribution. See Scott R. Bowman's discussion of "corporate individualism" in *The Modern Corporation and American Political Thought: Law, Power, and Ideology* (University Park: Pennsylvania State University Press, 1996). See also Jeffrey Sklansky's account of "the emerging jurisprudence of corporate property" through the work of jurist Thomas M. Cooley in *The Soul's Economy*, pp. 209–215.

34. Henry C. Adams, "Relation of the State to Industrial Action," *Publications of the American Economic Association* 1.6 (January 1887), 26; Thomas Whittaker, "Individualism and State-Action," *Mind* 13.49 (1888): 52. Raymond Jackson Wilson has noted that "a thorough account of the travail of the concept of the transcendent individual would come close to being a complete intellectual history of the period [1860 to 1920]." Wilson, *In Quest of Community: Social Philosophy in the United States, 1860–1920* (New York and Oxford: Oxford University Press, 1968), 15.

35. Kloppenberg, *Uncertain Victory*, 329. This discourse promoted reactionary agendas as well, as in George Fitzhugh's defense of slavery and the "communal values" of plantation culture, *Sociology for the South, or, The Failure of Free Society* (Richmond, VA: A. Morris, 1854).

36. Robert A. Nisbet, *The Sociological Tradition* (New York: Basic Books, 1966), 9.

37. The term derives from George Herbert Mead, "The Social Self," *Journal of Philosophy, Psychology and Scientific Methods* 10 (1913): 374–380, though the concept is evident in earlier pragmatist and feminist thought. See also, for example, John Dewey, *Reconstruction in Philosophy* (New York: Henry Holt and Company, 1920); George H. Mead, *Mind, Self, and Society: From the Standpoint of a Social Behaviorist* (Chicago: University of Chicago Press, 1972); William James, *Principles of Psychology* (New York: Henry Holt and Company, 1890). Feminist criticism of individualism was often explicitly political. Charlotte Perkins Gilman, for example, attacked the claims of "the Individualist" that socialism would destroy human individuality. See *Charlotte Perkins Gilman: A Nonfiction Reader,* ed. Larry Ceplair (New York: Columbia University Press, 1992), esp. 79–83. Julia Ward Howe concurred that the excesses of the individualistic worldview have amplified the social pathologies of poverty and class oppression, stating that "there is no monster like an exaggerated individual." Quoted in William Leach, *True Love and Perfect Union: The Feminist Reform of Sex and Society* (Middletown, CT: Wesleyan University Press, 1989), 133.

38. Sumner cited in Sklansky, *The Soul's Economy,* 131; Perkins cited in Robertson, *American Myth, American Reality,* 181; Rockefeller cited in Trachtenberg, *The Incorporation of America,* 86; Wilson cited in Martin J. Sklar, *The Corporate Reconstruction of American Capitalism,* 406.

39. Frederick Winslow Taylor, *The Principles of Scientific Management* (New York: Harper & Row, 1911), 7, 140. Taylor's first published statement of his ideas was "A Piece Work System Being a Step Toward Partial Solution of the Labor Problem," *Transactions of the American Society of Mechanical Engineers* 16 (1895): 859–903.

40. Robert Franklin Hoxie, *Scientific Management and Labor* (New York: D. Appleton, 1915), 104. As R. Jeffrey Lustig asserts, "The concentration of work authority Taylor proposed required more than a simple reassignment of tasks; it required the active taking of initiative away from work groups that had previously exercised it. . . . Scientific management now helped [industry] usurp the workers' authority over their crafts and, eventually, over productive intelligence itself." Lustig, *Corporate Liberalism,* 190. For an introduction to the "labor process theory" undergirding the new labor history, see Harry Braverman, *Labor and Monopoly Capital: The Degradation of Work in the Twentieth Century* (New York: Monthly Review Press, 1974); and David Montgomery, *Workers' Control in America* (Cambridge: Cambridge University Press, 1980), and *The Fall of the House of Labor: The Workplace, the State, and American Labor Activism, 1865–1925* (Cambridge: Cambridge University Press, 1987).

41. See, for example, Gary Cross, *An All-Consuming Century: Why Commercialism Won in Modern America* (New York: Columbia University Press, 2002); William Susman, *Culture as History: The Transformation of American Society in the*

*Twentieth Century* (New York: Pantheon, 1984); Susan Strasser, Charles McGovern, Matthias Judt, and Daniel S. Mattern, eds., *Getting and Spending: American and European Consumer Society in the Twentieth Century* (Cambridge: Cambridge University Press, 1998); and Lawrence B. Glickman, ed., *Consumer Society in American History: A Reader* (Ithaca: Cornell University Press, 1999).

42. Sidney Webb, "The Difficulties of Individualism," *Economic Journal* 1.2 (1891): 373.

43. See Mark Seltzer, *Bodies and Machines*. One supporter of Taylor claimed that Taylorism, with its attentiveness to the individual laborer, heralded "the beginnings of the restoration of individuality." C. B. Going quoted in Daniel T. Rodgers, *The Work Ethic in Industrial America, 1850–1920* (Chicago: University of Chicago Press, 1974), 56. Some thirty years later, another economist worried that "the workers by the millions in mills and factories are being shaped to meet the demands of this machine." Charles Reitell, "Machinery and Its Effect Upon the Workers in the Automotive Industry," *Annals of the American Academy of Political and Social Science* 116 (November 1924): 37.

44. See Foucault, *Discipline and Punish*, esp. chap. 3. On "responsible autonomy" of workers see Andrew L. Friedman, *Industry and Labour: Class Struggle at Work and Monopoly Capitalism* (London: MacMillan, 1977); and Michael Burawoy, *Manufacturing Consent: Changes in the Labor Process Under Monopoly Capitalism* (Chicago: University of Chicago Press, 1979).

45. Taylor is being quoted here by textile executive Richard A. Feiss, in a speech delivered to the Society to Promote the Science of Management. He prefaces this by asserting that it is necessary "that every member of the organization have a character sufficiently developed or capable of development to be in harmony with the character of the organization." Cited in Char Roone Miller, *Taylorized Citizenship: State Institutions and Subjectivity* (Westport, CT: Praeger, 2002), 17. Miller ties Taylorization to the progressive and capitalist objective of "creat[ing] within citizens the desire to behave" (16), an argument also elaborated in Barbara Townsley, *Reframing Human Resource Management: Power, Ethics, and the Subject at Work* (London: Sage, 1994).

46. Taylor, *Principles of Scientific Management*, 45–46.

47. Edward Cadbury, "The Case For and Against Scientific Management, *Sociological Review* 7 (1914): 104. James Scott echoes Cadbury in his estimation that high-modernist planning, of which Taylorism is one example, disdains "the skills, intelligence, and experience of ordinary people. . . . In the Taylorist factory . . . the logic of work organization is to reduce the factory hands' contribution to a series of repetitive, if practiced, movements—operations as machinelike as possible." Scott, *Seeing Like a State*, 346.

48. Rey Chow, "Postmodern Automatons," in Butler and Scott, eds., *Feminists Theorize the Political*, 105.

49. Consider the 1911 description, by advocates of Taylorism, of female textile workers' passive adoption of the discipline and ethos of scientific manage-

ment in Chris Nyland, "An Early Account of Scientific Management as Applied to Women's Work with Commentary by F. W. Taylor," *Journal of Management History* 6.6 (2000): 248–271. Such an account contrasts sharply with those of the introduction of Taylorist techniques on the male shop floor cited by Montgomery in *The Fall of the House of Labor*, esp. chapters 4 and 5.

50. James Livingston is making, in the first chapter of *Pragmatism, Feminism, Democracy*, a larger point about the latent patriarchal undertones haunting the recent critique of consumer culture. Arguing that this critique constitutes "merely a protest against proletarianization *from the standpoint of modern subjectivity*, in the name of possessive individualism" (23), Livingston asks that we resist being sutured into this primal scene, and look instead at what consumer culture and corporate capitalism made possible—specifically, the entry of greater numbers of women into the public sphere; and with it, a salutary reformulation of and archaic subjectivity; and the emergence of organizations and theories in and through which social democracy might be realized. Livingston is engaging Richard W. Fox, T. J. Jackson Lears, William Leach, and other cultural historians characterizing the transition from proprietary to corporate capitalism, and the decline of the sovereign self, as the Waterloo of American progressive politics. See Fox and Lears, eds., *The Culture of Consumption* (New York: Pantheon, 1983); Lears, *Fables of Abundance: A Cultural History of Advertising in America* (New York: Basic Books, 1994); Leach, *Land of Desire: Merchants, Power, and the Rise of a New American Culture* (New York: Vintage, 1993); and Sklansky, *The Soul's Economy*.

51. Schachter and others question the reliability of the Golden Age myth— *did* manual laborers enjoy autonomy before the midcentury control revolution? One might also ask what this putative autonomy did for these workers in terms of political power. Were they measurably better off than those workers who achieved agency—through collective actions such as coordinated line slowdowns and stints, bargaining, and strikes—in the mechanized and bureaucratic work environments of monopoly capitalism? See Hindy Lauer Schachter, *Frederick Taylor and Public Administration Community: A Reevaluation* (Albany: State University of New York Press, 1989), pp. 13–15. See also Daniel Nelson, *Frederick W. Taylor and Rise of Scientific Management* (Madison: University of Wisconsin Press, 1980); Peter F. Meiksins, "Scientific Management and Class Relations: A Dissenting View," *Theory and Society* 13.2 (March 1984): 177–209; and David Stark, "Class Struggle and the Transformation of the Labor Process: A Relational Approach," *Theory and Society* 9.1 (January 1980): 89–130. Also, it is important to remember that the discourse of possessive individualism and its loss had a mostly elite provenance. As Robert Wiebe notes, "If the national class imagined factory jobs as individualism lost, countless wage-earners decided otherwise." *Self-Rule: A Cultural History of American Democracy* (Chicago: University of Chicago Press, 1995), 195.

52. Barry Shank has noted that "the concept of republicanism . . . with its at-

tendant assumptions of economic self-sufficiency and autonomous subjectivity, has maintained its organizing power even as it has slithered out of its original time-frame and historiographical genre." Shank, "Subject, Commodity, Marketplace: The American Artists Group and the Mass Production of Distinction," *Radical History Review* 76 (Winter 2000): 31.

53. As Thomas Haskell has argued, from the "denial of the autonomy" in the late nineteenth century "there followed momentous consequences. . . . To the extent that the individual was viewed not as the autonomous creator, but the created product of society, nineteenth-century ethical views and the politics based on them would have to give way to a new welfare-oriented humanitarianism and a new politics." Haskell, *The Emergence of Professional Social Science: The American Social Science Association and the Nineteenth-Century Crisis of Authority* (Urbana: University of Illinois Press, 1977), 14.

54. See Kloppenberg, *Uncertain Victory;* Michael McGerr, *A Fierce Discontent: The Rise and Fall of the Progressive Movement in America, 1870–1920* (New York: Free Press, 2003).

55. Walter Lippmann, *The Good Society* (New York: Grosset & Dunlap, 1936), 45–53.

56. Livingston, *Pragmatism, Feminism, and Democracy,* 50–51.

57. William James cited in Zunz, *Making America Corporate,* 11; Woodrow Wilson cited in Sklar, *The Corporate Reconstruction of American Capitalism,* 407.

58. Otis L. Graham, *An Encore for Reform: The Old Progressives and the New Deal* (New York: Oxford University Press, 1967).

59. Croly called for the renewal of a "Hamiltonian" view of American life that emphasized the sovereignty of the public over against that of individual or corporate citizens. He asserted that "Jeffersonian individualism must be abandoned for the benefit of a genuinely individual and social consummation" and in its stead must be cultivated an individuality that enables "personal moral freedom." His conclusion, outlining constructive individualism, had about it an ecclesiastical tone, arguing that the individual was fulfilled "by the sincere and enthusiastic imitation of heroes and saints." Croly, *The Promise of American Life* (Cambridge, MA: Harvard University Press, 1965 [1909]), 153, 410, 454.

60. Sklansky, *The Soul's Economy,* 220.

61. Charles Horton Cooley, *Human Nature and Social Order* (Somerset, NJ: Transaction, 1983 [1902]), 351, 423.

62. John Dewey, "Individualism, Old and New," *The Later Works 1925–1953,* vol. 5, *1929–1930,* ed. Jo Ann Boydston (Carbondale: Southern Illinois University Press, 1988), 89.

63. Clifford Geertz, *The Interpretation of Cultures* (New York: Basic Books, 2000), 218.

64. William H. Whyte, *The Organization Man* (Garden City, NY: Doubleday Anchor Books, 1956), 5.

65. Quoted in Arieli, "Individualism and National Identity," 182. Roosevelt's

phrase should remind us, as Max Weber commented, that "the expression individualism includes the most heterogeneous things imaginable." Weber, *The Protestant Ethic and The Spirit of Capitalism,* trans. Talcott Parsons (New York: Charles Scribner's Sons, 1958), 222ff.

66. See, for example, Robert Lynd and Helen Lynd, *Middletown: A Study in Modern American Culture* (New York: Harcourt Brace and World, 1919). For an account of the intellectual ferment of the 1920s see Casey Blake, *Beloved Community: The Cultural Criticism of Randolph Bourne, Van Wyck Brooks, Waldo Frank, and Lewis Mumford* (Chapel Hill: University of North Carolina Press, 1990).

67. Hoover, *American Individualism* (Garden City, NJ: Doubleday Page & Company, 1922), 4, 5, 7, 14, 44.

68. Ibid., 68.

69. Walter Benn Michaels, "An American Tragedy, or The Promise of American Life," *Representations* 25 (Winter 1989): 73, 80–81.

70. For example, as Jay Fliegelman has argued regarding the Revolutionary era, the project of "declaring independence" required complex rhetorical, philosophical, and performative strategies that attempted to make explicit the connections between American political subjectivity and the larger Enlightenment goal of creating a society according to "natural law." Fliegelman, *Declaring Independence: Jefferson, Natural Language, and the Culture of Performance* (Stanford: Stanford University Press, 1993).

71. Winfried Fluck, "The Humanities in the Age of Expressive Individualism and Cultural Radicalism," *Cultural Critique* 40 (Fall 1998): 59–60. Expressive individualism has been described by Robert M. Bellah and his coauthors as the belief "that each person has a unique core of feeling and intuition that should unfold or be expressed if individuality is to be realized." Bellah et al., *Habits of the Heart: Individualism and Commitment in American Life* (Berkeley: University of California Press, 1985), 334.

72. Miller, *Taylorized Citizenship,* 10.

73. Gramsci quoted in Michaels, "An American Tragedy," 90–91.

74. Dimnet quoted in Irene Taviss Thomson, "The Transformation of the Social Bond: Images of Individualism from the 1920s Versus the 1970s," *Social Forces* 67.4 (June 1989): 861. The 1920s discourse also resembled that of the cold war for its condemnations of individualist expression that flouted social norms. See Thomson, "From Conflict to Embedment: The Individual-Society Relationship, 1920–1991," *Sociological Forum* 12.4 (December 1997): 631–658.

75. Wiebe, *Self-Rule,* 187.

76. This is not to say that consumption *precluded* political action. As Nan Enstad has argued, through their consumption of fashion and popular culture, young female garment workers in New York City laid claim to the symbolic status of "ladies." Their assumption of this dignified identity augmented rather than eclipsed the political subjectivity they developed as workers. Yet these workers' resistant ethos, a product of their symbolic class ascent through

consumption, can also be read as another example of the counterhegemonic appropriation of hegemonic rhetoric and iconography, a la working-class republicanism. Moreover, their refashioning of themselves as ladies is very much in keeping with the expressive individualist project of making conspicuous one's true interior self, which in this case of these immigrant workers meant a compensatory affectation of the taste and purchasing power of the middle class. Political activism of the picket-line and ballot-box variety was an occasional rather than a standard effect of the self-cultivation required under expressive individualism. See Enstad, *Ladies of Labor, Girls of Adventure.* At the same time, an explicit consumer identity animated a number of political causes in the twentieth century, through actions such as boycotts and pressure campaigns. See, for example, Kathryn Kish Sklar, "The Consumer's White Label Campaign of the National Consumer's League," *Getting and Spending,* 17–35; and Kathy M. Newman, *Radio Active: Advertising and Consumer Activism, 1935–1947* (Berkeley: University of California Press, 2004).

77. "Modern industrial production," Stuart Ewen writes, "required that workers be free to 'cultivate themselves' among the uncontestable fruits of the new industrial cornucopia." Ewen, *Captains of Consciousness* (New York: Basic Books, 2001), 27. One such tale of middle-class arrival, from a 1929 *True Story Magazine,* can be found cited in Lizabeth Cohen, "Encountering Mass Culture at the Grassroots: The Experience of Chicago Workers in the 1920s," *American Quarterly* 41.1 (1989): 6–7. Cohen notes the ideological nature of these accounts: most industrial workers did not enjoy the standard of living they depicted.

78. Charles McGovern, *Sold American,* 77.

## chapter two

1. Lewis Mumford, *The Highway and the City* (New York: Harcourt, Brace & World, 1963), 234.

2. U.S. Department of Transportation, Federal Highway Administration, Office of Highway Information Management, Chart MV-200, "Motor Vehicle Registrations, 1900–1995," *Highway Statistics Summary to 1995.*

3. Kristin Ross, *Fast Cars, Clean Bodies,* 29.

4. In his study of pollution control policy, Sudhir Chella Rajan notes the "systematic blindness" afflicting (and perpetuated by) the majority of technical or "political" accounts of automobility, which evade "the political problem of automobility." This blindness, Rajan observes, "gives us a unique opportunity to examine, in broader terms, an important domain of contemporary life. For indeed, we can discern a deep-seated cultural politics as having affected the way automobile policy is even *represented* in North America. It is a politics that eschews taking steps toward a critical discourse on the automobile." Rajan, *The Enigma of Automobility,* 16.

5. "The Spreading Automobile," *Harper's Weekly* July 1, 1899, 655, quoted in Patricia W. Lipski, "The Introduction of 'Automobile' into American English," *American Speech* 39.3 (October 1964): 178–179.

6. Wilson quoted in "Motorists Don't Make Socialists, They Say: Not Pictures of Arrogant Wealth, as Dr. Wilson Charged," *New York Times* March 4, 1906, 12; Sims's speech is referenced in "District of Columbia Legislating," *Automobile*, February 22, 1906, 414; review of Kremer production quoted in Frank Donovan, *Wheels for a Nation*, 17; statement on "the prejudice against motor cars" from "Motoring, The Favorite Sport of the Day," *Town & Country* September 29, 1906. A more lighthearted class politics found expression in many of the nearly two hundred automobile-themed popular songs published and recorded in automobility's first decade. These songs glamorized, even as they poked fun at, the moneyed figure of the car owner and driver. Many of their lyrics delighted in swells' dirtying their hands and clothes in the inevitable mechanical breakdowns they suffered. Vaudevillian Bobby North's 1913 "He'd Have to Get Under—Get Out and Get Under," for example, tells of a makeout session thwarted by mechanical trouble. Like many others, including perhaps the first of the genre, 1899's "Love in an Automobile," North's song merged these gentle class politics with suggestions of the sexual allure and amorous uses of cars. No mechanical problems afflicted the couple in 1905's "In My Merry Oldsmobile," who "love to 'spark' in the dark old park." Such songs (some of which were sponsored or promoted by the industry) as well as automobile-themed dime novels and early films, participated in the assimilation of the automobile, as they addressed and constituted an audience already receptive to the liberating energies of consumer modernity, even if car ownership was not (yet) within their reach. See Donovan, *Wheels for a Nation*, 14–15. See also Clay McShane's discussion of early automobile-themed popular culture in *Down the Asphalt Path*, 141–148.

7. Winthrop Scarrett, "The Horse of the Future and the Future of the Horse," quoted in Richard O. Davies, *The Age of Asphalt: The Automobile, the Freeway, and the Condition of Modern America* (Philadelphia: J. B. Lippincott Company, 1975), 8.

8. U.S. Department of Transportation, "Motor Vehicle Registrations, 1900–1995; "What It Costs to Run an Automobile," *Outing* (1910), in *Motoring in America: The Early Years*, ed. Frank Oppel (Secaucus, NJ: Castle Books, 1989), 472.

9. See Flink, *The Automobile Age* and *America Adopts the Automobile*; Rae, *The Road and the Car in American Life* and *The American Automobile*; and Michael L. Berger, *The Devil Wagon in God's Country*.

10. W. E. Roach Company, "Automobiles that Give Satisfaction," advertisement, *Saturday Evening Post* March 31, 1900.

11. "This anomaly," Laird continues, "seems especially salient because automobiles dominate both popular and scholarly memories of the 1920s, and

the decade's marketing specialists left a forceful legacy in their tools of persuasion. [Automaker] Jordan's novel invitation to step 'into the Playboy when the hour grows dull with things gone dead and stale' echoes the Roaring Twenties of legend, and automobile ads ever since. . . . As American culture assimilated automobility, the 1920s became the transition decade for the automobile industry, during which corporate operations increasingly distanced themselves from owners and founders, and their advertising followed suit." Pamela Walker Laird, "'The Car Without a Single Weakness': Early Automobile Advertising," *Technology and Culture* 37.4 (October 1996): 210. Since that time, Stan Luger notes, "billions have been spent on advertising to define freedom as equivalent to individual mobility, to equate a new car with success, and to imbue particular models with different social identities." Luger, *Corporate Power, American Democracy, and the Automobile Industry* (Cambridge: Cambridge University Press, 2000), 182.

12. See, for example, Flink, *The Automobile Age;* and Rae, *The American Automobile Industry* (Boston: Twayne, 1984), and *Henry Ford: Great Lives Observed* (New York: Prentice-Hall, 1969).

13. Laird, "'The Car Without a Single Weakness,'" 210.

14. Flink, *America Adopts the Automobile,* 100; M. M. Musselman, *Get a Horse!* (Philadelphia: J. B. Lippincott, 1950), 50.

15. On this dominant apologia for capitalism, see Ellen Meiksins Wood, *The Origins of Capitalism* (New York: Monthly Review Press, 1999).

16. Dunn, *Driving Forces,* 2, 184; Feldman, *Freedom as Motion,* 58.

17. Tim Cresswell, "The Right to Mobility: The Production of Mobility in the Courtroom," *Antipode* 38.4 (September 2006): 737.

18. *The Horseless Age* 1 (1895), quoted in Flink, *America Adopts the Automobile,* 22.

19. "The Future of the Motocycle," *Chicago Times-Herald* November 29, 1895.

20. David Gartman, *Auto-Opium,* 34, 11.

21. Peter J. Ling, *America and the Automobile,* 4.

22. Gartman, *Auto-Opium,* 41, 43.

23. Ling, *America and the Automobile,* 4–5.

24. Gartman, *Auto-Opium,* 43. "Perhaps," Leon Mandel has written, "[the American] climbs into his car and becomes a different man . . . perhaps what we understand as automobile-conferred privacy is only a refinement of the historical need to be mobile in a kind of ultimate way." Mandel, *Driven,* 21.

25. As Rudy Volti has observed, the automobile's "overwhelming commercial success was not exclusively due to the mobility it offered. . . . Much of the appeal of the automobile stems from its ability to confer a measure of insulation from the outside world while providing at least the illusion of power." Volti, "A Century of Automobility," *Technology and Culture* 37.4 (October 1996): 667. More than a mere conveyance, the automobile was seen as the "means for an individual to detach herself from an environment of givens and move out to an

environment of choice, a world of possibilities and unknowns." Lawrence M. Friedman, *The Republic of Choice: Law, Authority, and Culture* (Cambridge: Harvard University Press, 1990), 55. Clay McShane observes that "more than any other consumer good the motor car provided fantasies of status, freedom, and escape from the constraints of a highly disciplined urban, industrial order." McShane, *Down the Asphalt Path*, 148. David Rieff echoes that "the promise of the automobile was not transportation so much as solitude and independence." Rieff, *Los Angeles: Capital of the Third World* (New York: Simon & Schuster, 1991), 45.

26. Loren E. Lomasky, "Autonomy and Automobility," *Independent Review* 2.1 (1997): 8–9. This essay can also be found on the websites of various conservative and/or libertarian think tanks with which the author is affiliated, such as the Competitive Enterprise Institute and the Heartland Institute. Lomasky is cited, and erroneously credited with coining the term "automobility," by his Heartland Institute colleagues Joseph L. Bast and Jay Lehr in their fantastical essay, "The Increasing Sustainability of Cars, Trucks, and the Combustion Engine" (Chicago: Heartland Institute, 2000). Lomasky's essay was also quoted in automotive columnist Gary Washburn's "An Academic Polishes Car's Rusty Image," *Chicago Tribune* August 21, 1995.

27. Melvin M. Webber, "The Joys of Automobility," *The Car and the City: The Automobile, the Built Environment, and Daily Urban Life*, ed. Martin Wachs and Margaret Crawford (Ann Arbor: University of Michigan Press, 1991), 283; Ruth Brandon, *How the Car Changed Life* (London: Macmillan, 2002), 2; Sam Kazman, "Automobility and Freedom," essay published on Atlas Society and Objectivist Center website, September 1, 2001, www.objectivistcenter.org /showcontent.aspx?ct=303&printer=True, accessed September 1, 2006; Jeff Jacoby, "Our Passion for Automobility," *Boston Globe* August 10, 1995.

28. Foucault, "Technologies of the Self," in Luther H. Martin, Huck Gutman, and Patrick H. Hutton, eds., *Technologies of the Self: A Seminar with Michel Foucault* (London: Tavistock, 1988), 18.

29. Warren James Belasco, *Americans on the Road: From Autocamp to Motel, 1910–1945* (Cambridge: MIT Press, 1979), 8. As Eric Leed has observed, "The identity-defining travels of the medieval knight were . . . ostensibly voluntary and undertaken to no utilitarian purpose. The chivalric journey, which is the pattern and model for significant modern travel, is essentially self-referential, undertaken to reveal the character of the knight as "free." . . . The celebration of travel as a demonstration of freedom and means to autonomy becomes the clearly modern *topos*." Leed, *The Mind of the Traveler*, 12–13.

30. H. P. Burchell, "The Automobile as a Means of Country Travel," *Outing* 46.5 (August 1905): 536; Charles and Alice Williamson, *The Lightning Conductor* (1902), quoted in Lord Montagu of Beaulieu and F. Wilson McComb, *Behind the Wheel: The Magic and Manners of Early Motoring* (New York: Paddington Press, 1977), 171; Otto Birnbaum quoted in Winfried Wolf, *Car Mania* (Chicago: Pluto

Press), 194; 1909 *Harper's Weekly* cited in Flink, *America Adopts the Automobile*, 102; Ohio Representative Albert Douglas cited in Karl Raitz, "American Roads, Roadside America," *Geographical Review* 88.3 (July 1998): 376; Theodore Dreiser, *A Hoosier Holiday* (New York: Lane, 1916), 93.

31. John Keats, *The Insolent Chariots*.

32. Quoted in Musselman, *Get a Horse!*, 114. Catherine Bertho Lavenir has observed of the same moment in France that "early 'society motorists' ostentatiously ignored their opponents. These pioneers were fully aware of the pleasure they were taking in driving powerful cars. The feeling of power and freedom associated with motoring was in accordance with the values of the new ruling classes." Lavenir, "How the Motor Car Conquered the Road," in Miriam Levin, ed., *Cultures of Control* (Amsterdam: Harwood Academic Publishers, 2000), 120.

33. Jeffrey T. Schnapp, "Crash: Speed as Engine of Individuation," *Modernism/Modernity* 6.1 (1999): 3.

34. Michael L. Bromley, *William Howard Taft and the First Motoring Presidency* (Jefferson, NC: McFarland Publishing, 2003); Walter Longstreth, *Little Journeys by Automobile* 1.7 (April 1916): 9 (NMAH, Box 18, File 19).

35. Miriam R. Levin, "Contexts of Control," in Levin, ed., *Cultures of Control*, 25.

36. Kurt Möser, "The Dark Side of 'Automobilism': Violence, War, and the Motor Car," *Journal of Transport History* 24.2 (September 2003): 244–245.

37. Lee Strout White (E. B. White), "Farewell My Lovely," *New Yorker* May 16, 1936, 20. This essay would later that same year be published as *Farewell to the Model T: From Sea to Shining Sea* (New York: Little Bookroom, 2003 [1936]).

38. Leon Vandervort, "The Beginner and His Automobile," *Outing* 40.5 (August 1902): 618; Robert Bruce, "The Place of the Automobile," *Outing* 37.1 (October 1900): 65. In this vein, Sarah Jain has noted "a paradox . . . has been debated since the beginnings of automobility: car safety is dependent on everyone driving cautiously and attending to the sociality of the road, whereas car advertising has highlighted the individuality and the potential for infraction offered by the automobile." Jain, "Violent Submission," 189.

39. Kenneth Grahame's *The Wind in the Willows* quoted in Peter Marsh and Peter Collett, *Driving Passion: The Psychology of the Car* (Boston: Faber and Faber, 1987), 177; on Jordan Baker's driving sensibilities see chap. 3, F. Scott Fitzgerald, *The Great Gatsby* (New York: Scribner's, 1999 [1925]); Herbert Ladd Towle, "The Automobile and Its Mission," *Scribner's* 53 (1913): 150; F. T. Marinetti, "Manifeste du Futurisme," *Le Figaro* February 20, 1909. Tim Benton notes that the Futurists love cars not "as products of industry—the result of standardization, taylorization, the revolution which Ford offered and which Fiat and Citroën later took up. They preferred cars which could kill." Benton, "Dreams of Machines: Futurism and l'Esprit Nouveau," *Journal of Design History* 3.1 (1990): 29–30.

40. Wolfgang Schivelbusch notes that the locomotive's speed and the uniformity of the rails "made the landscape seen from the train window appear to be 'another world.'" Schivelbusch, *The Railway Journey*, 24. As with rail and earlier transportations revolutions, automobility "precipitated fundamental perceptual and psychic changes in human subjects and in the fantasies that governed their modes of interconnection with landscapes traversed and viewed." Schnapp, "Crash," 3.

41. Emily Post, *By Motor to the Golden Gate,* ed. Jane Lancaster (Jefferson, NC: McFarland & Company, 2004) [(New York: D. Appleton, 1916)], 255.

42. Montagu and McComb, *Behind the Wheel*, 172. "Who has not," asked Robert Bruce in *Outing*, "stood beside a modern greyhound of the rail and thought a kingdom all too small a price to pay for the privilege of just once being engineer?" Bruce, "The Place of the Automobile," 65.

43. Phil Patton, *Open Road*, 13.

44. Hiram Percy Maxim, "A Sample of American Automobiling," *The Automobile* 4.4 (April 1902), in Oppel, *Motoring in America*, 378.

45. W. B. Adams, quoted in Schivelbusch, *The Railway Journey*, 14

46. Erik Cohen, "Phenomenology of Tourist Experiences," *Defining Travel: Diverse Visions,* Susan L. Roberson, ed. (Jackson: University Press of Mississippi, 2001), 38. See also Dean McCannell, "Staged Authenticity: Arrangements of Social Space in Tourist Settings," *American Journal of Sociology* 79.3 (1973): 589–603.

47. See Lears, *No Place of Grace;* and Miles Orvell, *The Real Thing: Imitation and Authenticity in American Culture, 1880–1940* (Chapel Hill: University of North Carolina Press, 1989).

48. Post, *By Motor to the Golden Gate,* 141; Edith Wharton, *A Motor-Flight through France* (New York: Charles Scribner's Sons, 1908), 1; William Joseph Showalter, "The Automobile and the Pioneer," *Annals of the American Academy of Political and Social Science* 116 (November 1924): 22. Other examples of the genre include Vernon McGill, *Diary of a Motor Journey from Chicago to Los Angeles* (Los Angeles: Grafton, 1922); Paul E. Vernon, *Coast to Coast by Motor* (London: Black, 1930); Alice Huyler Ramsey, *Veil, Duster, and Tire Iron* (Covina, CA: Castle Press, 1961); and Jeannie Lippitt Weedar, *Rhode Island to California by Motor* (Santa Barbara: Pacific Coast, 1917). See also the overviews by Curt McConnell, *Coast to Coast by Automobile: The Pioneering Trips, 1899–1908* (Stanford: Stanford University Press, 2000), and *"A Reliable Car and a Woman Who Knows How to Drive It":  The First Coast-to-Coast Auto Trips by Woman, 1899–1916* (Jefferson, NC: McFarland, 2002); and T. R. Nicholson, *The Wild Roads: The Story of Transcontinental Motoring* (New York: Norton, 1969).

49. Chas. G. Percival, "Introductory" to pamphlet on his 1913 journey (NMAH, Box 18, File 28).

50. Fuessle quoted in Marguerite S. Shaffer, *See America First: Tourism and*

*National Identity, 1880–1940* (Washington, DC: Smithsonian Institution Press, 2001), 131.

51. Charles Horton Cooley, Journal 22, 105, entry of September 6, 1923, Charles Horton Cooley Papers, Box 6, Bentley Historical Library, University of Michigan. It is interesting that the enthusiasm with which mass automobility was greeted and assimilated by the state and industry found a parallel in the responses of many progressives and proponents of social selfhood such as Cooley. "All the world, it seems, are cheerfully driving automobiles," he noted approvingly in 1923. "I like travelling by your own will and means trusting somewhat to your own skill, not without some sense of danger" (Journal 22, 100–101, entries of June 3 and July 8, 1923). I am grateful to Hal Orbach for passing on to me Cooley's journal entries on driving.

52. Peck wrote, "Whether the people of the United States continue to pursue the purpose of Thomas Jefferson . . . or to strike out into an uncharted domain of human experience, the modern motor car is one of the forces that make for an acceleration of the pace." Harvey W. Peck, "Civilization on Wheels," *Social Forces* 7.2 (December 1928): 309.

53. Shaffer, *See America First*, 142.

54. M. H. James, "The Automobile and Recreation," *Annals of the American Academy of Political and Social Science* 116 (November 1924): 34.

55. Such narratives would feed what Jeffrey Schnapp has described as "a new nationalist mythology that envisaged roadway networks—be they English turnpikes, German *autobahnen*, Italian *autostrade*, or American freeways—as the arterial system of the nation's body and driving along them as a form of communion." Schnapp, "Crash," 17.

56. Ford Motor Company, *The Lady and Her Motor Car* (Detroit: Ford Motor Company, 1911), 2 (BFRC, Accession 175, Ford Motor Company 1909–1911 Folder).

57. This is not to say there were no women who undertook such a journey as drivers. Alice Huyler Ramsey, for example, drove herself on the 1909 journey from which *Veil, Duster, and Tire Iron* was drawn. Among the sights enthusiastically recounted by *National Geographic*'s William Showalter were "women without men in their parties . . . not one of them disheartened with the toils of the road behind them or awed by the miles ahead of them!" Showalter, "The Automobile and the Pioneer," 22.

58. Virginia Scharff, *Taking the Wheel*, 13.

59. McCluggage paraphrased in Mandel, *Driven*, 10.

60. Cited in Michael L. Berger, *The Automobile in American History and Culture*, 408.

61. Scharff, *Taking the Wheel*, 163.

62. Jain, "'Dangerous Instrumentality,'" 64.

63. Female drivers, Kathleen Franz asserts, "embodied the goals of New

Womanhood to make new space for women outside the home." Franz, *Tinkering*, 57. Sara Parchesky has similarly argued that "women's mastery of exciting new technologies (such as the car) offered a spectacular image of New Womanhood as both practical power and thrilling adventure." Parchesky, "Women in the Driver's Seat: The Auto-Erotics of Early Women's Films," *Film History* 18 (2006): 174.

64. See McGovern, *Sold American*, 79–80.

65. Quoted in O'Connell, *The Car in British Society*, 46.

66. Donovan, *Wheels for a Nation*, 13. For a republican critique of effeminate wealth, see, for example, John Brown's 1757 treatise, "An Estimate on the Manners and Principles of the Times," in *Commerce, Culture, and Liberty: Essays on Capitalism Before Adam Smith*, ed. Henry C. Clarke (Indianapolis: Liberty Fund, 2003), 424–447.

67. "Newport," *Harper's Bazar* [sic] July 29, 1899, 626, quoted in Lipski, "The Introduction of 'Automobile' into American English," 179.

68. Möser, "The Dark Side of 'Automobilism,'" 253.

69. "One of the great faults of the electric car," wrote M. M. Musselman in 1950, "was that by nature it was ladylike." Musselman, *Get a Horse!*, 240. See Virginia Scharff, "Gender, Electricity, and Automobility," in *The Car and the City*, ed. Wachs and Crawford, 75–85; and Gijs Mom, *The Electric Vehicle*.

70. McShane, *Down the Asphalt Path*, 155.

71. See Michael L. Bromley, *William Howard Taft and the First Motoring Presidency*, 12–21.

72. Jain, "Violent Submission," 196.

73. "The Vogue of Motoring for Women," *Town & Country* December 1, 1906 (NMAH, Box 22, File 9).

74. Michele Ramsey, "Selling Social Status: Women and Automobile Advertisements from 1910–1920," *Women and Language* 28.1 (Spring 2005): 28.

75. Quoted in Musselman, *Get a Horse!*, 241.

76. On the bicycle as the precursor to the automobile, see Sidney H. Aronson, "The Sociology of the Bicycle," *Social Forces* 30.3 (March 1952): 305–312; and David L. Herlihy, *Bicycle: The History* (New Haven: Yale University Press, 2006).

77. Ford Motor Company, *The Woman and the Ford* (Detroit: Ford Motor Company, 1911), 9 (BFRC, Accession 175, Ford Motor Company 1909–1911 Folder).

78. Quoted in ibid., 242.

79. Quoted in Franz, *Tinkering*, 56.

80. Ford Motor Company, *The Woman and the Ford* (Detroit: Ford Motor Company, 1911), 3 (BFRC, Accession 175, Ford Motor Company 1909–1911 Folder).

81. Franz, *Tinkering*, 45. See also Sherrie Inness, "On the Road and in the Air: Gender and Technology in Girls' Automobile and Airplane Serials," *Journal*

*of Popular Culture* 30.2 (Fall 1996): 47–60; and Nancy Tilman Romalov, "Mobile Heroines: Early Twentieth-Century Girls' Automobile Series, *Journal of Popular Culture* 28.4 (Spring 1995): 231–243.

82. Parchesky, "Women in the Driver's Seat," 176. See also William M. Drew, "Speeding Sweethearts of the Silent Screen, 1908–1921," http://www.welcome tosilentmovies.com/features/sweethearts/sweethearts.htm (accessed October 29, 2006). See also Nan Enstad, *Ladies of Labor, Girls of Adventure,* chap. 5.

83. Robert Sloss, "What a Woman Can Do With an Automobile," *Outing* 56.1 (April 1910): 62, 68–69.

84. Luellen Cass Teters, "Fair Woman as a Motorist," *Motor* January 1904, 19.

85. Vincent Bryan and Gus Edwards, *In My Merry Oldsmobile* (New York: M. Witmark and Sons, 1905).

86. Marvin Adelson, "The Car, The City, and What We Want," in *The Car and the City,* ed. Wachs and Crawford, 292.

87. C. H. Claudy, 1913, cited in Berger, *The Devil Wagon in God's Country,* 64–65.

88. Michael Warner, *The Letters of the Republic.*

89. As the historian Daniel Albert has observed, from the perspective of midcentury traffic engineers "the core of the 'traffic problem' were individual drivers who, although perhaps already citizens, could not safely be granted fully fledged citizenship in the new motorized society. As a motorized citizen, the driver would have to be held to a higher standard of behavior than was acceptable from the pedestrian citizen. Mental deficiencies which might not have been dangerous in the slower horse-and-buggy days or in a widely dispersed rural society, proved deadly in the urban motor age. . . . The very meaning of citizenship—the rights and responsibilities of the individual in relation to the group—would have to be rethought . . . in the new motorized world." Albert, "Primitive Drivers: Racial Science and Citizenship in the Motor Age," *Science as Culture* 10.3 (September 2001): 336–337.

90. "Road Building Far Behind the Automobile," Portland Cement Association advertisement, *Motor* November 1924, 109.

91. Arthur Fürst, quoted in Möser, "The Dark Side of 'Automobilism,'" 244.

92. "Anita King, Movie Actress Who Is Trying to Break 3000 Mile Auto Record," *San Francisco Call and Post* September 1, 1915.

93. Quoted in Musselman, *Get a Horse!,* 247–248. See also McConnell, "A Reliable Car and a Woman Who Knows How to Drive It," chap. 4.

94. Romalov, "Mobile Heroines," 232; Franz, *Tinkering,* 58–59. Franz further observes that the vacationing practice of motor camping gave rise to the category of the "motor wife," which encouraged women to take pride in their resourcefulness in on-the-road domesticity and to leave the driving and mechanical competence to men (58–66).

95. "The purposive agents of modernity," Nancy Cott has written, "had to take women's desires for and emblems of emancipation into account." Cott, *The*

*Grounding of Modern Feminism* (New Haven: Yale University Press, 1987), 174. See Ramsey, "Selling Social Status"; and Laura H. Behling, "The Woman at the Wheel: Marketing Ideal Womanhood, 1915–1934," *Journal of American Culture* 20.3 (Fall 1997): 13–30, and "Fisher's Bodies: Automobile Advertisements and the Framing of Modern Female Identity," *Centennial Review* 41.3 (1997): 515–528.

96. Romalov, "Mobile Heroines," 237.

97. Booth Tarkington, *The Magnificent Ambersons* (New York: Bantam Classics, 1994 [1918]), 173

98. See Foucault, *Security, Territory, Population.* As the sociologist Nikolas Rose explains, "govern*mentality* both extends the concerns of rulers to the ordering of the multitudinous affairs of a territory and its populations in order to ensure its wellbeing, and simultaneously establishes divisions between the proper spheres of action of different types of authority" (italics in original). Rose, "Governing 'Advanced' Liberal Democracies," in Barry, Osborne, and Rose, eds., *Foucault and Political Reason,* 42.

99. See, for example, McShane, *Down the Asphalt Path;* Lavenir, "How the Motor Car Conquered the Road"; and Jain, "'Dangerous Instrumentality.'"

100. S. H. Nerlove and W. G. Graham, "An Automobile Mortality Table for 1928," *Journal of Political Economy* 36.2 (April 1928): 280. See also Norman Damon, "The Action Program for Highway Safety," *Annals of the American Academy of Political and Social Science* 320.1 (November 1958): 15–26. Thirty-seven percent of those killed by cars in New York State in 1925 were under the age of fourteen; and a total of 15,821 children were struck by automobiles that year, 558 of them fatally. Quoted in Weaver Weddell Pangburn, "Playgrounds, a Factor in Street Safety," *Annals of the American Academy of Political and Social Science* 133 (September 1927): 178. The historian Peter Norton has analyzed the rededication of urban streets to the automobile in the early twentieth century, an achievement that required the delegitimation—in fact the criminalization—of pedestrianism, through the legal construct of "jaywalking." Norton, "Street Rivals: Jaywalking and the Invention of the Motor Age Street," 2006, unpublished paper provided to the author courtesy of Dr. Norton.

101. Public, Jürgen Habermas has written, "was synonymous with 'state-related'; the attribute no longer referred to the representative court of a person endowed with authority but instead to the functioning of an apparatus with regulated spheres of jurisdiction and endowed with a monopoly over the legitimate use of coercion." The concept of the public road, then, differs from an imperial road such as the Appian Way, which belonged to the emperor. Habermas, *The Structural Transformation of the Public Sphere: An Inquiry into a Category of Bourgeois Society,* trans. Thomas Burger with the assistance of Frederick Lawrence (Cambridge: MIT Press, 1989), 18.

102. Thomas Jefferson, among other American officials, envisioned public roads primarily as crucial ligatures between farm households and markets, but

also as signifiers of unity and aspiration, as evidenced by his administration's improvements to the Natchez Trace Trail and sponsorship of the 1803 expedition to explore the Louisiana Purchase. Henry Nash Smith claimed that "the Lewis and Clark expedition . . . gave tangible substance to what had merely been an idea, and established the image of a highway across the continent so firmly in the minds of Americans that repeated failures could not shake it." Smith, *Virgin Land: The American West as Symbol and Myth* (Cambridge: Harvard University Press, 1970), 17. By 1808, Jefferson and Treasury Secretary Albert Gallatin had successfully argued the need for a national road, a project that occupied the imagination and energy of myriad geographers, surveyors, engineers, merchants, laborers, politicians, and white settlers in the years between 1790 and 1840 (though it was never completed). This road, Joseph S. Wood has observed, "reflected the ideal of a rural, agrarian, and artisanal society seeking to expand itself over geographical space." Wood, "The Idea of a National Road," *The National Road,* ed. Karl Reitz (Baltimore: Johns Hopkins University Press, 1996), 121. In the 1950s, an advertisement for Portland Cement positioned an image of the signers of the Constitution next to a superhighway, stressing that the venerable document and the company's product were similarly effective in binding the nation together; a Ford Motor Company advertisement from the same decade declared that "the physical outline of [American] society is a map of the American Road. "The American Road III," Ford advertisement, *Life* February 25, 1952.

103. Aronson, "The Sociology of the Bicycle," 310, 311.

104. Moreover, Gutfreund notes, industry-supported advocacy groups succeeded, during the 1930s, in passing laws earmarking gasoline tax receipts for highway construction and maintenance exclusively. By 1940, the ever-louder demand for more roads could be seen merely as a call for progress; few apprehended "the inherent wealth transfer produced by spending money raised from *all* taxpayers for the benefit of the subset of the public described [by the highway lobby] as *the motoring public.* . . . Highway construction was now sheltered, at least partially, from the need to compete with education, law enforcement, prisons, or welfare program for scarce government funds, unlike virtually all other government endeavors." Gutfreund, *20th-Century Sprawl: Highways and the Reshaping of the American Landscape* (Oxford: Oxford University Press), 31, 34.

105. These engineers enjoyed virtually total discretion in early roadbuilding decisions, indirectly shaping decades of American domestic policy as they executed their ostensibly nonpolitical task. Bruce Seely, *Building the American Highway System.*

106. During the Depression, roadbuilding became a component of New Deal relief, as in the federal government's grant to the Pennsylvania Turnpike Authority in 1938. In that same year Congress and President Roosevelt asked the BPR to develop a plan for a network of six superhighways, and to determine the best option for financing such a network. MacDonald's vigorous opposition to

public-private partnerships and toll roads (such as Robert Moses's Triborough Bridge Authority, the Pennsylvania Turnpike, and the turnpikes eight states would develop over the next decade) stemmed, at least partly, from his desire to maintain full federal authority (his own) over national roadbuilding. The BPR's report, *Toll Roads and Free Roads* (1939), created the blueprint of interregional highways, radial expressways, and exurban beltways from which highway planners would realize the National System of Interstate and Defense Highways in the next decade; it also rejected the toll funding mechanism employed by the Pennsylvania Turnpike and other roads, claiming that most routes would be unable to support themselves by direct user fees alone. Wartime, while slowing the pace of road construction, impressed upon Roosevelt and other officials the need for better highways to speed troops and equipment around the country. See Gutfreund, *20th-Century Sprawl*; Mark Rose, *Interstate*; Tom Lewis, *Divided Highways*; Christy Borth, *Mankind on the Move: The Story of Highways* (Washington, DC: Automotive Safety Foundation, 1969), 191–228; and Stephen B. Goddard, *Getting There: The Epic Struggle between Road and Rail in the Twentieth Century* (New York: Basic Books, 1994).

107. Despite this rhetoric, there is a lack of "evidence in the past of a vigorous social movement having played an essential role in charting the course of automobility. Rather, whatever planning process was, and continues to be, responsible for creating the institutional order has involved very few of the users—the public—as participants." Rajan, *The Enigma of Automobility*, 13.

108. Even the BPR's MacDonald, who throughout his long tenure had advocated the continuing health of urban mass transit, described the choice facing congested urban centers as between more highways and getting along "with things as they are." Quoted in Davies, *The Age of Asphalt*, 14. "The fatal mistake we have been making," Lewis Mumford wrote in 1963, "is to sacrifice every other form of transportation to the private motorcar." Mumford, *The Highway and the City*, 237–238.

109. General Motors' conduct during this time—influencing the removal of some a hundred urban electric trolley systems and intraurban railroad lines (in various states of repair) from the 1930s through the 1950s—fit with a more general campaign pursued by the automotive industries to eliminate alternatives to driving. For example, GM purchased, and then retired, Los Angeles's functional if somewhat decrepit trolley system. The corporation was also censured in 1961 by the Interstate Commerce Commission for its undue influence in having lines removed from the New Haven Railroad.

110. James Scott, *Seeing Like a State*, 73–74.

111. See Gilles Deleuze and Felix Guattari, *A Thousand Plateaus: Capitalism and Schizophrenia*, trans. Brian Massumi (London: Athlone Press, 1988), 474–500.

112. Dodge and Kitchin, "Code, Vehicle, and Governmentality," 9. See U.S. Department of Transportation, Federal Highway Administration, Chart DL-1C,

"Licensed Drivers by Sex and Ratio to Population," *Highway Statistics 2005.* On early licensing and police, see also Flink, *America Adopts the Automobile,* 174–178.

113. Other elements of the apparatus of automobility appearing during this time were the centerline (1911); the electric traffic signal (1914); the stop sign (1915); federally mandated state highway departments (1916); official route signage (1918); and the three-color traffic light (1920). See U.S. Dept. of Transportation, Federal Highway Administration, "The Evolution of MUTCD," http://mutcd.fhwa.dot.gov/kno-history.htm (accessed March 18, 2007). See also Damon, "The Action Program for Highway Safety"; Government Accounting Office, "Auto Insurance: State Regulation Affects Cost and Availability" (1986), http://archive.gao.gov/t2pbat24/130972.pdf (accessed February 24, 2007); and Herbert J. Stack, *History of Driver Education in the United States* (Washington: National Education Association, 1966).

114. John Jerome, *The Death of the Automobile: The Fatal Effect of the Golden Era, 1955–1970* (New York: W. W. Norton, 1972), 14–15.

115. André Gorz, "L'Ideologie Sociale de la Bagnole," *Le Sauvage* September/October 1973.

116. Jain, "'Dangerous Instrumentality,'" 61; Dodge and Kitchin, "Code, Vehicle, and Governmentality," 2; U.S. Department of Health, Education and Welfare, "Report of the Secretary's Advisory Committee on Traffic Safety (Washington, DC: U.S. Government Printing Office, 1968), 6.

117. On the ways in which political thinkers justified this shift, see Gary G. Hamilton and John R. Sutton, "The Problem of Control in the Weak State: Domination in the United States, 1880–1920," *Theory and Society* 18.1 (January 1989): 1–46; and Stephen Skowronek, *Building a New American State: The Expansion of National Administrative Capacities, 1877–1920* (Cambridge: Cambridge University Press, 1982).

118. Jeremy Packer, "Disciplining Mobility," in Jack Z. Bratich, Jeremy Packer, and Cameron McCarthy, eds., *Foucault, Cultural Studies, and Governmentality,* 138, 153. Packer defines safety as "the positive steps taken to avoid the loss of production; the insurance of profitability; the maintenance of efficiency; or most generally any technique used in the disposition of things and wo/men that avoids loss. . . . Risk is something to be avoided, while safety is the positivity that organizes conduct" (150).

119. Catherine Bertho Lavenir, "How the Motor Car Conquered the Road," in Levin, ed., *Cultures of Control,* 125.

120. "Motor Driving as a Fine Art," *Town & Country* September 26, 1908, 28.

121. This term is inspired by Michael Sandel's definition of "the procedural republic, by which I mean a public life animated by the liberal vision and self-image." Sandel, "The Procedural Republic and The Unencumbered Self," in *Communitarianism and Individualism,* ed. Shlomo Avineri and Avner De-Shalit (Oxford: Oxford University Press, 1992), 25.

## chapter three

1. John Gray, *Two Faces of Liberalism* (New York: New Press, 2000), 123.

2. Dwight D. Eisenhower, Commencement Speech at Columbia University, June 1, 1949.

3. Haskell and Teichgraeber, introduction, *The Culture of the Market*, 33. Striving to differentiate between the two regimes, American rhetoric focused on the degree to which the Enlightenment conception of the human individual figured into the political calculus of each: were individual rights sacralized, or were they sacrificed to the will of the collective? Arthur Schlesinger, Jr., for example, isolated the "essential dynamic" of totalitarianism as "toward the unlimited domination and degradation and eventual obliteration of the individual." Schlesinger, *The Vital Center: The Politics of Freedom* (Boston: Houghton Mifflin, 1949), 87. This harrowing Manichaean vision—in part a holdover from the wartime binary of the war against fascism—informed policy-template documents such as the National Security Council's 1950 "United States Objectives and Programs for National Security" (NSC 68). That document's main author, Paul Nitze, portrayed the conflict as an apocalyptic choice "between the idea of freedom under a government of laws, and the idea of slavery under the grim oligarchy of the Kremlin." Nitze and his collaborators emphasized that "the free society values the individual as an end in himself," and extends to that individual "the opportunity to realize his creative powers." National Security Council, "NSC 68: United States Objectives and Programs for National Security," in *American Cold War Strategy: Interpreting NSC 68,* ed. Ernest R. May (Boston: Bedford Books, 1993), 27.

4. John Lewis Gaddis, *The Long Peace: Inquiries Into the History of the Cold War* (New York: Oxford University Press, 1987), 235–236.

5. T. J. Jackson Lears, "From Salvation to Self-Realization: Advertising and the Therapeutic Roots of the Consumer Culture, 1880–1930," in Fox and Lears, eds., *The Culture of Consumption,* 9.

6. Rupert Wilkinson, *The Pursuit of American Character* (New York: Harper & Row, 1988), 105. I am referring to men such as John Foster Dulles, Dean Acheson, Henry L. Stimson, and George F. Kennan. Guy Oakes has argued that Eisenhower Secretary of State Dulles, for example, saw in his fellow citizens "intellectual confusion, moral corrosion, a loss of the 'spiritual loyalties' that provided the basis for American individualism and its ethic of self-control, and a vulnerability to subversion by hostile forces that would eventually destroy the American way of life." Oakes, *The Imaginary War: Civil Defense and American Cold War Culture* (New York: Oxford University Press, 1994), 23. See also John C. Donovan, *The Cold Warriors: A Policy-Making Elite* (Lexington, MA: D. C. Heath, 1974).

7. National Security Council, "NSC 68," 42, 29; Geroid Tanquary Robinson, "The Ideological Combat," *Foreign Affairs* 27.4 (1949): 538.

8. John William Ward, *Red, White, and Blue,* 250.

9. Thomas L. Hartshorne, *The Distorted Image: Changing Conceptions of the American Character Since Turner* (Cleveland: Press of Case Western Reserve University, 1968), 152. Efforts to construct this "nonideological" propaganda included, for example, the "American Style" conference held at MIT in 1957 and attended by luminaries such as Kennan, J. Robert Oppenheimer, David Potter, and David Riesman. The conference sought "an account of our national purposes, intentions and hopes that is at once honest and inspiring." Oppenheimer, "Theory Versus Practice in American Values and Performance," *The American Style: Essays in Value and Performance,* ed. Elting E. Morrison (New York: Harper & Brothers, 1958), 111. It was the "very feeling that the hosts of Midian were on the prowl," Godfrey Hodgson has written, "that the United States was wrestling with the Evil One, and therefore needed to match the messianic beliefs of the adversary with an equivalent dogma, that made it so fashionable in the late 1950s to define the grand purposes of America." Hodgson, *America in Our Time* (New York: Vintage Books, 1976), 70. The encyclicals published to this end represented, Hodgson argues, "comprehensive attempts . . . to codify the ideological and political beliefs of a nation's elite" (505–506). Though phrased in national terms, it was important that the rhetoric of the "equivalent dogma" be universal, with "America" as a synecdoche for freedom and human dignity. Hence Murray Dyer's assertion that "until we can find 'the common purposes, the common interests, the common values of the free world,' and express them in terms capable of firing the hearts of men and then prove by action that these common denominators are the mainspring of our endeavor, our political communication is unlikely to be more than counterpropaganda. As counterpropaganda the struggle must take on the character of the survival of our nation against the Soviet. This will not be a victory of the heritage of the Western world in conflict with forces denying the dignity of men." Dyer, *The Weapon on the Wall,* quoted in John B. Whitton, "The American Effort Challenged," *Propaganda and the Cold War,* ed. John B. Whitton (Washington: Public Affairs Press, 1963), 113n.

10. As W. Scott Lucas has noted, U.S. propaganda during the cold war "rested upon the mobilization of a superior culture." Lucas, *Freedom's War: The American Crusade Against the Soviet Union* (New York: New York University Press, 1999), 93.

11. Dorothy Lee, *Freedom and Culture* (New York: Prentice-Hall, 1959), 57. The rhetoric of freedom, Eric Foner has written, "suffused American politics, culture, and society" during the cold war. Foner, *The Story of American Freedom* (New York: WW. Norton, 1998), 252. Most Western political philosophers characterized freedom as "the protection of the individual against tyranny," whereas their Soviet and Chinese counterparts asserted the historical-materialist doctrine of freedom as "an actor's conscious control over the necessity which dictates one's actions." William A. Glaser, "The Semantics of the Cold War,"

*Public Opinion Quarterly* 20.4 (1957): 709–710. Noting the plasticity of the term, Sir Percy Spender, Australian ambassador to the U.S., told an audience of Union College graduates that "today Freedom—political, economic and individual freedom—lies destroyed or is in the course of being destroyed over great areas of the globe. And it has been destroyed and is being destroyed in the name of Freedom." Spender, "Liberty and the Individual: 'Know the Truth and the Truth Shall Make You Free,'" *Vital Speeches* August 1955, 1407.

12. Arthur Larson, *What We Are For* (New York: Harper & Brothers, 1959), 102; Gabriel Hauge, *Is the Individual Obsolete?* (Pittsburgh: Carnegie Institute of Technology, 1964), 24.

13. Kim McQuaid, *Uneasy Partners: Big Business in American Politics, 1945–1990* (Baltimore: Johns Hopkins University Press, 1994), 77. Philip M. Taylor has similarly noted that "the permeation of Cold War themes extended impercepti-bly into a wide range of activities from the Space Race to science fiction movies, from the Olympic Games to comic books, and from medical research to May Day parades." Taylor, "Through a Glass Darkly? The Psychological Climate and Psychological Warfare of the Cold War," in *Cold War Propaganda in the 1950s*, ed. Gary D. Rawnsley (New York: St. Martin's Press, 1999), 225. Paul N. Edwards has echoed these claims: "the struggle as a whole went on everywhere and perpetu-ally." Edwards, *The Closed World* (Cambridge, Mass.: MIT Press, 1996), 11.

14. Lawrence Halprin, *Freeways* (New York: Reinhold, 1966), 12.

15. Howard Brick, "The Reformist Dimension of Talcott Parsons' Early Social Theory," in Haskell and Teichgraeber, eds., *The Culture of the Market*, 362. Charles Beard attributed the Depression to a foolish societal commitment to the creed. Beard, "The Myth of Rugged American Individualism," *Harper's* December 1931.

16. Harold Laski, *American Democracy: A Commentary and an Interpretation* (New York: Viking Press, 1948), 69.

17. F. A. Hayek, *The Road to Serfdom* (Chicago: University of Chicago Press, 1944), 20. See also Hayek, *Individualism and Social Order,* and Max Lerner, *Ideas Are Weapons: The History and Uses of Ideas* (New York: Viking Press, 1939). For an analysis of the individualist-collectivist dichotomy from this period, see Abraham Kaplan, "American Ethics and Public Policy" in Morrison, ed., *The American Style,* 3–110.

18. Hence erstwhile socialist Max Lerner's approving observation in 1937 that "our intellectuals have moved toward Marxian thought; in our institutional life ' we have within our own framework borrowed some of the elements of the Rus-sian Revolution." Lerner, *Ideas are Weapons,* 535.

19. Daniel Lerner quoted in Zygmunt Bauman, *Intimations of Postmodernity* (New York: Routledge, 1991, 78. Dorothy Ross has explained this "mainstream-ing" of sociology and other social sciences as a concession to anti-socialistic forces by most early American practitioners, who, perhaps by virtue of their class origin and "respectable" sensibilities, were willing to trade radicalism for

social and academic legitimacy. See Ross, *The Origins of American Social Science* (Cambridge: Cambridge University Press, 1991).

20. As Terence Ball has noted, social scientists in the postwar period were "likened repeatedly to technicians, to engineers, even to physicians concerned with the 'health' of American society." Ball, "The Politics of Social Science in Postwar America," *Recasting America: Culture and Politics in the Age of Cold War*, ed. Lary Mary (Chicago: University of Chicago Press, 1989), 82. See also Ellen Schrecker, *No Ivory Tower: McCarthyism and the Universities* (New York and Oxford: Oxford University Press, 1986).

21. See Ron Robin, *The Making of the Cold War Enemy: Culture and Politics in the Military-Intellectual Complex* (Princeton: Princeton University Press, 2001). For an example of this type of work, see Margaret Mead, "On Methods of Implementing a National Morale Program," *Applied Anthropology* 1.1 (1941): 20–24. For retrospective analyses see Gene M. Lyons, *The Uneasy Partnership: Social Science and the Federal Government in the Twentieth Century* (New York: Russell Sage Foundation, 1969); Rebecca S. Lowen, *Creating the Cold War University: The Transformation of Stanford* (Berkeley: University of California Press, 1997); and Ellen Herman, *The Romance of American Psychology: Political Culture in the Age of Experts* (Berkeley: University of California Press, 1995). Some social scientists, however, rebuffed the proffered hand of power. C. Wright Mills, for example, warned his colleagues of the perils of such alliances: "To *appeal* to the powerful, on the basis of any knowledge we now have, is utopian in the foolish sense of the term. Our relations with them are more likely to be only such relations as they find useful, which is to say that we become technicians accepting their problems and aims, or ideologists promoting their prestige and authority." Mills, *The Sociological Imagination* (New York: Grove Press, 1959), 193.

22. See, for example, Talcott Parsons, *The Structure of Social Action* (New York: McGraw-Hill, 1937).

23. Georgia Representative E. E. Cox quoted in Lyons, *The Uneasy Partnership*, 278. These investigatory bodies were the 1952 House of Representatives Cox Committee and the 1954 Reese Committee.

24. Paul Jones, "Human History Is Made by Men, Not 'Trends,'" *Saturday Evening Post* December 10, 1955, 10–12

25. Arthur Larson, *What We Are For* (New York: Harper & Brothers, 1959), 112; Robert Lindner, *Prescription for Rebellion* (New York: Rinehart & Company, 1952), 22; Abraham Kaplan, "American Ethics and Public Policy," in Morrison, ed., *The American Style*, 87. These claims were not necessarily false: one Soviet psychologist famously dismissed the idea of individual autonomy by arguing that an individual could not "by direct force control his behavior any more than a shadow can carry stones." Quoted in Robert Conquest, *The Politics of Ideas in the U.S.S.R.* (New York: Frederick A. Praeger, 1967), 27.

26. David M. Potter, *People of Plenty: Economic Abundance and the American Character* (Chicago: University of Chicago Press, 1954), xvii. Informing this

compromise was an anthropological notion of culture as a complex, though discernible, web of beliefs and practices that governed the symbolic, social, and political life of a given society. The mediating concept character derived largely from the work of Erich Fromm, who defined it as "the specific form in which human energy is shaped by the dynamic adaptation of human needs to the particular mode of existence of a given society." Fromm, *Escape From Freedom* (New York: Henry Holt and Company, 1941), 276.

27. See Michael McGiffert, "Selected Writings on American National Character," *American Quarterly* 15.2, part 2: supplement (1963): 271–288. Examples include Henry Steele Commager, *The American Mind: An Interpretation of American Thought and Character Since the 1880s* (New Haven: Yale University Press, 1950); Seymour Martin Lipset, *The First New Nation* (New York: Basic Books, 1963); Geoffrey Gorer, *The American People: A Study in National Character* (New York: W. W. Norton, 1948); D. W. Brogan, *The American Character* (New York: Time, Inc., 1944; 1956); Perry Miller, "The Shaping of the American Character," *New England Quarterly* 28.4 (1955): 163–186; and David M. Potter, "The Quest for the National Character," in John Higham, ed., *The Reconstruction of American History* (New York: Harper & Row, 1962).

28. See David C. McClelland, *The Achieving Society* (Princeton: D. Van Nostrand Company, 1961).

29. Herman, *The Romance of American Psychology,* 171. The malleable self was certainly nothing new to the advertising industry. The most effective propaganda techniques, one analyst wrote, "can be obtained . . . from Madison Avenue and from the sociologists as guides for the wording of the output." Donald Dunham, *Kremlin Target U.S.A.: Conquest by Propaganda* (New York: Ives Washburn, 1961), 204. After World War II, the "scientization" of the advertising industry added to its legitimacy and therefore increased its value to producers of consumer products. Works such as Edward Bernays's *The Engineering of Consent* (Norman: University of Oklahoma Press, 1955) treated the cultivation of consumption as merely another scientific puzzle to be solved. Vance Packard's *The Hidden Persuaders* (New York: Cardinal Editions, 1958), by contrast, condemned the apparent contempt that ad agencies showed the human individual. Adoption of scientific models of advertising (given a social-scientific twist as "marketing"), however, complemented rather than revolutionized the central vision that historically powered advertising, namely, that the human self was environmentally formed and conditioned, and that its capacities for transformation were untold.

30. Margaret Mead, "The Traditional Character and the Bolshevik Ideal," *American Appraisals of Soviet Russia, 1917–1977,* ed. Eugene Anschel (Metuchen, NJ: Scarecrow Press, 1978) 284, 286.

31. Raymond A. Bauer, Alex Inkeles, and Clyde Kluckhohn, "Soviet Society vs. the National Character," in Anschel, ed., *American Appraisals of Soviet Russia,* 290–291. Geroid T. Robinson similarly noted that "the 'individual' in the great

Russian novels is not the rugged, independent individual who deliberately and joyfully transcends his group ties, but the lonely, lost man who is individualistic in that he is out of touch with his culture." Robinson, in Carl J. Friedrich, ed., *Totalitarianism: Proceedings of a Conference Held at the American Academy of Arts and Sciences* (Cambridge, MA: Harvard University Press, 1953), 81.

32. See also Margaret Mead, "What Makes the Soviet Character?," *Natural History* 60 (1951): 396–303, 339; Ada Siegel, "The New Soviet Man," *American Mercury* (November 1950): 524–532; Thomas A. Bailey, *America Faces Russia: Russo-American Relations From the Early Times to Our Day* (Ithaca: Cornell University Press, 1950). Another valuable source is the 1951 collection of essays *Soviet Attitudes Toward Authority*, recently republished as Mead, Geoffrey Gorer, and John Rickman, *Russian Culture* (New York: Berghahn Books, 2000). For an interesting comparison of American character and that of the Chinese, the U.S.'s other cold war antagonists, see Francis L. K. Hsu, *Americans and Chinese: Two Ways of Life* (New York: Abelard Schuman Ltd., 1953).

33. The "Crisis of the Individual" series that ran in *Commentary* in 1945 and 1946 featured articles by luminaries such as John Dewey, Hannah Arendt, William A. Orton, Reinhold Niebuhr, and Pearl S. Buck. The essays generally called for, in Orton's words, "the reassertion of the individual against the mob." Orton, "Everyman Amid the Stereotypes," *Commentary* 1.7 (May 1946): 10.

34. Wilfred M. McClay, *The Masterless*, 224; Robert Booth Fowler, *Believing Skeptics: American Political Intellectuals, 1945–1964* (Greenwood, CT: Greenwood Press, 1978) 233. "If Americans are so receptive to diagnoses of changing and declining character," John Hewitt has observed, "it is not because of a penchant for self-flagellation, but because of a belief that what is broken can be repaired." Hewitt, *Dilemmas of the American Self* (Philadelphia: Temple University Press, 1989), 45.

35. Archibald MacLeish, "Loyalty and Freedom," *American Scholar* 22.4 (Fall 1953): 395; Wallace Stegner, "Variations on a Theme by Conrad," *Yale Review* 39.3 (1950): 522; R. W. B. Lewis, *The American Adam* (Chicago: University of Chicago Press, 1955), 91; Harold W. Dodds, "The Importance of Being an Individual: Conformity Versus Non-Conformity," *Vital Speeches* August 1, 1955, 1405; State Department Policy Planning Staff quoted in W. Scott Lucas, "Beyond Diplomacy: Propaganda and the History of the Cold War," in Rawnsley, ed., *Cold War Propaganda in the 1950s*, 18; see, for example, Horkheimer's *Eclipse of Reason* (New York: Oxford University Press, 1947).

36. Irving Louis Horowitz, *C. Wright Mills: An American Utopian* (New York: Free Press, 1983), 227. See David Riesman (with Nathan Glazer and Reuel Denney), *The Lonely Crowd: A Study of the Changing American Character* (New Haven: Yale University Press, 1965 [1950]); Betty Friedan, *The Feminine Mystique* (New York: W. W. Norton, 1963); C. Wright Mills, *White Collar: The American Middle Classes* (New York: Galaxy/Oxford University Press, 1951); and William Whyte, *The Organization Man*. See also Erik Erikson, *Childhood and Society* (New York:

Norton, 1950); Robert Lindner, *Must You Conform?* (New York: Rinehart, 1956); and Vance Packard, *The Status Seekers* (New York: D. McKay Co., 1959).

37. This menace was captured perhaps most compellingly by Theodor Adorno and his coauthors in their 1951 study *The Authoritarian Personality* (New York: W. W. Norton, 1982), which ominously observed that many Americans "are no longer, or rather never were, 'individuals' in the sense of traditional nineteenth-century philosophy" (349).

38. Shawn Perry-Giles, *The Rhetorical Presidency, Propaganda, and the Cold War, 1945–1955* (Westport, CT: Praeger, 2002), 186.

39. William Graebner, *The Age of Doubt: American Thought and Culture in the 1940s* (Boston: Twayne, 1990), 122.

40. Stegner, "Variations on a Theme by Conrad," 520–521. Daniel Belgrad has thematized the postwar artistic program as one of "spontaneity" in *The Culture of Spontaneity: Improvisation and the Arts in Postwar America* (Chicago: University of Chicago Press, 1998). See also Carl N. Degler's treatment of postwar art and literature in *Affluence and Anxiety: 1945–Present* (Chicago: Scott, Foresman and Company, 1968).

41. See Eva Cockcroft, "Abstract Expressionism, Weapon of the Cold War," *ArtForum*, June 1974, 39–41; and David Craven, "The Disappropriation of Abstract Expressionism," *Art History* 8.4 (1985): 499–513.

42. Suzanne Clark, *Cold Warriors: Manliness on Trial in the Rhetoric of the West* (Carbondale: Southern Illinois University Press, 2000), 2. Wendy Kozol examines the way the cold war was represented in the pages of *Life* magazine "through gender-coded signs of power and weakness." She writes, "Depicting the enemy as male, and the United States as female, intensifie[d] Cold War dangers not only by conceding power to the enemy but by emasculating the signifier of the nation." Kozol, *Life's America: Family and Nation in Postwar Photojournalism* (Philadelphia: Temple University Press, 1994), 110–111.

43. Quote is from Philip Wylie, *Generation of Vipers*, 2nd ed. (New York: Rinehart, 1942), xii. "Momism" derives from Erikson, *Childhood and Society*. Elaine Tyler May has analyzed the postwar conflation of communism and emasculation, and the consequent "containment" of femininity, in *Homeward Bound: American Families in the Cold War Era* (New York: Basic Books, 1988). On the effect of gender anxieties on cold war literature, film, and cultural criticism, see Nina Baym, "Melodramas of Beset Manhood," *American Quarterly* 33.2 (1981): 123–139; David Savran, *Communists, Cowboys, and Queers: The Politics of Masculinity in the Work of Arthur Miller and Tennessee Williams* (Minneapolis: University of Minnesota Press, 1992); and Michael Rogin, "Kiss Me Deadly: Communism, Motherhood, and Cold War Movies," *Representations* 6 (Spring 1984): 1–36.

44. K. A. Cuordileone, "'Politics in an Age of Anxiety': Cold War Political Culture and the Crisis in American Masculinity, 1949–1960," *Journal of American History* 87.2 (September 2000): 522–523.

45. Aaron L. Friedberg, *In the Shadow of the Garrison State: America's Anti-Statism and Its Cold War Grand Strategy* (Princeton: Princeton University Press, 2000), 74.

46. Lucas, *Freedom's War*, 3.

47. See Robert Griffith, "Dwight D. Eisenhower and the Corporate Commonwealth," *American Historical Review* 87.1 (February 1982): 87–122.

48. "'Policy culture' refers to the values, norms and customs that are displayed by actors and organizations engaged in the development of public policy and that are, in other words, disseminated in the public domain." Frank Hendriks, *Public Policy and Political Institutions: The Role of Culture in Traffic Policy* (Cheltenham, UK: Edward Elgar, 1999), 34.

49. How the term "People's Capitalism" arrived in the lexicon of the admen is unclear, though it is certain that they did not coin it. It had been around at least as early as 1945, when Louis Menchini published his *The People's Capitalism* (San Francisco: Hallesint, 1945). According to George V. Allen, who headed the USIA from 1957 to 1960, People's Capitalism was intended "to help our Latin American friends understand that private enterprise in the United States is a far cry from the exploitative picture painted by Karl Marx." Allen, "What the U.S. Information Program Cannot Do," in John Boardman Whitton, ed., *Propaganda and the Cold War* (Washington: Public Affairs Press, 1963), 60.

50. The speaker here is William C. Stolk of National Can Company. "National Campaign to Sell Capitalism Urged on Industry," press release, October 24, 1956 (Lambie Files, DDEL, Box 31). "Indoctrination in democracy" comes from Truman administration Attorney General Tom C. Clark, quoted in Robert Griffith, "The Selling of America: The Advertising Council and American Politics, 1942–1960," *Business History Review* 57.3 (Fall 1983), 398. Griffith quotes a speaker at a 1941 advertisers' conference charging the industry with its wartime mission: joining "the vast, world-wide struggle between two philosophies, the totalitarian idea, with people as the vassals of the state against the American philosophy of free enterprise and free competition and free opportunity for the individual to realize his own destiny under free institutions" (390). In the postwar era, the "repetitious, pervasive, and unchallenged" propaganda of the Advertising Council, Griffith writes, "surround[ed] Americans in all walks of life with an omnipresent and distorted reflection of their society and thus help[ed] shape, to a degree no less real for being difficult to measure, the political culture of postwar America" (412).

51. Edward J. Bermingham to Dwight D. Eisenhower, March 14, 1951, quoted in Griffith, "Dwight D. Eisenhower and the Corporate Commonwealth," 98. "The important thing to do," wrote USIA director Theodore Repplier to his deputy, "is to make it clear that something new in the way of how men make a living collectively has come about and then to describe the differences between people's capitalism and old-world capitalism. . . . By gum, we have brought about something completely unique in the world's history in that we have

abolished the system where a small group of fat cats sit on top of the great mass of the underpaid and we should darn well tell the world about it." The letter, it should be noted, is chastising in tone, as Repplier felt the USIA's recent People's Capitalism booklet to be "a pretty poor effort." He suggests that it acknowledge the existence of poverty in America—at one point adding that "our negroes in many cases live in squalor"—as a corrective to the campaign's current "boastful" tone. Repplier to Abbott Washburn (Lambie Files, DDEL, Box 31). Boosting the campaign, *Reader's Digest* explained in 1956 that American capitalism regarded employees as "part of the enterprise, not enemies," and that each consumer was "a citizen of the national economy." "A Fresh View of Capitalism," *Reader's Digest* July 1956, 137–138; Max Eastman, "The False Promise of Socialism," *Reader's Digest* November 1955, 158–160.

52. People's Capitalism asserted that the nation had produced an economy of such widespread participation and bounty that it rendered notions of exploitation and class conflict superfluous. These claims echoed the convictions of the chief executive, who had written in his diary of the need to contradict Lenin's claim that "there were no restraints upon the power of the . . . great corporations and syndicates." Eisenhower diary, July 2, 1953, quoted in David Green, *Shaping Political Consciousness: The Language of Politics in America from McKinley to Reagan* (Ithaca: Cornell University Press, 1987), 12. Predictably, People's Capitalism's champions obviated any mention of the collective and often bloody struggles through which American capitalism had evolved, and denied the importance of collectivities such as those based on class. Instead, they emphasized that "intelligent reform," presumably by enlightened managers, had created something which the freighted term capitalism did not describe fully or fairly.

53. Asserting that "the opportunity of the individual to participate in the operation of the economy is an important attribute of people's capitalism," roundtable members estimated (using data on stockholding and farm and business ownership) that "something like one-third of all American families share in the ownership of the nation's most productive assets and economic enterprises." "The American Round Table: Discussions on People's Capitalism," pp. 8–9, 6 (Lambie Files, DDEL, Box 12). By the logic of this roundtable (and a subsequent one held at Columbia in 1957), life insurance policies, pensions, and even savings accounts also made millions of people "indirect owners of industry." Among the panelists were historian David Potter, *Fortune* editor John Davenport, law professor and behavioralist Harold Lasswell, George T. Brown of the AFL-CIO, *Collier's* editor Roy Price, and Liston Pope, dean of Yale's Divinity School. Sending the conference digest report to Eisenhower's propaganda chief, Repplier attached a note that enthused, "At last, our intellectual foundation for Peter Charlie." The "Peter Charlie" code name suggests the program's status as what the Truman administration more transparently called "psychological warfare." Repplier to James M. Lambie, January 28, 1957 (Lambie Files, DDEL,

Box 38). The 1956 and 1957 conference proceedings were both published as books in 1957 by the Advertising Council.

54. Report of the People's Capitalism Committee, Cloud Club, May 15, 1956 (Lambie Files, DDEL, Box 31). At least one scholarly monograph was published: Jacob M. Budish's boosterish *People's Capitalism: Stock Ownership and Production* (New York: International Publisher, 1958). See also T. V. Smith, "People's Capitalism," *House Beautiful* November 1956, 226.

55. Victor Perlo, "'People's Capitalism' and Stock-Ownership," *American Economic Review* 48.3 (1958): 347. See also the proceedings of a Soviet conference on People's Capitalism, *People's Capitalism: New Social Order or New Depression?* (Toronto: Northern Book House, 1957).

56. A December 1956 *Time* article labeled People's Capitalism "The New Conservatism," suggesting it was merely traditional conservative economic rhetoric in a shiny new wrapper. See "New Conservatism: Bold Creed for Modern Capitalism," *Time* November 26, 1956, 98–99. Theodore Repplier complained to James A. Linen, *Time's* publisher, that he had read the article "with a sinking heart . . . If TIME, LIFE, FORTUNE were put behind a move to call our unique American economy 'the new conservatism,' it would be nothing short of a tragedy from a propaganda standpoint." Repplier to Linen, December 1956 (Lambie Files, DDEL, Box 31). More favorable views included those of H. Hazlitt, "People's Capitalism," *Newsweek* September 17, 1956, 95; and F. G. Clark and R. S. Rimanoczy, "What Marxism Promises, U.S. Capitalism Delivers," *Reader's Digest* February 1957, 173–174.

57. Allen, "What the U.S. Information Program Cannot Do," 60–61. The central elements of People's Capitalism resurfaced, however, in Arthur Larson's 1959 *What We Are For,* under the moniker "Enterprise Democracy," and have resurfaced perennially in conservative rhetoric.

58. Lucas, *Freedom's War,* 93. In the sentimental rhetoric of the People's Capitalism, "Crusade for Freedom," and "People-to-People" campaigns, the charitable activities of common citizens could determine the course of history; the government's role was merely to encourage and coordinate individual endeavor. The Crusade for Freedom, for example, rallied each citizen to "be a front-line fighter in the battle for freedom" by contributing to the Voice of America. American Heritage Foundation, "Your Crusade for Freedom" (Lambie Files, DDEL, Box 12). The People-to-People program encouraged the formation of personal bonds between Americans and foreigners through travel, student exchange, and letter writing.

59. Robinson, "The Ideological Combat," 527–528.

60. Volker Berghahn, *America and the Intellectual Cold Wars in Europe: Shepard Stone Between Philanthropy, Academy, and Diplomacy* (Princeton: Princeton University Press, 2001), 290.

61. Bel Geddes, *Magic Motorways* (New York: Random House, 1940), 293.

62. *Red Nightmare* (film), dir. George Waggner, perfs. Jack Kelly, Jeanne Cooper, Peter Brown (Warner Bros. Pictures, 1962). "Any interference with the freedom to travel," asserted William D. Patterson in the *Saturday Review,* should concern the American people to no less an extent than interference with speech, press, religion, or assembly." Patterson, "The Freedom to Travel," *Saturday Review* January 10, 1959, 24. And yet that freedom was restricted by the cold war state. See Helen Nearing and Scott Nearing, *Our Right to Travel* (Harborside, ME: Social Science Institute, 1959); and Frederick G. Whelan, "Citizenship and the Right to Leave, *American Political Science Review* 75.3 (September 1981).

63. Clark, *Cold Warriors,* 2.

64. George W. Pierson, "A Restless Temper . . . " *American Historical Review* 69.4 (July 1964): 989.

65. George W. Pierson, *The Moving American* (New York: Knopf, 1973) 118. See also Pierson, "The M-Factor in American History," *American Quarterly* 14.2, part 2, supplement (1962): 275–289; and Everett Lee, "The Turner Thesis Reexamined," *American Quarterly* 13.1 (1961): 77–83.

66. Handlin, *The Uprooted: The Epic Story of the Great Migrations That Made the American People* (New York: Grosset & Dunlap, 1951); John Steinbeck, *Travels With Charley: In Search of America* (New York: Viking, 1961), 93; Lewis Mumford, *The Golden Day: A Study in American Literature and Culture* (New York: Dover Publications, 1968 [1926]), 26.

67. David Riesman, in collaboration with Nathan Glazer, *Faces in the Crowd: Individual Studies in Character and Politics* (New Haven: Yale University Press, 1952), 739.

68. Jack Kerouac, *On the Road* (New York: Viking, 1957), 133. On the road's depiction in American literature, see John A. Jakle, *The Tourist: Travels in Twentieth-Century North America* (Lincoln: University of Nebraska Press, 1985); Ronald Primeau, *Romance of the Road: The Literature of the American Highway* (Bowling Green: Bowling Green State University Popular Press, 1996); and Kris Lackey, *RoadFrames.*

69. Riesman and Glazer, *Faces in the Crowd,* 739–740.

70. Riesman et al., *The Lonely Crowd,* 260. However hoary its thesis, *The Lonely Crowd* refrained from the polemic and moralizing that usually attended claims, scholarly and otherwise, of Americans' growing conformity. Instead, Riesman and his coauthors developed an ostensibly less normative terminology of American social character, redescribing the much-lamented "conformity" as a shift in social character resulting from the experience of political and economic consolidation.

71. Daniel Lerner, "Comfort and Fun: Morality in a Nice Society," *American Scholar* 27.2 (Spring 1958): 157–158.

72. Ford sent this highway-booster pamphlet, *Freedom of the American Road* (Dearborn, MI: Ford Motor Company, 1956), to libraries, members of Congress, magazines, newspapers, dealerships, colleges and universities, schools, cham-

bers of commerce, etc. Ford also produced a film with the same title. It was sent in January 1956 to President Eisenhower by Henry Ford II, who commended the president on his leadership in roadbuilding initiatives. Eisenhower acknowledged the gift and wrote that he was "delighted to know of the initiative the Ford Motor Company is taking in helping solve the highway problem." Cross Reference Sheet, January 26, 1956 (DDEL, Official Files 141-B). AAA produced in the same year a pamphlet, *The AAA Motorists' Program for Better Highways* (Washington: AAA, 1956), focusing more explicitly on highway funding.

73. Foner, *The Story of American Freedom*, 265; Elizabeth Janeway, *The Early Days of Automobiles* (New York: Random House, 1956), 21; Pierson, "The M-Factor in American History," 282; "Construction: March of the Monsters," *Time* June 24, 1957, 92; Ilya Ilf and Eugene Petrov, *Little Golden America: Two Soviet Humorists Survey These United States* (New York: Farrar and Rinehart, 1937), 76; Bellamy Partridge, *Fill 'Er Up! The Story of Fifty Years of Motoring* (New York: McGraw-Hill, 1952), 217–218. The propaganda utility of mass automobility also derived from its signification of social mobility; it could be read in the apocryphal account of the incredulous response of visiting Soviet dignitaries when told that the legions of parked cars outside a Detroit factory belonged not to executives but to workers. "Americans are such liars," one visitor apparently said to another. See Reginald M. Cleveland and S. T. Williamson, *The Road Is Yours: The Story of the Automobile and the Men Behind It* (New York: Greystone Press, 1951).

74. See Michael L. Berger, "Women Drivers!: The Emergence of Folklore and Stereotypic Opinions Concerning Feminine Automotive Behavior," *Women's Studies International Forum* 9 (1986): 257–263. "Don't let the sneering masculine commonplace 'woman driver' deter or frighten you," *Independent Woman* magazine told its readers in 1939. Quoted in Franz, *Tinkering*, 72.

75. *Fifty Years on Wheels: A Broadcast Commemorating the 50th Anniversary of the Automobile Industry in America*, New York: Columbia Broadcasting System (transcript) (NMAH, Box 23, File 9).

76. *The Passing Scene: The Travelers 1954 Book of Street and Highway Accident Data* (BFRC, Accession 841, Fletcher Platt Files, Box 3, Clippings and Booklets File).

77. Roland Marchand has argued that one response to the postwar "domestication" of American manhood "was to reassert a compensating image of masculinity that conceded nothing to feminine limitations." Marchand, "Visions of Classlessness, Quests for Dominion: American Popular Culture, 1945–1960," in *Reshaping America: Society and Institutions, 1945–1960*, ed. Robert H. Bremner and Gary W. Reichard (Columbus: Ohio State University Press, 1982), 172.

78. Enloe quoted in Janet Wolff, "On the Road Again: Metaphors of Travel in Cultural Criticism," *Cultural Studies* (1993): 229; Mary Gordon, *Good Boys and Dead Girls and Other Essays* (New York: Viking, 1991).

79. Lindner, *Prescription for Rebellion*, 285–286.

80. John Brinckerhoff Jackson writes that "the European metaphorical use

of the words *road* or *way* or *path* emphasized the difficulties encountered by the average wayfarer in the course of his or her journey through life. . . . As long as the average person had to confront the indignities and complications of traveling on foot, the metaphorical message remained most important. But over the last century and a half, two developments have taken place: we have produced a new kind of road and a new metaphor, a vast network of smooth, efficient highways leading to every conceivable destination." Jackson, *A Sense of Place, a Sense of Time* (New Haven: Yale University Press, 1994), 204.

81. Jeffrey Schnapp, "Crash," 34–35.

82. Pierson, *The Moving American*, 186–187; M. M. Musselman, *Get a Horse!*, 22; Daniel Boorstin, *The Image, or, What Happened to the American Dream* (New York: Athenaeum, 1962), 77, 117.

83. Sidonie Smith, *Moving Lives*, 177.

84. Steinbeck, *Travels With Charley*, 20.

85. Marchand, "Visions of Classlessness," 172.

86. Musselman, *Get a Horse!*, 246.

87. For examples of articles extolling woman's competence, see "Female Drivers: Less Deadly Than the Male," *New York Times Magazine* March 27, 1955, 26; "Woman Driver: A Myth Exploded," *New York Times Magazine* November 4, 1951, 18; "Men Better Drivers Than Women?" *New York Times Magazine* October 1956, 33; "Battle of the Sexes Takes to the Highway," *Science Digest* November 1954, 36; "More Women Drivers, But Men Still Hold Edge," *Science Digest* September 1953, 96; "So You Think That Women Can't Drive," *Saturday Evening Post* April 14, 1951, 34; "Practical Tribute to Those Women Drivers," *Saturday Evening Post* June 18, 1955, 12; "Who's the Better Driver?," *American Mercury* March 1956, 24–27; and "The First Woman Driver," *Life* September 8, 1952, 83.

88. A. R. Lauer, *The Psychology of Driving: Factors of Traffic* Enforcement (Springfield, IL: Charles C. Thomas, 1960), 73, 77–78.

89. Of this "highly select group" one analyst wrote, "they tend to resent authority and restrictions upon their behavior; generally speaking, they seem to be hostile toward those who enforce it." Quoted in Herbert J. Stack, "Improving the Behavior of Drivers," *American Journal of Public Health* 47 (April 1957): 451.

90. Acknowledging the insurance company statistics that showed women having fewer accidents, Marble observed that the statistics did not reflect the number of the accidents in which women were an *indirect* cause. Alice Marble, "Plea: 'Don't Be a Woman, Driver,'" *New York Times Magazine* October 30, 1955, 30. Moreover, female drivers were deemed more "unstable, impulsive, infantile, anxious, and irritable" than their male counterparts by the Detroit Recorder's Court Psychopathic Clinic, which was charged with evaluating traffic offenders. Cited in Daniel Albert, "Psychotechnology and Insanity at the Wheel," *Journal of the History of the Behavioral Sciences* 35.3 (Summer 1999): 300.

91. "For Drivers Only," *Reader's Digest* December 1956, 232.

92. Ward, *Red, White, and Blue*, 260–261.

93. The Defense Highway Act of 1941 expanded the federal government's stake to 75 percent for those highways defined as "strategic." In 1943, the President's National Interregional Highway Committee (dominated by BPR officials) produced *Interregional Highways*, a study that again expressed the need for and delineated a proposed system of multilane, long-distance, limited-access highways. The committee's recommendations made their way, in somewhat diluted form, into the Federal-Aid Highway Act of 1944, which allocated $1.5 billion in funds for both highways and the previously neglected urban primary road systems, and which specifically designated the "National System of Interstate Highways." The Federal-Aid Highway Act of 1952, signed by President Truman, was the first highway legislation to specifically allocate funds (a measly $25 million on a 50/50 matching scheme) for the construction of this system. See Gutfreund, *20th-Century Sprawl;* and Tom Lewis, *Divided Highways.* Many scholars attribute Eisenhower's strong interest in the interstate project to his military experiences, not only his time as Allied Supreme Commander in Europe, but also with the 1919 transcontinental army convoy that traveled from Washington to San Francisco. Whatever the origin of Eisenhower's interest in transcontinental highways, they were clearly the public-works priority of his administration. According to official biographer Stephen Ambrose, the interstates were Eisenhower's favorite project. See Ambrose, *Eisenhower: The President* (New York: Simon & Schuster, 1984).

94. Davies, *The Age of Asphalt,* 138.

95. Eisenhower diaries, quoted in Griffith, "Dwight D. Eisenhower and the Corporate Commonwealth," 92.

96. *Address by the President Delivered at the 11th Annual Dinner of the National Security Industrial Association, October 25, 1954* (Clay Committee Records 1954–55, DDEL, Box 3).

97. Philip Rieff, "A Character Wrecked By Success," *Partisan Review* 24.2 (1957): 305.

98. Alonzo L. Hamby, *Liberalism and Its Challengers: FDR to Reagan* (Oxford: Oxford University Press, 1985), 120; William E. Robinson, quoted in Griffith, "Dwight D. Eisenhower and the Corporate Commonwealth," 91.

99. "As an economic fact," Mills wrote, "the old independent entrepreneur lives on a small island in a big new world; yet, as an ideological figment and a political force he has persisted as if he inhabited an entire continent. He has become the man through whom the ideology of utopian capitalism is still attractively presented to many of our contemporaries." *White Collar,* 34–35.

100. Editors of *Fortune* and Russell W. Davenport, *U.S.A.: The Permanent Revolution* (New York: Prentice-Hall, 1951), 205–206.

101. Eisenhower quoted in Ward, *Red, White, and Blue,* 259–260. By this view, society was, indeed, the "joint-stock company" that Ralph Waldo Emerson had warned against in "Self-Reliance"; but rather than being "in conspiracy against the manhood of its members," society enabled and conferred identity.

It also harked back to George Perkins's 1908 assertion that individuals derived a sense of achievement and purpose by interacting with one another "within the limits of the same organization." Quoted in James Oliver Robertson, *American Myth, American Reality*, 180.

102. A. B. Zalkind, quoted in Conquest, *The Politics of Ideas in the U.S.S.R.*, 28.

103. Raymond A. Bauer, *The New Man in Soviet Psychology* (Cambridge: Harvard University Press, 1959), 48.

104. As Bauer and Alex Inkeles observed of the Soviet system, "The official formulation of the relationship of the individual to the state has been given an appearance of spurious continuity by adroit verbal manipulation. Throughout the history of the Soviet Union the regime stressed the harmony, in a socialist society, between the needs of the individual and the needs of the state. In the early period, for approximately the first decade after the revolution, the meaning of this statement was that a social order would be developed to serve the needs and interests of the individual citizen. Since the inauguration of the First Five Year Plan, however, it has come to mean that a type of citizen will be developed who serves the needs and interests of the state." Alex Inkeles and Raymond A. Bauer, *The Soviet Citizen: Daily Life in a Totalitarian Society* (Cambridge: Harvard University Press, 1959), 257.

105. Hauge, *Is the Individual Obsolete?*, 24.

106. Robinson, "The Ideological Combat," 534–535; 531–532.

107. Barry Hindess has discussed liberalism's ambiguity on autonomy, its status as both natural and artifactual, in "Liberalism, Socialism, and Democracy: Variations on a Governmental Theme," in Barry, Osborne, and Rose, eds., *Foucault and Political Reason*, 65–80.

108. Address of Vice President Richard Nixon to the Governors' Conference, Lake George, New York, July 12, 1954 (Clay Committee Records 1954–55, DDEL, Box 4).

109. Quoted in Richard F. Weingroff, "Broader Ribbons Across the Land," *Public Roads* Special Edition (1996): 10.

110. In the interwar era, planners and experts such as Bel Geddes and Moses had found a cultural climate increasingly sympathetic to their visions of rationally ordered land- and cityscapes, and to the forceful integration of the automobile. They shared with the industrial members of the highway lobby— who were often their sponsors—an overwhelming faith in automobility. According to John Burby, one expert "believed that there should be a road leading to nearly any place an American with an automobile might want to go, an attitude shared by other highway engineers who called the proposed highway routes they draw on maps 'desire lines.'" Burby, *The Great American Motion Sickness*, 90–91. See also Bruce Seely, *Building the American Highway System*.

111. Wilburn Cartwright quoted in Goddard, *Getting There*, 151. Planning and construction of the *Autobahn* had begun not under Hitler's regime but in

the 1920s under the state highway agency *Stufa*. See Thomas Zeller, *Driving Germany: The Landscape of the German Autobahn, 1903–1970* (Oxford: Berghahn Books, 2007).

112. Hamilton and Sutton, "The Problem of Control in the Weak State," 1.

113. Ford averred that his industry, in championing federal expenditures for highway construction, was merely trying to give the American people "what they so clearly want." Automobility's dominance was a settled issue: "Sometimes people vote with their dollars; sometimes with ballots. But the goal is always the same—providing what people want. As far as urban transportation is concerned, what people want is clear. They have voted overwhelmingly in favor of the automobile." Henry Ford II quoted in Davies, *The Age of Asphalt,* 70. The American commitment to automobility continues to be explained as a matter of preference. Describing the debate around the Federal-Aid Highway Act of 1956, William O'Neill writes, "Critics complained that highways were killing passenger rail service, an alternate and environmentally superior form of transportation. This was true but irrelevant, for most Americans prefer highways to railways, and if Eisenhower had gone against the grain of public opinion, he would have ended up with neither." O'Neill, "Eisenhower and American Society," in *Eisenhower: A Centenary Assessment,* ed. Gunter Bischof and Stephen E. Ambrose (Baton Rouge: Louisiana State University Press, 1995), 107–108. Mark I. Gelfand has similarly argued that in the face of political pressures, the national government had little choice but to go along with consumers, who were spending billions for automobiles." Gelfand, "Cities, Suburbs, and Government Policy," in *Reshaping America: Society and Institutions, 1945–1960,* eds. Robert H. Bremner and Gary W. Reichard (Columbus: Ohio State University Press, 1982) 274. More recently, Sam Kazman has claimed that "automobile use is a matter of people voting with their tires." Kazman, "Automobility and Freedom."

114. Address of Vice President Richard Nixon to the Governors' Conference; Cleveland and Williamson, *The Road Is Yours,* 17; George Romney, "The Motor Vehicle and the Highway: Some Historical Implications," in *Highways in Our National Life: A Symposium,* ed. Jean Labatut and Wheaton J. Lane (Princeton: Princeton University Press, 1950), 221.

115. Letter from Fletcher N. Platt of Ford Traffic Safety and Highway Improvement Department to Edward T. Jetter of the *West Side Times* in Buffalo, New York, enclosed with a copy of *Freedom of the American Road* (BFRC, Accession 841, Fletcher Platt Files, Box 1, Introductory Letters File). The company sent a myriad of letters with the same content, some signed by Henry Ford II instead of Platt.

116. Romney, "The Motor Vehicle and the Highway," 220–221. These supposedly fundamental differences did not prevent a *Science Monthly* writer from describing the Interstate plan as "*autobahn,* U.S.A." See P. E. Griffin, "Blueprint for *autobahn,* U.S.A.," *Science Monthly* June 1954, 380–387.

117. Dunn, *Driving Forces,* 190.

118. Riesman, *Abundance For What? and Other Essays* (Garden City, NY: Doubleday, Inc., 1964), 288.

119. Vikki Bell, "The Promise of Liberalism and the Performance of Freedom," in Barry, Osborne, and Rose, eds., *Foucault and Political Reason,* 90.

120. Mark Rose, *Interstate,* 95.

121. See Lewis, *Divided Highways;* Rose, *Interstate;* Leavitt, *Superhighway—Superhoax;* Goddard, *Getting There;* Borth, *Mankind on the Move;* Weingroff, "Broader Ribbons Across the Land." In September 1954, Eisenhower appointed the President's Advisory Committee on a National Highway Program, headed by retired General Lucius D. Clay. Joining Clay on the committee were financier Sloan Colt, head of Bankers Trust; William Roberts of Allis Chalmers (makers of bulldozers and other heavy equipment); Dave Beck of the International Brotherhood of Teamsters; and Stephen Bechtel of the Bechtel civil-engineering corporation. BPR deputy Frank Turner sat in as secretary (the new BPR chief was Francis V. DuPont; Eisenhower had fired Thomas MacDonald in 1953). Clay's opening remarks at the first hearings in October 1954 rehearsed the crisis theme of the highway lobby and the administration—who were now officially joined together on this advisory committee. "We accept as a starting premise the fact that the penalties of an obsolete road system are large," Clay said, "and that the price in inefficiency is paid not only in dollars, but in lives lost through lack of safety, and also in national insecurity." Quoted in Leavitt, *Superhighway—Superhoax,* 29–30. All of the Clay Committee members stood, directly or indirectly, to gain financially from highway funding: testifying before a Senate subcommittee on highway funding in 1955, BPR director Francis DuPont was asked if he thought that the Interstate Highway System would merely whet what would become an insatiable appetite in American citizens for roadbuilding projects and improvements. DuPont responded, "I hope so." In addition to their ownership of the mammoth chemical concern, DuPont's family owned some 63 million shares in General Motors. Leavitt, *Superhighway—Superhoax,* 45. Not surprisingly, the 1954 hearings featured no testimony from defenders of mass transit. Among those testifying were Robert Moses, the American Automobile Manufacturers Association, the American Petroleum Institute, AAA, Associated General Contractors of America, AASHO, and the American Road Builders Association.

122. Herbert Brean, "Dead End for U.S. Highway," *Life* May 30, 1955, 109. The following year, Brean speculated, accurately, that the interstate system "by 1970 will stretch into every corner of the U.S. and profoundly shape the nation's future social and economic progress." Herbert Brean, "New Vistas of the Road," *Life* November 19, 1956, 75. See also R. Moley, "The Clay Highway Plan," *Newsweek* March 21, 1955, 112; H. K. Evans, "Here's the President's Highway Plan," *Nation's Business* February 1955, 58–62; and "Here's Ike's Highway Plan," *U.S.*

*News and World Report* March 4, 1955, 64. *The Nation* playfully demurred: "The President's a Piker," December 25, 1954, 541.

123. H. W. Brands, *The Strange Death of American Liberalism* (New Haven: Yale University Press, 2001), 77–78. I disagree with Brands' assertion that an initially reluctant Eisenhower had been won over to the Interstate plan by "the argument that good roads would enhance national defense" (77).

124. See Richard Weingroff, "Federal-Aid Highway Act of 1956: Creating the Interstate System," *Public Roads* 60.1 (Summer 1996): 10–17.

125. Brean, "Dead End for the U.S. Highway," 109; "Why Motorists Blow Their Tops," *Reader's Digest* June 1952; "Neurotics at the Wheel," *Time* November 2, 1953; "Highwaymen," *Collier's* January 26, 1952, 35. See also "How New Jersey Built Its Dream Road," *Saturday Evening Post* December 8, 1951, 36; "Good Highways: When?," *U.S. News and World Report* March 28, 1952; "Modern Cars Ride Ancient Roads," *Nation's Business* July 1952; "Roads We Could Have Bought," *Nation's Business* December 1952; "Gigantic Highway Program: Imperative and Costly," *Newsweek* December 15, 1952; and "Time to Clear the Road," *Collier's* January 12, 1952.

126. The highway crisis became the justification for the many roadbuilding projects proposed by the highway lobby's members or solicited from private citizens. The Litchfield quote is from a pamphlet entitled "New Frontiers," authored by a group calling itself The Avenue of Tomorrow, Ltd. ("Trustees of the American Dream"). It proposed a system of "U.S. Monumental Highways," which, in addition to the interstates, conceived of planned suburban communities, businesses, hospitals, churches, libraries, monorails, pneumatic mail tubes, and so on. The Avenue of Tomorrow, Ltd. ("Trustees of the American Dream") envisioned a "fully engineered—expertly planned" nation, anchored by automobility. "New Frontiers," Avenue of Tomorrow, Ltd., 1951, 2–3 (Clay Committee Records 1954–55, DDEL, Box 4). In 1953, General Motors sponsored a contest inviting proposals for "building better highways for America." These ranged from suggestions of public-private partnerships in building and administering highways, to schemes for the total privatization of automobile travel. Robert Moses won the $25,000 prize for his dramatically pro-public works essay (Clay Committee Records 1954–55, DDEL, Box 3). For more on the "highway crisis," see Rose, *Interstate*, 41–54.

127. *Freedom of the American Road*, 1, 120.

128. Even visionary highway planners such as Norman Bel Geddes spoke in terms of feasibility, common sense, safety, and historical continuity, not radical transformation. Bel Geddes attributed the popularity of the Futurama exhibit at the 1939 New York World's Fair to the fact "that its boldness was based on soundness. The plan it presented appealed to the practical engineer as much as to the idle day-dreamer. The motorways which it featured were not only desirable, but practical." *Magic Motorways*, 6.

129. Brean, "New Vistas of the Road," 76.

130. Bel Geddes, *Magic Motorways,* 10.

131. Romney, "The Motor Vehicle and the Highway," 221, 226; George Humphrey quoted in Davies, *The Age of Asphalt,* 4; Francis E. Merrill, "The Highway and Social Problems," in *Highways in Our National Life,* 136.

132. This advertisement occasioned a letter from Peter D. Gellatly, editor of the *Saturday Evening Post,* to President Eisenhower, calling the chief executive's attention to the "enlightened vision of such companies as Republic Steel" and informing him that identical reprints were being sent to various elected officials as a means of helping the interstate project along. The White House responded by acknowledging that the Republic Steel ad "is certainly a good one" and that "such institutional advertising can give a life to the road program by increasing the public's awareness of the need for better roads." Peter D. Gellatly to Dwight D. Eisenhower, April 28, 1955 (DDEL, DDE Central Files, General File, Box 1230); James C. Hagerty to Peter D. Gellatly, May 4, 1955 (DDEL, DDE Central Files, General File, Box 1230).

133. "We Can Do Something About Highways, Traffic, and Safety: Notes for a Talk" (BFRC, Accession 579, Box 12, Public Relations "Freedom of the American Road" 1956 Campaign File).

134. "People's Capitalism—This IS America," *Collier's* January 6, 1956, 74; Theodore H. White, "Where Are Those New Roads?," *Collier's* January 6, 1956, 46. *Collier's* editor Roy Price would attend the November 1956 People's Capitalism conference at Yale.

135. George F. Will, "Gotta Love Those Cars," *Washington Post* June 16, 1996.

136. "Every Man a Capitalist," *Collier's* August 17, 1956, 82.

137. "The Freedom Train," *New Republic* September 20, 1948, 7.

138. Halprin, *Freeways,* 17.

139. Jeremy Packer, "Disciplining Mobility," in Jack Z. Bratich, Jeremy Packer, and Cameron McCarthy, eds., *Foucault, Cultural Studies, and Governmentality,* 140.

## chapter four

1. E. L. Doctorow, *Ragtime* (New York: Penguin, 1974), 256. Doctorow adapted the character of Walker from Heinrich von Kleist's 1808 novella, "Michael Kohlhaas," which recounted the tale of a sixteenth-century merchant who seeks justice for wrongs suffered at the hands of a Saxon *Junker.* The novella documents the tension between the emancipatory forces of modernity—individualism and the "contractual" forms of association, equality under the law, free mobility—and a feudal order based on arbitrary privilege. The lesson Doctorow appears to impart through his retelling of the Michael Kohlhaas story is that for African Americans, modernity arrived late, if it arrived at all. See Richard Sterne, "Reconciliation and Alienation in Kleist's 'Michael Kohlhaas'

and Doctorow's *Ragtime*," *Legal Studies Forum* 12.1 (1988): 5–22. Moreover, as Katalin Orbán notes, "both Kleist's and Doctorow's texts focus, with great ambivalence, on the potential for transcending pervasive difference, for the dissolving of borders and the merging of divisions." Orbán, "Swallowed Futures, Indigestible Pasts: Post-Apocalyptic Narratives of Rights in Kleist and Doctorow," *Comparative American Studies* 1:3 (2003): 328.

2. For examples of scholarship on black automobility, see Paul Gilroy, "Driving While Black"; Kathleen Franz, "The 'Open Road': Automobility and Racial Uplift in the Interwar Years"; Howard L. Preston, *Automobile Age Atlanta: The Making of a Southern Metropolis, 1900–1935* (Athens: University of Georgia Press, 1979); and Mark S. Foster, "In the Face of 'Jim Crow': Prosperous Blacks and Vacations, Travel and Outdoor Leisure, 1890–1945," *Journal of Negro History* 84:2 (Spring 1999): 130–149.

3. Philip Fisher, "Democratic Social Space: Whitman, Melville, and the Promise of American Transparency," *Representations* 24 (Fall 1988): 64–65.

4. Barbara Klinger, "The Road to Dystopia: Landscaping the Nation in *Easy Rider*," in Steven Cohan and Ina Rae Hark, eds., *The Road Movie Book* (New York: Routledge, 1997), 188.

5. Charles W. Mills, *Blackness Visible: Essays on Philosophy and Race* (Ithaca: Cornell University Press, 1998), 155.

6. Bruce Burgett, *Sentimental Bodies*, 14. Keith Faulks notes that "because liberals start with the assumption that the individual is a rational, atomistic actor, they tend towards agency-centered explanations of human behaviour: we shape our own lives through the choices we make. . . . This ignores the nature of constraints that structures of power such as race, class, and gender place upon the individual." Faulks, *Citizenship* (London: Routledge, 2000), 58.

7. Joyce W. Warren, *The American Narcissus*, 4; Jörg Beckmann, "Mobility and Safety," 84. "Hence," Mark Simpson asserts, "the need to recognize, in the very hegemony that holds mobility to be a flatly common condition in America, the power of mobility as a differential resource" (*Trafficking Subjects*, xxix); and Doreen Massey's inquiry into "whether our relative mobility and power over mobility and communication entrenches the spatial imprisonment of other groups" (*Space, Place, and Gender*, 151).

8. Kathleen Franz, "'The Open Road,'" 135.

9. William Cohen, *At Freedom's Edge: Black Mobility and the Southern White Quest for Racial Control, 1861–1915* (Baton Rouge: Louisiana State University Press, 1991), 13. Regarding the Great Migration, it is important to remember that "no one went north because he simply wanted to. . . . All were forced north by terror and violence or some form of racist practice." Donald R. Gibson, "Individualism and Community in Black History and Fiction," *Black American Literature Forum* 11.4 (Winter 1977), 124.

10. Virginia Scharff, *Twenty Thousand Roads*, 143. Kenneth L. Karst further notes that "our civic culture is, among other things, a constant stream of mes-

sages encouraging individuals to take action to advance their conditions and those of their families. Blacks living under the Jim Crow system were not insulated from those messages, and yet they were denied the opportunity to act on them." Karst, *Belonging to America* (New Haven: Yale University Press, 1989), 67.

11. Philip Wylie, *Tomorrow!* (New York: Rinehart & Company, 1954), 272–273.

12. "Prized designations like 'independence,' 'autonomy,' and 'free will,'" Hartman further notes, "are the lures of liberalism, yet the tantalizing suggestion of the individual as potentate and sovereign is drastically undermined by the forms of repression and terror that accompanied the advent of freedom." Saidiya Hartman, *Scenes of Subjection*, 117, 122.

13. Manuel Castells, *The City and the Grassroots* (Berkeley: University of California Press, 1983), 311–312.

14. Sharon Willis, "Race on the Road: Crossover Dreams," in Cohan and Hark, eds., *The Road Movie Book*, 287.

15. Andrew Wiese, *Places of Their Own: African American Suburbanization in the Twentieth Century* (Chicago: University of Chicago Press, 2004), 291.

16. Howard L. Preston, in his study of early twentieth-century Atlanta, argues that the rise of automobility reinforced segregation by both race and class: whatever the significance of increased individual mobility, car ownership both separated whites from blacks and divided the black community along lines of affluence. "The land-use pattern which automobility brought about in Atlanta . . . laid the ground work for the easy exploitation of blacks via the 'separate-but-equal' doctrine. . . . By 1930 . . . racism could be measured by miles and minutes." Preston, *Automobile Age Atlanta*, 111–112.

17. Quoted in Flink, *The Automobile Age*, 131.

18. Quoted in *Crisis* (November 1910): 8.

19. Albert, "Primitive Drivers," 337.

20. Gilroy, "Driving While Black," 84.

21. Franz, "'The Open Road,'" 139.

22. See Todd Gould, *For Gold and Glory: Charlie Wiggins and the African-American Racing Car Circuit* (Bloomington: Indiana University Press, 2002).

23. Arna Bontemps, "A Summer Tragedy," in Langston Hughes, ed., *The Best Short Stories by Black Writers* (Boston: Little, Brown, 1967), 62.

24. Quoted in Franz, "'The Open Road,'" 135.

25. See *African-American Masters: Selections from the Smithsonian American Art Museum* (New York: Harry N. Abrams, 2003). See also Stanley Crouch, *One-Shot Harris: The Photographs of Teenie Harris* (New York: Harry N. Abrams, 2002).

26. Chester Himes, *If He Hollers Let Him Go* (New York: Thunder's Mouth Press, 1986 [1945]), 31, 13, 14.

27. Courtland Milloy, "Black Highways: Thirty Years Ago in the South, We

Didn't Dare Stop," *Washington Post* June 21, 1987; Eddy Harris, *South of Haunted Dreams: A Ride through Slavery's Old Backyard* (New York: Simon & Schuster, 1993), 25.

28. John Jerome, *The Death of the Automobile: The Fatal Effect of the Golden Era, 1955–1970* (New York: W. W. Norton, 1972), 14; Lackey, *RoadFrames*, 114,130.

29. bell hooks, *Wounds of Passion: A Writing Life* (New York: Owl Books, 1999), 47.

30. Harold R. Isaacs, *The New World of Negro Americans* (New York: Viking, 1963), 16.

31. J. Robert Oppenheimer, "Theory Versus Practice in American Values and Performance," in Morrison, ed., *The American Style: Essays in Value and Performance,* 111.

32. Editors of *Fortune* and Russell W. Davenport, *U.S.A.: The Permanent Revolution,* 167, 170; George Schuyler, "The Phantom American Negro," *Reader's Digest* July 1951, 52.

33. On the effect of the cold war on race relations, see Thomas Borstelmann, *The Cold War and the Color Line: American Race Relations in the Global Arena* (Cambridge: Harvard University Press, 2001); and Mary L. Dudziak, *Cold War Civil Rights: Race and the Image of American Democracy* (Princeton: Princeton University Press, 2001).

34. Albert Q. Maisel, "The Negroes Among Us," *Reader's Digest* September 1955, 106.

35. Eisenhower confined his administration's civil rights objectives "to areas of clear federal jurisdiction, greatest international propaganda value, and minimum risk of political fallout or domestic unrest." For example, "nondiscrimination plans for the military resembled more closely the scripting of a modern morality play, staged for the benefit of foreign and domestic observers rather than benefiting the black serviceman himself." Robert Burk, *The Eisenhower Administration and Black Civil Rights* (Knoxville: University of Tennessee Press, 1984), 23–24.

36. Foremost among these "model Negroes" put on display for their instrumental value in the cold war was political scientist Ralph Bunche, whose "status proved that American democracy works . . . . Bunche's success in the 1950s Cold War proved that the United States was indeed the land of opportunity despite what the Communists said." Charles P. Henry, *Ralph Bunche: Model Negro or American Other?* (New York: NYU Press, 1999), 4, 160. The Department of State sponsored a number of "Goodwill Ambassador" tours by African American speakers, jazz musicians, and dance troupes. See Penny M. Von Eschen, *Satchmo Blows Up the World: Jazz, Race, and Empire in the Cold War* (Cambridge: Harvard University Press, 2004).

37. Adam Clayton Powell, "The President and the Negro," *Reader's Digest* October 1954, 61–64. By contrast, Arthur Larson, a key White House advisor, concluded in 1968 that "President Eisenhower, during his presidential tenure,

was neither emotionally nor intellectually in favor of combating segregation in general." Quoted in Charles C. Alexander, *Holding the Line: The Eisenhower Era, 1952–1961* (Bloomington: Indiana University Press, 1975), 119.

38. "Negroes Have Their Own Wall Street Firm," *Saturday Evening Post* October 29, 1955, 12; Frank M. Snowden, "They Always Ask Me About Negroes," *Saturday Evening Post* March 10, 1956, 32–33, 105–106; USIA press release quoted in John David Skrentny, "The Effect of the Cold War on African-American Civil Rights: America and the World Audience, 1945–1968," *Theory and Society* 27.2 (April 1998): 248.

39. According to Christopher Newfield, the liberal dream holds that "the market will provide the mechanism that decides which individuals become equal, at what time, and to what extent without penalizing anyone for their group identity." Newfield, *The Emerson Effect*, 181.

40. Godfrey Hodgson, *America in Our Time*, 76. A hybrid of classical and progressive liberalism, the vital center consensus remained rooted in a vision of the market as producing "a natural harmony of interests," yet was amenable to Keynesian regulation of that market by the state. See Arthur M. Schlesinger, *The Vital Center*.

41. Booker T. Washington, "The Atlanta Exposition Address," in John Hope Franklin and Isidore Starr, eds., *The Negro in Twentieth Century America: A Reader on the Struggle for Civil Rights* (New York: Vintage Books, 1967), 88.

42. Powell, "The President and the Negro," 61.

43. Maisel, "The Negroes Among Us," 104.

44. E. Franklin Frazier, *Black Bourgeoisie: The Rise of a New Middle Class* (New York: Free Press, 1957), 186.

45. "St. Alban's: New York Community is Home for More Celebrities than Any Other U.S. Residential Area," *Ebony* September 1951, 34, cited in Wiese, *Places of Their Own*, 148.

46. Warren Belasco, "Motivatin' With Chuck Berry and Frederick Jackson Turner," in *The Automobile and American Culture*, ed. David L. Lewis and Laurence Goldstein (Ann Arbor: University of Michigan Press, 1980), 266.

47. Gilroy, "Driving While Black," 90.

48. Herbert Hoover, "Let's Say Something Good About Ourselves," *Reader's Digest* February 1956, 41. The piece was an excerpt of Hoover's essay, "Saying Something Good About Ourselves," published in *U.S. News and World Report* six months earlier.

49. Lester B. Granger, "Last of Pioneers," 1947 (Butler Papers, Box 1).

50. "Democracy Defined at Moscow" (editorial), *Crisis* (April 1947): 105.

51. hooks, *Wounds of Passion*, 48.

52. The Chesnutt and Mamie Garvin Fields anecdotes are quoted in Mark S. Foster, "In the Face of Jim Crow," 143, 141. Leslie Perry of the NAACP cited the Mallard murder in his statement before Congress' Antilynching and Protection of Civil Rights Hearings in 1949. Subcommittee of the Committee on the Judi-

ciary, House of Representatives, 81st Congress, 1st and 2d Sessions, June 1949; January 1950 (Washington, DC: U.S. Government Printing Office, 1950).

53. Lizabeth Cohen, *A Consumer's Republic* (New York: Vintage, 2003), 188.

54. The reconciliation of these values is particularly fraught for African Americans. As Loren Schweninger has argued, antebellum free blacks "created a type of individualism recognizable to whites but also consistent with their particular history of moving from slavery to freedom." Schweninger, "From Assertiveness to Individualism: The Difficult Path from Slavery to Freedom," in *American Chameleon: Individualism in Trans-National Context*, eds. Richard O. Curry and Laurence B. Goodheart, 129.

55. *The Negro Motorist Green Book* (New York: Victor H. Green & Co., 1938, 1941, 1940). Presumably Green named the book after himself, or to associate it with the AAA's *Blue Book*, which had provided a similar service to white travelers for much of the century.

56. Eulogy for Billy Butler by Marion Cumbo, St. Joseph's Church, March 23, 1981 (Butler Papers, Box 1).

57. "Billy Butler to Publish Travel Guide," *Pittsburgh Courier* April 5, 1947; "Musician and Guide to His Bedeviled Race," *New York Post* August 5, 1947; Granger, "Last of Pioneers" (Butler Papers, Box 1).

58. Mabel A. Roane, *Travelguide* (1947), back cover.

59. Cleveland *Gazette* column, 1895, quoted in Henry Louis Gates, "The Trope of a New Negro and the Reconstruction of the Image of the Black," *Representations* 24 (Fall 1988): 136.

60. I borrow this term from Frazier's 1957 polemic *Black Bourgeoisie*. Andrew Wiese documents the near-doubling of the national African American population in census-defined suburbs between 1940 and 1960. See Wiese, *Places of Their Own*, 110–142. On the leisure opportunities available to affluent African Americans earlier in the century, see Foster, "In the Face of 'Jim Crow.'"

61. *The Negro Motorist Green Book* (New York: Victor H. Green & Co., 1937). The guidebook ran from 1937 to 1959, though I could find no physical record of its publication from 1942 to 1946. Green also acknowledged Jewish travel guides to a restricted America as an inspiration.

62. Others profiled in either the "Travelguide Salutes" or "People (or Things) You Should Know About" sections during periodical's eleven years included Philippa Duke Schuyler, W. C. Handy, Ralph Bunche, Roy Campanella, Radio Corporation of America, Mollie Moon, William R. Hudgins, Philip Morris & Co., CBS, Schenley Industries, Justice Harold A. Stevens, Randolph A. Wallace, and the United Negro College Fund.

63. See Cohen, *A Consumer's Republic*, 166–191.

64. Among the other guidebooks, most of which appeared after *Green Book* and *Travelguide*, were *Go: Guide to Pleasant Motoring*, *Hackley & Harrison's Hotel and Apartment Guide for Colored*, and *The Afro-American's Travel Guide* (published today as *The African-American Travel Guide*).

65. These covers featured both professional "sepia" models and African American women of note, such as Rachel Robinson (Jackie's wife) and Elaine Robinson (wife of Bill). The layouts were often done by James Drake, art director for the Pittsburgh *Courier*.

66. Letter from Dickinson, North Dakota, in "Replies from Our Correspondents," *The Negro Motorist Green Book* (1948), 5.

67. Marguerite Cartwright, "A Thought From a Friend," *Travelguide* (1947).

68. *The Negro Motorist Green Book* (1948), 1.

69. *Travelguide* (1955), 5

70. Hutchinson further notes that "you didn't need the 'Green Book' to travel through the South. You knew that you couldn't eat in a roadside cafe or stay overnight in a roadside motel. The book was primarily for travel in the North and the West." Earl Hutchinson Sr. with Earl Ofari Hutchinson, *A Colored Man's Journey Through 20th-Century Segregated America* (Los Angeles: Middle Passage Press, 2000), 87.

71. Scharff, *Twenty Thousand Roads*, 143.

72. Arthur F. Raper, *Preface to Peasantry: A Tale of Two Black Belt Counties* (Chapel Hill: University of North Carolina Press), 174–175; Jack Temple Kirby, "Black and White in the Rural South, 1915–1954," *Agricultural History* 58 (July 1984). Both Raper and Kirby are quoted in Cory Lesseig, *Automobility: Social Changes in the American South, 1909–1939* (New York: Routledge, 2001), 112–114.

73. Chester Himes, *The Quality of Hurt* (New York: Paragon House, 1990), 123.

74. Warren Brown, "For Many, the Road Still Represents Freedom," *Washington Post* April 10, 2005. "I've always viewed cars," Brown wrote in a previous column, "as freedom machines." Brown, "Automobile Played Role in Long Ride to Freedom," *Washington Post* September 5, 2004.

75. See Raymond A. Mohl, "Planned Destruction: The Interstates and Central City Housing," in *From Tenements to the Taylor Homes*, ed. John F. Bauman, Roger Biles, and Kristin M. Szylvian (University Park: Pennsylvania State University Press, 2000), 226–245; Robert D. Bullard et al., eds., *Highway Robbery: Transportation Racism & New Routes to Equity* (Cambridge: South End Press, 2004); Thomas J. Sugrue, *The Origins of the Urban Crisis: Race and Inequality in Postwar Detroit* (Princeton: Princeton University Press, 1996); Milan Dluhy, Keith Revell, and Sidney Wong, "Creating a Positive Future for a Minority Community: Transportation and Urban Renewal Politics in Miami," *Journal of Urban Affairs* 24:1 (Spring 2002): 75–95; and Charles E. Connerly, "From Racial Zoning to Community Empowerment: The Interstate Highway System and the African-American Community in Birmingham, Alabama," *Journal of Planning Education and Research* 22:2 (2002): 99–114.

76. Tom Lewis, *Divided Highways*, 270.

77. Scharff, *Twenty Thousand Roads*, 140.

78. See George Ritzer, *The McDonaldization of Society* (Thousand Oaks, CA: Pine Forge Press, 2004).

79. Lawrence Halprin, *Freeways*, 12.

80. Newfield, *The Emerson Effect*, 218.


## chapter five

1. Alexis de Tocqueville, *Democracy in America*, trans. George Lawrence, 2 vols. (New York: Harper & Row, 1966), vol. 1, 273.

2. Giorgio Agamben, *Che Cos'è un Dispositivo*, 22.

3. In a way "that few would have dreamed of in 1956," Lewis writes, "the builders of the Interstates were helping to forge a new social order, in which women as well as men were able to leave home. In this new world Janis Joplin would record a song about hitchhiking across the country, and Huck Finn, Walt Whitman, Woody Guthrie, and Jack Kerouac would eventually have to share the road with Thelma and Louise." Tom Lewis, *Divided Highways*, 272–273. See also Lisa St. Albin DeTeran, *Indiscreet Journeys: Stories of Women on the Road* (London: Virago, 1989).

4. It is interesting that Elinor Nauen opens her anthology, *Ladies, Start Your Engines: Women Writers on Cars and the Road* (Boston: Faber and Faber, 1996), with Emerson's maxim. Responding to a female transportation researcher's comment that "owning their first car frees women," Jane Holtz Kay muses, "Ah, Freedom, mobility, Ah, the open road. I mull over her words. How familiar . . . how romantic . . . how like a—man." Kay, *Asphalt Nation*, 23. Yet as the trade magazine *Autoweek* reported in 2003, "while women in America are legally identical with men as vehicle operators, their experiences of automobility in some ways radically differ from men's." Steve Thompson, "Improving Drivers, Female-Style," *Autoweek* 53.25 (June 23, 2003): 10.

5. Jean Baudrillard, *America*, 54.

6. John Dewey, "Individualism, Old and New," 57.

7. Jay Fliegelman, *Declaring Independence*, 3.

8. Barry Hindess, "Liberalism, Socialism, and Democracy: Variations on a Governmental Theme," in Barry, Osborne, and Rose, eds., *Foucault and Political Reason*, 65.

9. See Immanuel Kant, *Foundations of the Metaphysics of Morals*, trans. Lewis White Beck, 2nd ed. (New York: Macmillan/Library of Liberal Arts, 1990). Joel Feinberg has observed that in addition and perhaps prior to the definition of "autonomy" as "an expression to label the realm of inviolable sanctuary most of us sense in our own beings," the term's synonyms (such as "self-rule," "self-determination," "independence," etc.) "are all familiar to us from their more frequent, and often more exact, application to states and institutions. Indeed, it is plausible that the original applications and denials of these notions were

to states and that their attribution to individuals is derivative, in which case 'personal autonomy' is a political metaphor." Feinberg, "Autonomy," in *The Inner Citadel*, ed. John Christman (New York and Oxford: Oxford University Press, 1989), 27.

10. David Riesman, *Individualism Reconsidered* (Glencoe, IL: Free Press, 1954), 33.

11. Riesman's understanding of autonomy was informed by Erich Fromm's theorization of "productive orientation." See Erich Fromm, *Man for Himself: An Inquiry into the Psychology of Ethics* (New York: Rinehart, 1947).

12. Riesman, *Individualism Reconsidered*, 17, 166.

13. Cicero, from *Paradoxa Stoicorum*, quoted in Felix A. Oppenheim, *Dimensions of Freedom: An Analysis* (New York: St. Martin's Press, 1961), 168. Feminist political theorists such as Christine Di Stefano have emphasized the "rule-governed habitat" in which subjects choose and make themselves. See Di Stefano, "Resymbolizing Autonomy: Feminism in Search of a Vanishing Concept," Institut für die Wissenschaften vom Menschen (IWM) Working Paper 10 (Vienna: IWM, 1997).

14. "Freedom—New Style," *Time* September 27 1954, 24.

15. John Gray has defined autonomy as "the condition in which a person can be at least part author of his life, in that he has before him a range of worth-while options." Gray observes, however, that the choice of options is limited by the necessity for uniformity in liberal institutions. Gray, *The Moral Foundations of Market Institutions* (London: IEA Health and Welfare Unit, 1992), 22.

16. Charlotte Montgomery, "How to Drive on Express Highways," *Good Housekeeping* April 1955, 118.

17. On this distinction see Hindess, "Liberalism, Socialism, and Democracy," 65–73.

18. Albert Whitney, *Man and the Motor Car* (New York: Prentice-Hall, 1954), 319.

19. Jeremy Packer distinguished as a safe subject "a self that reflects upon various practices and discourses regarding safety in the construction of ethical subjectivity. There are guidebooks, prescriptions, codes, warnings, guilt-producing car commercials, education programs, and so forth, which help individuals prepare a regimen that will ensure that they are free from risk." Packer, "Disciplining Mobility," in Jack Z. Bratich, Jeremy Packer, and Cameron McCarthy, eds., *Foucault, Cultural Studies, and Governmentality*, 155.

20. American Automobile Association, *Sportsmanlike Driving* (Washington, DC: AAA, 1955), 92; "As It Looks," *Motor* August 1931, 46.

21. Clifford, *Routes*, 34–35.

22. Whitman, "Song of the Open Road," 299.

23. John Steinbeck, *Travels With Charley*, 81.

24. Baudrillard, *America*, 53.

25. John Urry, "The System of Automobility," 27.

26. Ian Leong, Mike Sell, and Kelly Thomas, "Mad Love, Mobile Homes, and Dysfunctional Dicks: On the Road with Bonnie and Clyde," in Steven Cohan and Ina Rae Hark, *The Road Movie Book*, 72.

27. "As It Looks," 46.

28. Quoted in Borth, *Mankind on the Move*, 296. He identifies the source only as "a speaker at a national conference on driving simulation."

29. William Phelps Eno, *The Motor-Vehicle Driver: His Nature and Improvement* (Saugatuck, CT: Eno Foundation for Highway Traffic Patrol, 1949), 4; American Automobile Association, *Sportsmanlike Driving*, chap. 5.

30. Cited in Packer, "Disciplining Mobility," 149.

31. Lauer, *The Psychology of Driving*, 62. Kennan saw in the motorization of American life an infantilizing process that destroyed the virtues on which citizenship depended: the rambling modern motorist was a far cry from the pioneer who had won the west, and would, by extension, win the cold war. Once the force behind American dynamism and strength, mobility had, in Kennan's view, degenerated into a practice of caprice, evasion, and flight rather than mission. See Kennan, *Memoirs: 1950–1963*, vol. 2 (Boston: Little, Brown, 1972), 80–83. A minority in the postwar era were similarly suspicious of automobility. Loretta Reilly of the Business and Professional Women's Club of Albany, for example, wrote to Henry Ford II in 1956 stating, "I am not making America a nomad nation such as the Indians were before the Pilgrims arrived and that is what the motor car has done." BFRC, Accession 841, Fletcher Platt Files, Box 1, Thank-You Letters File.

32. Bel Geddes, *Magic Motorways*, 47, 56–57. Bel Geddes's patronizing, delighted tone is typical of planners of high-modernist projects. Highways engineering tends to presuppose subjects who—"like the 'unmarked citizens' of liberal theory—have, for the purposes of the planning exercise, no gender, no tastes, no history, no values, no opinions or original ideas, no traditions, and no distinctive personalities to contribute to the enterprise." James Scott, *Seeing Like a State*, 346.

33. Brean, "New Vistas of the Road," 76. These visions are now beginning to find purchase on the public imagination, as members of a highway lobby even more influential than its 1950s predecessor repackages its postwar pitch for the interstates as a call for automation. "Although the public may be loath to admit it," writes one commentator, "the unimpeded mobility of the automobile— considered a birthright for many Americans—is threatened by traffic-choked roadways." A transportation consultant quoted in the same article notes that, in an age of highway gridlock, "somehow we need to better meet the seemingly unsatisfiable demand for the freedom and mobility provided by cars and other vehicles." Steven Ashley, "Smart Cars and Automated Highways," *Mechanical Engineering* May 1998, 58–62. One robotic "smart-car" system currently under review by the State of California bears the particularly ironic appellation "Free Agent." See C. Thorpe, T. Jochem, and D. Pomerleau, "Automated Highways

and the Free Agent Demonstration," *International Symposium on Robotics Research* October 1997. See also "Automobility: Cars that Drive Themselves," *Omni* 15.6 (April 1993): 38–42.

34. Roy E. Babcock, "Surface for the Mounted," proposal (Clay Committee Records 1954–55, DDEL, Box 3, File 9).

35. Mark Simpson, *Trafficking Subjects*, 93.

36. As Jörg Beckmann has suggested, the discourse of automotive safety that figures the latter as "occupying a stable position within traffic network space" translates to a politically resonant privileging of the *immutability* of subjects. Beckmann, "Mobility and Safety," 96.

37. Philip Fisher, "Appearing and Disappearing in Public: Social Space in Late Nineteenth-Century Literature and Culture," in *Reconstructing American Literary History*, ed. Sacvan Bercovitch (Cambridge, MA: Harvard University Press, 1986), 178.

38. Larry McMurtry, *Roads* (New York: Touchstone, 2000), 184; Simone de Beauvoir, *America Day by Day* (New York: Grove Press, 1953), 161; Baudrillard, *America*, 53; Steinbeck, *Travels With Charley*, 85; Merle Haggard, "White Line Fever," *Okie from Muskogee* (Capitol Records, 1969 [CD, 2001]); Catherine R. Stimpson, foreword to *Women and the Journey: The Female Travel Experience*, ed. Bonnie Frederick and Susan H. McLeod (Pullman: Washington State University Press, 1993), ix.

39. Morse, *Virtualities: Television, Media Art, and Cyberculture* (Bloomington: Indiana University Press, 1998), 107. Other writers have linked highway driving to the passivity of television viewing, claiming that the windshield is simply another screen of images.

40. Didion, *The White Album* (New York: Simon and Schuster, 1979), 83; *Play It As It Lays* (New York: Farrar, 1970), 9–10.

41. Williams quoted in Gilroy, "Driving While Black," 81.

42. Henri Lefebvre, *Everyday Life in the Modern World* (New Brunswick: Transaction, 1994), 100.

43. Raymond Jackson Wilson, *In Quest of Community*, 4. "Emerson became 'Emerson,'" Quentin Anderson observed, "in a period in which there was an acute and widely diffused emotional demand for a new mode of self-validation." Anderson, *The Imperial Self: An Essay in American Literary and Cultural History* (New York: Alfred A. Knopf, 1971), 236. The literary critic Richard Poirier lauds Emerson's "predilection for what he calls 'abandonment'"; he suggests that the Emersonian genius is a "phenomenon of energy." Poirier, *The Renewal of Literature: Emersonian Reflections* (New York: Random House, 1987), 74–75.

44. Christopher Newfield, *The Emerson Effect*, 218, 4, 217.

45. Richard Sennett, "What Tocqueville Feared," in *On the Making of Americans: Essays in Honor of David Riesman*, ed. Herbert J. Gans et al. (Philadelphia: University of Pennsylvania Press, 1979), 124. Philip Slater has similarly noted that "Americans have an unfortunate tendency to assume that freedom means

being left alone. We are surprised and outraged when we stumble across the mammoth bureaucracies we have created through our abdication of personal responsibility." Slater, *A Dream Deferred: America's Discontent and the Search for a New Democratic Ideal* (Boston: Beacon Press, 1991), 21.

46. In these quotations I have drawn from three different translations of Tocqueville's *Democracy in America*, vol. 2, part 4, chap. 6.

47. John W. Draper, quoted in Arieli, *Individualism and Nationalism in American Ideology*, 326.

48. George W. Pierson, "A Restless Temper," 972.

49. Beckmann, "Mobility and Safety," 88; Lefebvre, *Everyday Life in the Modern World*, 101.

50. Tocqueville, *Democracy in America*, vol. 2, part 4, chap. 6. Tocqueville's dystopian predictions of the subject's atomization and loss of agency through individualism have been revisited and pronounced fulfilled by those thinkers loosely grouped under the banner of communitarianism. See Edward W. Lehman, ed., *Autonomy and Order: A Communitarian Anthology* (Lanham, Md.: Rowman & Littlefield, 2000); Bellah et al., *Habits of the Heart*; Amy Gutmann, "Communitarian Critics of Liberalism," in *Communitarianism and Individualism*, ed. Shlomo Avineri and Avner De-Shalit 120–136; Alasdair MacIntyre, *After Virtue: A Study in Moral Theory*, 2nd ed. (Notre Dame: University of Notre Dame Press, 1984); and Michael Sandel, "The Procedural Republic and the Unencumbered Self," in *Communitarianism and Individualism*, ed. Avineri and De-Shalit.

51. Indeed, Newfield's thesis in *The Emerson Effect* descends from Foucault's insistence, most clearly articulated in *The History of Sexuality*, on the individual as a product of various discourses—economic, theological, political, juridical, and medical—that affirm and perpetuate the very idea of the individualized self. The political philosopher George Kateb has pejoratively described Foucault's schematics of subjectivity as follows: "Foucault alleges that modern individualism is, appearances notwithstanding, the result of techniques of discipline. The more each person regards himself or herself as distinct from others, as special, as acting spontaneously, as living in response to the deep promptings of one's unique inner life, the more one is being victimized by the disciplinary and docility-inducing techniques of modern power. . . . [Their result] is the creation or 'fabrication' of an individual identity, an identity acquired by docile absorption of the habits and, above all, of the words and meanings implanted by technicians." Kateb, *The Inner Ocean: Individualism and Democratic Culture* (Ithaca: Cornell University Press, 1992), 233, 239. See also, for example, Theodor Adorno and Max Horkheimer, *Dialectic of Enlightenment*, trans. John Cumming (New York: Herder & Herder, 1972); and Herbert Marcuse, *One-Dimensional Man: Studies in the Ideology of Advanced Industrial Society* (Boston: Beacon Press, 1964).

52. Adorno et al., *The Authoritarian Personality* (New York: W. W. Norton, 1982), 349. This begs the question of the Frankfurt School's fraught position

on individualism more generally. Martin Jay notes that, though the Frankfurt School recognized the bourgeois individual as a liberal-capitalist fiction, Adorno in particular mourned its demise. This was, after all, the subject who crafted and appreciated the aesthetic innovations of modern art, literature, and music, not to mention revolutionary thought such as Marxism. Both Adorno and Horkheimer treated the passing of the bourgeois individual "in a highly nuanced way, both mourning its loss and recognizing its limitations." Jay, *Adorno* (Cambridge, MA: Harvard University Press, 1984), 37. In the wake of this individual's passing, Adorno theorized a subject that was, in one sense, like Riesman's autonomous individual: a nonconformist, but possessed of a more clear-eyed and courageous understanding of the determining factors which structure her life. Yet, unlike Riesman's autonomous individual, Adorno's ideal subject did not *identify with* or *adjust to* the world as it appeared before her; nor did she seek in its amenities and marketed eccentricities—such as automobility—deliverance from conformity or alienation. Such a subject, however, was not the one Adorno saw rising to replace the moribund bourgeois individual in the middle of the twentieth century. Instead, he saw an emerging society of highly tractable, potentially aggressive automatons. Of course, the vision of Nazi Germany informed Adorno's sensibilities; but he did not see the United States as qualitatively different in terms of the obliteration of individuality.

53. Adorno, *Minima Moralia: Reflections from a Damaged Life,* trans. E. F. N. Jephcott (New York: Verso, 1991), 59. The literary scholar Nico Israel writes that, "in Adorno's view, capitalist modern technology, which offers up ever-newer, ever-faster means of 'transport' . . . moves the subject of technology (viewer, reader, rider) further towards subjection, and more quickly too." Israel, "Damage Control: Adorno, Los Angeles, and the Destruction of Culture," *Yale Journal of Criticism* 10.1 (1997): 99.

54. "Thus," Packer writes, "to be mobile is to be free to govern oneself." "Disciplining Mobility," 140.

55. *Society's Responsibilities* (Washington, DC: AAA, 1937), 99.

56. Christopher Newfield, "Corporate Pleasures for a Corporate Planet," *Social Text* 44 (Fall–Winter 1995): 37.

57. Gilles Deleuze, *Two Regimes of Madness: Texts and Interviews 1975–1995* (New York: Semiotext(e), 2006), 322. See also Deleuze, "Postscript on the Societies of Control," *October* 59 (Winter 1992): 3–7. This control attends the newer and much-heralded technologies of individual agency and mobility, particularly the information superhighway; one can hear its voice in the Microsoft ad campaign that asks its users, "Where do you want to go today?"

58. Art Buchwald, *Have I Ever Lied to You?* (New York: Putnam, 1968), 197–198.

59. Ford Motor Company Research and Information Department, "Trails to Turnpikes" poster for promotional *The American Road* campaign (BFRC, Accession 1859, Box 12, Background Materials and Research Notes File).

60. Karl Raitz, "American Roads, Roadside America," *Geographical Review* 88.3 (July 1998): 364.

61. Sudhir Chella Rajan, *The Enigma of Automobility*, 19.

62. Adelson, "The Car, the City, and What We Want," 292, 286.

63. Stephen Moore, "The War Against the Car," *Wall Street Journal* November 11, 2005: A10.

64. Raymond Williams, *The Country and the City* (London: Chatto and Windus, 1973), 296.

65. See Raymond Williams, *Television*, chap. 1. See also Sheller and Urry, "Mobile Transformations of Public Life," *Theory, Culture, and Society* 20.3 (2003): 107–125.

66. See Beckmann, "Mobility and Safety," on this contrast.

67. See Lefebvre, *Everyday Life in the Modern World*, 100–104.

68. Gorz, "The Social Ideology of the Motor Car." As the psychologist Raymond A. Novaco similarly notes, "being in a car is to inhabit a microenvironment that can be easily geared for frustration and anger." Novaco, "Automobile Driving and Aggressive Behavior," in *The Car and the City*, 235.

69. Steinbeck, *Travels With Charley*.

70. Updike seems to be describing here the anomic suburban world of his fiction, the Rabbit novels in particular. Updike, "Emersonianism," *Odd Jobs: Essays and Criticism* (New York: Alfred A. Knopf, 1991), 158, 160.

71. John Dunn, *The Politics of Socialism: An Essay in Political Theory* (Cambridge: Cambridge University Press, 1984), 94.

72. Lefebvre, *Everyday Life in the Modern World*, 100–101.


## epilogue

1. Nikolas Rose, *Powers of Freedom: Reframing Political Thought* (Cambridge: Cambridge University Press, 1999), 66.

2. Anthony Giddens quoted in Beckmann, "Automobility," 600. "Whatever the fate of the high-minded sense of individuality that was the dream of the eighteenth-century philosophers," writes the theorist Nick Mansfield, "we can see ourselves, in the absolute desperation with which we attempt to grasp, express and sell our subjectivity, very much in their wake, even if the type of freedom we enjoy looks like a parody of what they expected." Mansfield, *Subjectivity: Theories of the Self from Freud to Haraway* (New York: New York University Press, 2000), 22.

3. Calum MacLeod, "China's Highways Go the Distance," *USA Today* January 29, 2006. See also Ted Conover, "Capitalist Roaders," *New York Times* July 2, 2006; and Heather Timmons, "Saturday Interview with Andrew Coslett; Holiday Inn Sees Replay of the 50's in China," *New York Times* July 1, 2006.

# index

*Page numbers in italics refer to figures.*

National System of Interstate and Defense Highways, 14, 65, 71, 94, 125; naming of, 98

*Nation's Business,* 200n122, 201n125

Native Americans, 23

Nauen, Elinor, 209n4

Nearing, Helen, 194n62

Nearing, Scott, 194n62

Negro League baseball, 124

*Negro Motorist Green Book,* 15, 106, 111, 115–117, *116,* 118–120, 124–125, 127, 128; vs. AAA *Blue Book,* 207n55

Nelson, Daniel, 168n51

Nerlove, S. H., 180n100

New Deal, 72–73, 90, 94, 181n106

Newfield, Christopher, 128, 140–141, 144, 146, 159n29, 206n39

"new individualism," 31, 33, 91, 141

New Jersey Turnpike, 139

Newman, Kathy M., 171n76

*New Republic,* 104

*Newsweek,* 80, 200n122, 201n125

*New View of Society, A* (Owen), 23

"New Womanhood," 13–14, 51, 59, 60

New York *Daily News,* 97

New York *Post,* 118

*New York Times,* 88–89, 215n3

*New York Times Magazine,* 196n87

Nicholson, T. R., 176n48

Nisbet, Robert A., 166n36

Nitze, Paul, 184n3

Nixon, Richard M., 93, 95

North, Bobby, 172n6

Norton, Peter, 180n100

Novaco, Raymond A., 215n68

"NSC 68" ("United States Objectives and Programs for National Security"), 70–71

Nyland, Chris, 168n49

Oakes, Guy, 184n6

O'Connell, Sean, 160n30

Office of Road Inquiry, Department of Agriculture, 64

Oldfield, Barney, 109

Oldsmobile advertising, 45

*Omni,* 212n33

O'Neill, William, 199n113

*On the Road* (Kerouac), 82, 87, 139

"open road," 14, 43, 107; in advertising, 100; and gender, 13, 52, 209n4; as oxymoron, 133; in Whitman, 13, 22, 134–135

Oppenheimer, J. Robert, 111, 185n9

Orbán, Katalin, 203n1

*Organization Man, The* (Whyte), 77

Orton, William A., 189n33

Orvell, Miles, 176n47

Osborne, Thomas, 158n22

O'Toole, Randal, 156n3

*Outing* magazine, 38, 43, 45, 55

Owen, Robert: *A New View of Society,* 23

Packard, Vance, 188n29, 190n36

Packer, Jeremy, 12, 67, 133, 143, 202n139

Pangburn, Weaver Weddell, 180n100

Parchesky, Sara, 56, 178n63

Parsons, Talcott, 187n22

Partridge, Bellamy, 85

Patel, Cyrus R. K., 163n16

Pateman, Carole, 162n6

Patterson, William D., 194n62

Patton, Phil, 46, 159n28

Peck, Harvey W., 49

Pennsylvania Department of Highways, 49

Pennsylvania Turnpike, 95, 181n106

*People of Plenty* (Potter), 74

People's Capitalism campaign, 79–80, 101, 104

Percival, Chas. G., 48

Perkins, George, 25, 198n101

Perlo, Victor, 193n55